Data Driven Marketing

FOR DUMMIES®

A Wiley Brand

by David Semmelroth

FOR DUMMIES®

A Wiley Brand

Data Driven Marketing For Dummies®

Published by: **John Wiley & Sons, Inc.,** 111 River Street, Hoboken, NJ 07030-5774, www.wiley.com

Copyright © 2013 by John Wiley & Sons, Inc., Hoboken, New Jersey

Published simultaneously in Canada

For general information on our other products and services, please contact our Customer Care Department within the U.S. at 877-762-2974, outside the U.S. at 317-572-3993, or fax 317-572-4002. For technical support, please visit www.wiley.com/techsupport.

Wiley publishes in a variety of print and electronic formats and by print-on-demand. Some material included with standard print versions of this book may not be included in e-books or in print-on-demand. If this book refers to media such as a CD or DVD that is not included in the version you purchased, you may download this material at http://booksupport.wiley.com. For more information about Wiley products, visit www.wiley.com.

Library of Congress Control Number: 2013946293

ISBN 978-1-118-61584-3 (pbk); ISBN 978-1-118-61576-8 (ebk); ISBN 978-1-118-61583-6 (ebk); ISBN 978-1-118-61601-7 (ebk)

Manufactured in the United States of America

10 9 8 7 6 5 4 3 2 1

Contents at a Glance

Table of Contents

Introduction

Welcome to *Data Driven Marketing For Dummies!*

But … what do I mean by data driven marketing? All marketing disciplines are fundamentally concerned with attracting and retaining customers. They're also all driven by data, in some sense. Marketers don't just haphazardly develop communications. They take as much information into account as they have available.

Database marketing, or data driven marketing, is a discipline which takes the use of information to an extreme. *Data driven marketing,* as I use the term in this book, can be characterized by three things:

- **It's a form of direct marketing:** Database marketers develop communications that are delivered directly to consumers. This has traditionally been done through direct mail and e-mail. But the principles of direct marketing are being used with increasing sophistication to deliver marketing messages via text messages, social media, web content, and other electronic channels.

- **It's fundamentally focused on individual customer information:** The *database* in database marketing refers to a customer database which contains purchase history, demographics, and other information about each customer. This level of detail forms the basis for highly relevant, personalized, and customized messages. This relevance drives the effectiveness of database marketing campaigns.

- **It's measurable:** And it's measurable in very precise financial terms. This measurability gives the database marketer the ability to create a marketing laboratory. Audiences, offers, messages, communication channels, and anything else related to a database marketing campaign can be tested to see how well they perform.

About This Book

Database marketing requires a variety of skill sets ranging from the technical to the creative. For this reason, database marketing departments tend to be made up of a diverse set of people. This makes them fun places to work. But it also poses some communication challenges.

I wrote this book partly to help fill that communication gap. I try to address the broad spectrum of work that needs to be done in the day-to-day operations of a database marketing department. In that regard, I've written this book with database and direct marketers in mind.

But customer information has grown and continues to grow more central to all sorts of business decisions and strategies. For this reason, this book will appeal to anyone in the business world who takes an interest in customer data and how it can be used to your advantage.

A small note: Within this book, you may see that some web addresses break across two lines of text. If you're reading this book in print and want to visit one of these web pages, simply type in the web address exactly as it appears in the text, pretending as though the line break doesn't exist. If you're reading this as an e-book, you've got it easy — just tap or click the web address to be taken directly to the web page.

Foolish Assumptions

I assume that if you're reading this, you have an interest in database marketing. Though I try to define marketing-specific terms as I use them, it would be helpful for you to have a passing familiarity with basic marketing terms like *target audiences* and *marketing channels.* Plenty of introductory marketing books can give you that basic level of understanding if you don't already have it, including Alexander Hiam's *Marketing For Dummies* (Wiley, 2009).

I also assume that you're not *too* put off by numbers. Database marketing involves a great deal of quantitative measurement. That doesn't mean that you need to have an accounting background, though. Being able to calculate percentages is sufficient.

Though this subject can get somewhat technical, I make no assumptions about your knowledge of either technology or advanced mathematical methods. I attempt to explain in simple terms what the basic ideas are about. My focus is on helping you to communicate with your technical teams and vice versa. If you can add up a column of numbers in a spreadsheet, then you're more than adequately prepared to read this book.

Some of the subjects in this book, particularly those that relate to building databases, assume that you have a fairly significant technology budget. Databases, software, and even maintenance require some level of investment. But even if this is not the case, the parts of this book that relate to developing and analyzing campaigns will still be relevant.

Icons Used in This Book

Look for these symbols to help you navigate through the text.

I use this icon to highlight specific suggestions for how to deal with a given situation.

This icon is used to point out information that you need to be aware of. I use it sometimes to summarize a point that I'm making in a section. I also use it to point out information that's fundamental to a given topic.

There are a number of common traps that you can fall into when it comes to database marketing. What you don't know can hurt you. I use this icon to point out situations where you need to tread carefully.

Beyond the Book

In the Part of Tens, I point out a number of websites and organizations that can provide you with information and support. Because I don't have room to cover related topics in detail, I also refer through this book to other *For Dummies* books that do. In particular, *Marketing For Dummies, Web Marketing For Dummies,* and *Social Media Marketing For Dummies* (all published by Wiley) contain more detailed discussions of some of the topics in this book.

There is also some juicy, free, extra material for this book online. The cheat sheet and several companion articles can be found at `www.dummies.com/extras/datadrivenmarketing/`.

Where to Go from Here

I've worked hard to make the parts and even chapters of this book self-contained. You should be able to start anywhere in the book and feel comfortable that you haven't missed too much to grasp what's going on. Part I provides a good introduction to the topic of database marketing from an infrastructure perspective and might be helpful for Information Technology folks who are trying to understand how to meet the needs of their database marketing group.

In Part III, I focus on tying various database marketing strategies to specific business problems. This is a good place to go if you're looking for ideas about how to address a specific goal.

Parts II and IV are largely concerned with the analysis of data. These are useful to non-technical marketers who want to better understand what sorts of things can be achieved through data analysis. They're also useful to technical folks who understand advance statistics but have minimal experience in database marketing applications. For the non-technical marketers, I would recommend starting with Chapter 6 to ground yourself before moving on to other chapters.

To get the full flavor of everything, and for anyone who is starting fresh with this topic, you can go old-school and head directly for Chapter 1.

Part I

Getting Started with Data Driven Marketing

 For Dummies can help you get started with lots of subjects. Visit www.dummies.com to learn more.

In this part . . .

✔ Find out how database marketing campaigns are organized.

✔ Explore the various types of customer data that are used in marketing campaigns.

✔ Learn how to manage and protect your customer contact information.

✔ Get to know your responsibilities regarding opt-outs and unsubscribe requests from customers.

✔ Understand the critical steps in database marketing campaign execution.

Chapter 1

Data Driven Marketing 101: It's All About the Customer

In This Chapter

▶ Understanding what data driven marketing is

▶ Compiling, managing, and analyzing customer data

▶ Understanding the components of database marketing campaigns

▶ Measuring and learning from your marketing campaigns

ata driven marketing means using data about customers to drive marketing communications. The use of consumer data in advertising was pioneered back in the 1930s by Arthur Nielsen of TV ratings fame. Nielsen's data was, and still is, largely derived from survey research. In this book, I approach the subject of data driven marketing primarily, though not exclusively, from the perspective of database marketing.

Database marketing uses direct communication to individuals, like direct mail and e-mail campaigns. What sets database marketing apart is, not surprisingly, the data it uses. Even though the phrase *data driven marketing* refers more broadly to all types of marketing, I often use the phrase interchangeably with *database marketing.*

Database marketers rely on customer databases that contain more than just customer contact information. These databases typically contain purchase history, age, income, and a host of other customer attributes. These attributes are analyzed with an eye toward understanding how to effectively drive sales to different types of customers.

Everything you do as a database marketer begins and ends with the customer. Your effectiveness at driving sales is fundamentally dependent on your understanding of your customer base. This understanding is driven not by intuition or guesswork but by rigorous analyses of facts. Virtually every decision you make is rooted in what your database says about your customers.

Database marketing involves a hybrid set of skills. It requires some level of understanding of database technology. It also involves some degree of analytic capability, particularly some familiarity with statistics. Business acumen is also key. And finally, it requires having some degree of appreciation for the psychology of the consumer. This diversity of skill sets is reflected in the teams that populate database marketing departments. They tend to be very interesting places to work.

In this chapter, I present an overview of the various components of an effective database marketing strategy. Clearly the database is one important component. Your approach to designing communications, or campaigns, is another. And one of the defining characteristics of database marketing is the use of analytic methods to measure and learn from your campaigns. But first, I want to prevent some potential confusion about the focus of this book.

What Data Driven Marketing Is (and Isn't) About

A number of marketing sub-disciplines involve the use of customer data. Web marketing and social media marketing come to mind. I touch briefly on some aspects of web marketing in this book. And I touch even more briefly on social media marketing. Both of these subjects are explored in depth in their own *For Dummies* volumes.

Small business marketing and business-to-business marketing have also evolved to include substantial use of data. Many of the ideas in this book can be applied in these arenas. In this book, however, I focus specifically on business-to-consumer marketing. I outline my reasons for that in this section.

Database marketing versus direct marketing

Database marketing, as I've said, is a sub-discipline of direct marketing. *Direct marketing* refers broadly to any communication that is sent directly to a consumer. It does not imply any sophisticated, or even unsophisticated, targeting or audience selection. The "coupon clipper" circulars that show up in your mailbox every week are an example of direct marketing that is not database marketing. Sure, they're sent directly to your mailbox. But they're sent to everyone else's as well.

I call this approach to direct marketing *carpet bombing*. Its online equivalent is *spam*. And it's probably the easiest way to distinguish direct marketing in general from database marketing as I use the terms. Database marketing is the opposite of carpet bombing.

These carpet bombing campaigns typically involve low-quality mail pieces and messages. They're frequently addressed to *Resident* rather than to an individual. And they're not targeted.

Database marketing campaigns on the other hand reflect the use of customer data in all these areas. The mail piece is personalized and often customized to resonate with the recipient. And most importantly, these campaigns are targeted at specific audiences rather than entire zip codes.

Database marketing and customer relationship management

Customer relationship management, more commonly shortened to *CRM,* has become a marketing industry staple. You hear about CRM in the context of systems, software, sales force automation, and corporate marketing strategies. It refers generally to the use of customer data throughout the enterprise.

In this sense, database marketing is a component of a company's CRM strategy. By definition, if you're doing database marketing, you're using customer data. But CRM also involves other forms of customer contact. Salespeople, call center agents, customer service reps, and company employees all have contact with customers. CRM attempts to use customer data to support all these functions.

This book focuses on only the database marketing component of customer contacts. Most of the discussion and examples I give stress communications through direct mail or e-mail or other electronic media. The only exception to this is a short section in Chapter 17 where I talk about integrating customer data with your company's broader CRM strategy.

Marketing to businesses

As I say earlier, I don't focus on business-to-business marketing in this book. One reason for this is that it's not my area of expertise. But I do know enough to know that business-to-business marketing differs in many significant ways from consumer marketing.

For one thing, in consumer marketing the fundamental notion is a household. Communications are targeted at and customized around individual households. On the business side, one business can have multiple contacts that you need to keep track of.

This difference affects fundamentally the way a business-to-business database needs to be structured. The consumer database model won't work. And the types of data that's available on businesses differs dramatically from that on the consumer side. Presence of children and marital status — typical marketing variables — don't make any sense in context of businesses.

For another thing, the different contacts in a business need to be treated differently when designing communications. For example, when trying to get a mail piece read by an executive, you need to think about how to keep the assistant who screens the mail from throwing it in the recycling bin.

That's not to say that the ideas in this book are completely irrelevant to business-to-business marketing. The basic structure of database marketing campaigns is the same in both contexts. Much of my discussion on analytics and measurement also applies.

Database marketing and small businesses

Again, many of the ideas in this book are applicable to small businesses. But small businesses have some features that make robust database marketing difficult, if not impossible.

First, small businesses are often geographically limited in their customer base. This makes the use of simpler and less expensive direct-mail programs more feasible than targeted programs. It's more cost effective for them to just carpet bomb zip codes than spend a lot of money on buying targeted lists.

Small businesses also have limited marketing and technology budgets. The cost of setting up elaborate databases, purchasing customer demographic data, and buying analytic tools can be prohibitive.

Having said that, it's possible for a clever and industrious business owner to take a more low-budget approach. The typical suite of office software contains presentation software along with spreadsheet and database software. Moreover, the spreadsheet software is a fairly powerful reporting and statistical tool if you know what you're doing. You could go a long way with just a PC and the occasional college intern.

Focusing on the Customer

Everything you do as a database marketer depends on understanding your customers. This in turn depends on having clean and accurate customer information. Customer databases aren't static entities. You don't just build one and hang up the tool belt. These databases require constant maintenance.

Getting customer data from your companies systems

Your customer data is spread out across a variety of sources. You have transaction systems that keep track of sales, orders, service requests, customer complaints, and everything else it takes to run your business. These systems include call center databases, cash registers, your website, and your e-commerce system.

When building a customer database, you face two main challenges. The first is simply getting the data out of these systems and collected in one place. Because the data is always being updated, this is an ongoing process.

Most customer databases that I've seen involve regularly scheduled data downloads from various source systems. I've seen this done monthly, weekly, and even daily or hourly. The frequency of these downloads defines how fresh the data in your database is.

It's important for you to understand how fresh your data is. Very likely, not all systems are loaded to your database on the same schedule, so this freshness factor may vary depending on what data you're looking at. The freshness of you data limits what you can do with it. For example, you can't send daily thank you e-mails for purchases if your purchase data is only loaded to your database on a weekly basis.

Integrating data at the customer level

The second, bigger, challenge is integrating the data. Database marketing focuses on the customer. Your database needs to be organized around your customers as well. Everything needs to tie back to individual customers.

One thing that makes this difficult is that much of the transaction data in your company's operational systems is anonymous. It's not actually associated with customers at all. If I go into a grocery store and hand the cashier a dollar bill for a candy bar, that sale can't be tied back to me.

Throughout this book, I talk about a number of ways to overcome this challenge. Technology — particularly the Internet and other electronic media — are making it much easier to get information about your customers' behavior, attitudes, and preferences. In the Part of Tens, I include a chapter specifically about this and other ways of linking data to customers.

Managing contact information

Your database marketing campaigns involve contacting your customers directly. That means your customer contact information needs to be accurate. Whether it's e-mail addresses, home addresses, or mobile device numbers, if these addresses aren't accurate, you're wasting your time.

Address quality

Managing your customer contact information is an ongoing maintenance chore. People move all the time. So addresses need to be regularly updated. The U.S. Postal Service can help with this. The USPS maintains and makes available a mover database that contains the change of address information it receives.

E-mail addresses aren't as easy to update, though a growing number of services can help with this. It *is* important, however, to recognize when an e-mail address is no longer in use. You can tell when one of your e-mails *bounces,* or is returned as undeliverable. These need to be removed from your database. If not, you risk the nasty repercussions of being labeled a spammer.

Respecting opt-outs

Customers can and do request to be taken off mailing lists. Another ongoing maintenance chore involves managing these *opt-outs.* Active management is required because these opt-outs can come from a variety of sources.

In the case of physical mail, there's a national database that contains global opt-outs. By *global* I mean these are folks who've asked to be excluded from any direct-marketing campaign. This database is managed by the Direct Marketing Association (of which you should be a member.) But people can also contact you directly to ask that you not market to them.

In the case of e-mail, legislation requires you to provide customers with the ability to opt out of hearing from you. Another piece of legislation applies to phone numbers. A national Do Not Call registry is operated by the FTC.

You need to respect opt-out requests. In some cases, you're legally obligated to do so. In the case of mail, the Direct Marketing Association takes a dim view of database marketers who don't comply with their standards. If the DMA blackballs you, you'll have a difficult time finding credible vendors to help with your direct mail. Plus, bottom line, it's just good business. Why waste money communicating with people who don't want to hear from you?

Communicating with the household

Most database marketing campaigns are directed at households rather than individuals. This is partly to reduce mailing costs. It usually doesn't make sense to mail multiple copies of your message to the same address.

But focusing on the whole household serves another purpose as well. Many of the demographic traits that drive the way you target and communicate your marketing messages are household-level traits. Things like presence of children and household income are classic examples. In fact, all the data collected by the U.S. Census Bureau is collected at the household level.

Actually building a household record is a little bit tricky. It involves a good bit of data cleansing and data processing to group customers together. Luckily, a variety of companies out there can do this for you. In fact, because they have a lot more data than you do, they can do it far more effectively than you can. I talk about householding services in Chapter 19.

The Database Marketing Campaign

Database marketing campaigns all have the same basic structure. And as the title of this chapter suggests, that structure revolves around the customer. As you develop your campaigns, you'll be using customer data to answer four basic questions about your campaign:

- ✔ Who?
- ✔ What?
- ✔ How?
- ✔ When?

Your attention needs to stay focused on the customer. A common trap that marketers fall into is to start with an offer or promotion and attempt to find an audience to sell it to. This "I've got something to sell, find me someone to buy it" approach is completely backwards and not particularly effective. The power of database marketing comes from an understanding of the customer's needs, preferences, and even financial means. An understanding of your customer's perspective is what drives effective offers.

The target audience

Your database marketing campaigns begin with a particular business challenge or opportunity in mind — a *goal*. Typically your goal involves generating revenue. But sometimes your goal may not generate revenue directly. For example, you may be asked to increase web registrations, with the thought that these registrants may be more likely to make purchases in the future.

Once you're presented with this goal, you need to figure out whom you're going to communicate with. This *target audience* will drive everything else you do in your campaign development process. Much of this book revolves around techniques for defining this target audience. The heart and soul of database marketing is the ability to use data and analytic techniques to choose audiences that will help you meet your business goal.

 Through the process of selecting your target audience, you'll develop a clear picture of the traits that are shared by that audience. You'll have a profile of that audience which might include past purchases, age, income, marital status, presence of children, and a host of other characteristics that describe them. This profile — your understanding of the who — will be used in answering the what, how, and when questions about your campaign.

The offer

The core of your marketing message is the offer that you put in front of the customer. Your goal is to make this offer relevant to members of your target audience. The audience profile is key in designing the offer.

You'll probably find, for example, that you have two distinct groups of customers as it relates to discounts. You have some that are extremely price sensitive and others who are more interested in getting premium benefits. By understanding which is which, you can design different offers that will appeal to different groups.

The price-sensitive group is probably going to need a discount. So you might offer them 20 percent off their next purchase. But the benefit-driven customer may be enticed by simply informing them of your new top-of-the-line product, no discount needed.

 Whatever your offer, you need to make it clear and concise. It's generally a bad idea to make several offers in a single communication. The offer needs to be the star of the show.

Closely related to your offer is the *call to action*. It's not enough to make the offer. You need to explicitly tell the customer how to take advantage of it. *Visit our website now* or *Visit our store today.* Like your offer, your call to action should be simple and prominent. It should also be crafted to convey a sense of urgency.

Your marketing message

The *how* of your database marketing campaign involves what you're sending them. This is frequently referred to as your marketing *collateral.* The first decision you have to make is how you're going to deliver it. For example, will it be an e-mail or direct mail piece?

Again, your database can help. By looking at past campaigns, you can get a sense of who is responding through which channels. People who often purchase online may be enticed by an e-mail with a link to your site. Those who typically buy in stores may respond better to a direct-mail piece that includes a coupon.

Once you've selected the channel, you can proceed with designing your communication. Here, yet again, the profile of your target audience can help you. You can craft your message with that particular audience in mind. Often you do that with the help of an advertising or creative partner. But that partner will definitely want to understand the target audience profile.

Timing your message

Your database marketing campaigns may be executed in conjunction with broader marketing initiatives, like mass media advertising. In these cases, they clearly need to be timed to take full advantage of the combined effects.

But you also need to understand when the message is most likely to be effective. If you're announcing a weekend sale, when is the right time to be in market? You don't want to wait until the last minute, but should you send your communication a week in advance? Two weeks?

These same sorts of questions arise when you're marketing products that require some degree of planning on the part of the customer. Things like vacations and mortgages don't tend to be last-minute impulse purchases. If you're trying to fill empty hotel rooms, you can't wait until the last minute to drop a campaign.

Your database can help yet again. By looking at past campaigns, you can get a sense of where the sweet spot lies. In the case of hotel reservations, your database can tell you exactly how far in advance reservations are typically made.

Analyzing Customer Data

A good portion of this book is about the types of analysis that are performed in database marketing. Much of this analysis requires some advanced knowledge of mathematics and statistics.

In this book, I largely avoid the more technical aspects. I concentrate instead on pointing out some pitfalls to look out for and how to evaluate the results of advanced analysis. In this section, I introduce you to a couple of the more common types of insights that can be coaxed from your customer data.

Grouping customers into segments

Database marketing relies fundamentally on the process of identifying the target audience. This is essentially an exercise in finding groups of customers who share similar traits.

A great deal of the analytic work that goes on in marketing in general has to do with finding such groups, called *segments*. Such work is generally referred to as *segmentation*. In this section, I outline a few approaches to segmentation that are commonly used in database marketing.

Geographic segments

Perhaps the easiest to understand is geographic segmentation. Households in the U.S. are divided up into a hierarchy of geographic groupings. These groups are defined by the Census Bureau. They range from individual city blocks, to block groups all the way up to what are called *Metropolitan Statistical Areas,* or MSAs, which are essentially large population centers.

The reason that these segments are important to marketers is that they reflect the way mass media is distributed. The viewership of local TV network affiliates is closely aligned with these MSAs. The same is true of radio audiences and the subscription bases of local newspapers.

What's more, these are the groupings that the Census Bureau uses to report census data. That means that marketers have access to a wealth of demographic and economic data on these areas.

 Weather, culture, and even school calendars vary geographically. This means that you'll often have reason to use geography in developing your marketing campaigns. Regional differences can help drive decisions about what products to offer, how to craft your message, and even when to communicate.

Demographic segmentation

Demographic data is a core part of your database. This data generally needs to be purchased if you want to have it at the individual customer level. There are a number of vendors out there who provide a wide range of customer level information.

Lifestage traits such as age, marital status, and number of children all affect the product needs of consumers. They also affect the types of messages that will make an emotional connection. Income drives affordability and price sensitivity. Homeowners need a wide range of products and services that aren't needed by renters.

As an ongoing part of your job as a database marketer, you'll be involved in trying to define and refine a demographic segmentation scheme for your customers. Because every business is different, there really isn't a one-size-fits-all segmentation scheme you can universally apply. By combining your customer purchase history with demographic data, you can develop a segmentation scheme tailored for your particular business needs.

Behavioral segmentation

Another common approach to segmentation involves analyzing transaction data. The idea is to group customers together based on the way they interact with you.

A standard behavioral segmentation in the credit-card industry involves looking at how customers use their cards. They're grouped into *transacters, revolvers,* or *inactive* according to how much they use the card and whether they pay off their balance every month. This is a useful distinction, because the nature of the revenue these groups generate is very different. Marketing campaigns are dramatically different depending on which group is being targeted.

Behavioral segmentation is particularly fruitful with web data. When customers visit your website, they generate a huge virtual paper trail. You can tell what pages they're looking at, what they're searching and shopping for, and even how long they stay on your site. This data is extremely useful in developing relevant database marketing campaigns.

Building response models

It's possible to use the results of past campaigns to define target audiences for future campaigns. This exercise is known as *response modeling*. It involves looking at the various customer attributes of responders. Some of these attributes turn out to be closely associated with how likely a customer is to respond to a given campaign.

When advanced statistical techniques are applied, it's actually possible to throw a bunch of different attributes into the mix all at once. These statistical procedures then tease out the combination of attributes that best predicts a customer response.

Again, I avoid getting into the deep statistical detail that underlies the model building process. Instead I focus on how to approach working with a statistician to build models. I also give you some tools to help interpret and evaluate response models.

Measuring Results

As I say at the beginning of this chapter, your job as a database marketer begins and ends with the customer. Focus on the individual customer is the defining principle of database marketing.

But there's another defining characteristic of database marketing that's a close second. Database marketing is *measurable*. Everything about it is measurable. Messages, offers, response rates, and even revenue can all be measured.

I don't mean to imply that every one of these things can be measured for every marketing campaign. You need to pick and choose your battles, so to speak. But there is nothing about these campaigns that you can't measure or test if you so choose.

There is an age-old adage among marketing executives that laments their inability to really understand marketing effectiveness. They know, so the saying goes, that only half their marketing is working. They just don't know which half. This adage does not apply to the database marketer.

The secret lies in the fact that you *know* who is responding to your campaigns. You can tie responses back to individuals in your target audience. This allows you to essentially design marketing experiments.

These experiments can test the success of one offer over another. You can scientifically compare the response rates of different messages. And you can even confidently calculate the revenue that is specifically due to your efforts.

In this book, I give you a primer on how to use the scientific method to go about designing your marketing experiments. By properly setting up your campaigns as experiments, you can not only learn a great deal about what works and what doesn't — you can also take credit for quantifiable contributions to your company's bottom line.

Chapter 2

Communicating Directly with Your Customers

In This Chapter

▶ Understanding the key components of a campaign

▶ Using data to focus your efforts

▶ Crafting your message with your data

▶ Getting the timing right

*Y*ou have no doubt pulled hundreds, if not thousands, of database marketing communications from your mailbox in your lifetime. From glossy catalogs to dull postcards addressed to *Occupant,* these mailings vary widely in quality. Some go directly into the recycling bin. Others get opened and read before being tossed. A precious few may actually capture your interest. This variation in quality and effectiveness is the result of the attention, or lack thereof, that was paid by the sender to the basics of database marketing.

In this chapter, I discuss the core components of database marketing campaigns. Your business model, marketing budget, and the quality of your marketing database may all limit how much you can do with a campaign. But regardless of your limitations, all database marketing campaigns have the same basic structure.

So, What Is a Database Marketing Campaign?

Database marketing campaigns are communications that are intended to get your customers to do something specific, like buy a widget. Often, these campaigns are designed to address a specific business opportunity. For example, you may be asked to help counteract a shortfall in projected sales. Or you may be asked to expand the customer base for a specific product.

When presented with such a task, you need to ask yourself some questions:

- ✔ Who is likely to buy said product?
- ✔ What would make them more likely to buy the product?
- ✔ How should I communicate with them?
- ✔ When should I communicate with them?

The answers to these questions form the basis for your database marketing campaign development.

Throughout this book, I stress the importance of staying focused on the customer. When developing marketing campaigns, it's particularly important to start with understanding your audience. It is easy to fall into the trap of thinking "I have something to sell — find someone on the database to buy it." It's much more productive to start by trying to understand who's in your database and what they've purchased in the past. This approach will help you to answer the what, how, and when questions in a much more meaningful way.

I recommend always taking an audience to offer approach rather than falling into the trap of offer to audience that happens so many times. The next section is an example of *audience to offer,* which means starting with the target audience, not your product or service.

Narrowing your focus to the target audience

One thing that distinguishes the discipline of database marketing from that of mass mailings is the way in which you go about deciding whom you communicate with. This decision is known as identifying the *target audience*.

In the case of mass mailings, the target audience is typically very large. Little or no effort is made to identify and exclude customers who are unlikely to respond to your communication. I've been known to refer to this strategy as *carpet bombing.*

Such mass mailings usually have very low response rates. I've personally seen campaigns that only got 1 response for every 400 pieces mailed. As you get more sophisticated in your targeting, you can invest more of your marketing budget in developing higher quality communications. In the case of direct mail, where postage and printing costs are high, this is particularly valuable.

Narrowing your target audience also makes it more likely that your message is relevant to your customer. You would craft a very different message to a family with young children than you would to a retired couple, for example. Relevant messages are far more likely to lead to customers doing business with you.

Showcasing what you have to offer

Many database marketing campaigns are designed to communicate discounts. You may want to announce an upcoming sale, for example. Or you may be offering a bargain on discontinued inventory. This enticement to your customer is known as an *offer* or *promotion.* An offer does not necessarily need to involve a discount. You may be offering information on how to use your new website or about the location of your new store. You may be offering to set up an appointment to look at new cars.

Setting up an appointment to look at new cars highlights another distinguishing aspect of database marketing: Your database may be able to tell you who's ready to buy a new car. Such information would give you an opportunity to make that sale without having to entice the customer with a steep discount.

It's not enough just to communicate your offer. You need to tell the customer how to respond. The *call to action* is a critical component of all of your marketing communications.

> *Visit our website at . . .*
>
> *Stop into our store on Saturday . . .*
>
> *Call now to receive . . .*

are examples of calls to action. Always be clear and explicit about what you want the customer to do.

Deciding how you will communicate

How you will communicate is actually a two-part question. First, you need to decide on your communication *channel.* Traditionally, direct mail and e-mail have been the most common database marketing channels. But a growing number of electronic channels are also available to you, ranging from social media to text messaging. Your website can even be customized to serve up content based on what you know about your customers.

Chapter 4 talks about the pros and cons of some common database marketing channels. Timing, budget, and the nature of your message all play a role in which channel you chose. Some marketers like to use multiple channels in a communication stream. For example, they may send direct mail and follow up with an e-mail. I talk a little more about this later in this chapter.

Once you know what marketing channel you're using, you need to develop the actual (or virtual) mail piece, which is commonly called *collateral*. This process is known as *creative development*. Creative development is a mix of art and science. It requires graphic design expertise and expertise in writing marketing copy. Many companies farm this work out to marketing agencies. A detailed discussion of the creative development process is beyond the scope of this book, but you can read about it in Alexander Hiam's *Marketing For Dummies* (Wiley, 2009).

You likely will not be doing creative development yourself. But you will be providing guidance to your designers by providing them with a *creative brief*. This is where you tell your creative team what you're trying to accomplish. Learning how to communicate your marketing strategy and business goals in a well-written creative brief is key to your success as a database marketer — for a lot more on this topic, see *Marketing For Dummies*.

Determining when to send it

Many database marketing campaigns are very time sensitive. Discount offers are valid for a limited time. Special events, like clearance sales, have specific dates associated with them, and so on. Your customers are busy people and typically cannot respond immediately to your call to action. They need planning time.

You need to get your message *in market* at the time that it's most likely to have an impact. This timing depends quite a bit on the nature of your offer and on your business itself. A vacation to Australia requires a good bit of planning and saving by your customer. A new pair of shoes is more of an impulse buy.

You want to be in market early enough that the customer has time to respond to your offer. But you don't want to be so early that the customer forgets about it. The Australia vacation offer probably needs to be in market several months before the offer is valid. A one day shoe sale promotion might only need a week or two of lead time.

The key building blocks of your database marketing campaign consist of the answers to the who, what, how, and when questions. Here is a summary of these building blocks:

✔ **The target audience** is whom you are communicating with.

✔ **Your offer or promotion and the associated call to action** are what you are communicating.

✔ **Your marketing collateral and marketing channel** are how you are communicating.

✔ **Your in market date** is when you are communicating.

Your database can help you in all four of these areas. In the following sections, I discuss in general terms using your database to plan your campaigns.

Hitting the Bull's-eye: The Target Audience Isn't Everyone

Even if you were so inclined, you probably can't afford to mail everyone in your database. You want to focus your marketing efforts on those who are likely to buy. Your database has a good deal to say on this subject. In this section, I provide an overview of some basic ideas related to choosing your audience. In Part II, particularly in Chapter 7, I go into much more detail on this aspect of database marketing.

Some customers have requested that you not send them marketing messages. They can do that in a number of ways. In some cases, you're legally obligated to honor these requests, which are generally referred to as *opt-outs*. Chapter 4 talks about opt-outs in more detail.

Understanding your customer base

You may have a pretty good sense of who is buying your product. Does your product appeal to a specific group of people? If you're marketing wedding gowns, you probably don't want to be communicating with young married couples. Your database can help you identify the niche groups that might be interested in your product.

There are a couple of ways of getting at these niche groups of potential buyers. One is to look for patterns that might distinguish past purchasers. Do they come from a narrow age range? Is there an income threshold that allows them to afford your product? Do they buy at the same time every year?

When exploring your data for common traits among your customers, don't pre-judge what's important. Look at all the data you have available. Something might surprise you. Those surprises are valuable insights. I learned this lesson early in my banking career. It was widely understood at the time that a large percentage of the accounts held by our customers were simply unprofitable. I was asked to take a look at profitability at the customer level. What I found was that, contrary to popular belief, our unprofitable accounts were held disproportionately by very profitable customers. This discovery pointed out the potential dangers of trying to address profitability by taking a product-centric pricing approach. Raising fees on unprofitable accounts was just as likely to drive away profitable customer as it was to increase individual product revenue.

Another way to understand your customers better is to just ask them. Customer surveys are a great way to learn about who is buying and why. They also may give you some insight on why people aren't buying. Your company may do surveys that serve a wide array of purposes beyond your specific database marketing needs. Advertising, pricing, and product development all benefit from survey research. Chapter 17 discusses how you can help with your company's research efforts.

Get involved in the development of customer surveys. In particular, push for questions that match up with the kind of customer data you have. You want to be able to connect as much survey data back to your database as you can. Knowing that your best customers tend to sleep late may help in figuring out when to run TV commercials. But it won't help you if that information is not in your database.

Suppose, for example, that you have household income data in your database. That income data comes in the form of income ranges: $20–$30K, $30–$40K, and so on. If you get survey research back that contains different ranges — say $20–$35K, $35–$50K, and so on — you can't effectively line up the survey results with the data you have on hand. This sort of misalignment of data is actually pretty common. But it's easy to avoid if you get involved up front.

Sizing your audience

By focusing your attention one whether customers share key traits, you also gain some flexibility in the number of people you contact. If your budget is limited, for example, you may want to tighten some of your audience selection criteria to produce fewer contacts.

For example, including customers with household incomes above $50K may produce too many names for you to mail. Increasing this threshold will naturally reduce the number of names in your mail file.

Your set of selection criteria can become quite complex. You may want to consider such criteria as the following:

- ✔ Age
- ✔ Income
- ✔ Family size
- ✔ Home value
- ✔ Geography

You can also use a host of other information in selecting your audience. In Chapter 7, I describe several common types of data that can be used to identify useful customer traits. You choose some threshold or range for each of these *variables*, which qualifies a customer to be included in your mailing.

It's often very helpful to understand how each of these variables affects the size of your mail file. An easy way to do this is to produce a report that shows how much the target audience shrinks as each individual variable is considered. This is known as a *waterfall report*. Table 2-1 is a simple example of such a report.

Table 2-1	A Basic Waterfall Report		
Selection rule	*Excluded Contacts*	*% Excluded*	*Included Contacts*
Greater metro region zip codes		n/a	400,000
Household income over $50K	200,000	50	200,000
Age at least 25 years	40,000	20	160,000
Children present in household	70,000	44	90,000
Final target audience size			90,000

Waterfall reports help you understand which of your selection criteria exclude the most customers. They also help you see which criteria are really not excluding anyone and might be candidates for more restrictive thresholds.

There will be times when your selection criteria produce an audience smaller than you would have liked. You may have a budget that assumes 100,000 contacts, but you only find 50,000 customers who fit the profile you're looking for. You may be tempted to expand the audience by loosening some of your thresholds.

Tread carefully here. If you set your thresholds based on a solid understanding of your customers, then loosening the thresholds will reduce your response rates. Just mailing to a larger audience may not significantly increase the overall effectiveness of your campaign. Consider other ways to use the extra budget money. You may find that first-class postage, a higher quality mail piece, or even spending your money on a different campaign better serves your goals.

Crafting Your Offer

Your database probably has less to say about this component of your campaign than it does about the other three. Often what you are promoting and the discount, if any, are already defined by the time you are asked to execute a campaign. Pricing is beyond the scope of this book, but I'll mention a couple ways in which your database can help.

For one thing, you're in a position to understand price sensitivity. Some customers always wait for discounts or sales. Others tend to buy either on impulse or when they need something. Your database can help in deciding when and if a discounted offer is really necessary.

Your database can also help in defining the appropriate call to action. Knowing that a customer typically buys online, for example, means you should probably be directing them to your website.

It's always tempting for businesses to try to drive customers to purchase points that are less costly. Banks would rather you use their online services than walk into a branch, for example. But changing established customer behaviors is extremely difficult to do and impossible to do quickly. In the world of database marketing, it's generally a good idea to go with the flow and send your customers where they are already comfortable. At least give them that option.

Talking Directly to Your Customer: Using Data to Tailor Your Message

You spent a great deal of time and effort understanding and selecting your target audience. You can use that insight in crafting a message that resonates with your customer. I only hint here at the ways in which your data can help you craft messages — see Chapter 12 for much more on this. The simplest way to do this is to use your selection criteria in your message. If you're targeting families with young children, for example, mention children in your message or include them in your imagery. If you're targeting customers in a particular geographic region, use that fact in your message. Tell people from the panhandle that you "Don't mess with Texas."

It's not necessary to talk to everyone the same way. You can have several different versions of your message. Your target audience may have several traits in common, but they don't have everything in common. Look beyond just your selection criteria for information about your customers that might help you get through to them.

If you're marketing baby supplies like bottles and pacifiers, you may find that your primary target audience is women in their 20s and 30s. But you may also find that it's useful to distinguish between women who are buying these supplies for their own children and women who are buying them as baby shower gifts for their friends and colleagues. The latter group may be much more willing to buy higher-end, more expensive products, for example. By taking into account marital status and presence of children, you can fashion offers and messages that resonate differently with the two groups.

Taking versions to the extreme, it's also possible to craft messages that are completely customized down to the level of the individual you're speaking to. Include specific details about the last product they bought. Mention the date of their last stay at one of your hotels. Digital printing and the world of e-mail make this sort of customization increasingly easy and affordable. I address this topic in more detail in Chapter 12. The marketing channel you use is also important. When selecting a marketing channel, looking at your campaign history is important. Simply put, check to see who has responded to direct mail or e-mail in the past. As I discuss in Chapter 4, you can even encourage your customers to tell you how to contact them.

Don't Sell Snow Shovels in July: Timing Your Message

Message timing depends on a couple of different factors. Seasonality is a big one. You want to be marketing products to your customers when they actually need them. Not selling snow shovels in July, at least in most places, may seem obvious. But seasonality may not always be so obvious.

Christmas specialty stores puzzled me for years. How could these places stay open all year around? Isn't Christmas the ultimate seasonal marketing opportunity? It finally dawned on me that I almost always ran across these stores when I was on vacation, usually at a very touristy destination.

The attraction of these stores has as much to do with preserving the memory of a vacation as it does with Christmas. It's not the holiday season that makes them relevant — it's the timing of the customer's vacation. Another factor to consider is how long it takes your customer to make a purchase decision. As mentioned earlier in this chapter, impulse buys require far less lead time than international vacations do.

Understanding how your customers make purchase decisions is a popular topic for survey research. You can also learn something from looking at past campaigns to see how long it took for people to respond. You can actually get quite sophisticated in timing your campaigns. In Chapter 10, I talk more about some ways to let your database choose the timing for you.

Using Database Marketing Effectively: The Tactical Advantage

Database marketing campaigns are rarely done in a vacuum. Your company has marketing campaigns on TV and radio and in magazines and various other places. Each of these campaigns has an audience, offer, message, and in-market date. These campaigns all have slightly different purposes and may reach different audiences.

Your database marketing campaigns need to be coordinated with your company's wider marketing efforts. Your brand is most effective if it's represented consistently. You don't want your database marketing offer to be undercut by an offer being advertised on TV. Ideally, your company's overall marketing strategy should be reinforced across your entire media presence.

That said, there are some things that database marketing is particularly good at. You have insight into what individual customers are doing. This insight gives you a powerful tactical advantage over broader advertising campaigns.

Customer-retention tactics

You can lose customers in a number of different ways. They move out of your company's footprint. They have a bad experience and walk out in a huff. A product wears out, and they replace it with your competitor's product. They make a reservation and then cancel it.

In many cases, your database signals that a customer is about to leave. The customer may have logged a complaint. You know when the customer bought a particular product and when the product needs to be replaced. This advanced knowledge gives you the opportunity to intervene before the fact.

You can contact the customer to address the complaint. You can communicate about the latest and greatest replacement for the one that's wearing out. Chapter 10 gives some more detailed examples of customer-retention tactics.

Cross-sell tactics

If you've ever bought anything online, you're familiar with the "People who bought that also bought this" pitch. This is a classic example of *cross-selling*. The basic idea is that there are natural product bundles: pen and paper, beer and peanuts, airline tickets and hotel reservations. When I read a book that I enjoy, I frequently proceed to find everything else the author has ever written.

By analyzing your past purchase data, you can identify naturally occurring product bundles. This is a particularly powerful technique in consumer goods industries. Even a specialty retail store, such as a pet store, has a wide array of products. Knowing that someone bought a dog collar or a litter box or a ferret cage is powerful information that can predict what they're likely to buy in the future. Once you understand your product bundles, you can put that knowledge to work by monitoring future purchases. When a customer purchases a product that's part of a bundle, you offer them other products in that bundle.

Product bundles aren't unique to consumer goods industries. People often open bank accounts in bundles — an overdraft protection line of credit with a checking account, for example. Insurance companies often bundle auto and homeowners policies together.

Any industry that offers an array of products can benefit from understanding their product bundles. Cross-selling to customers who buy into these bundles is an effective way to increase sales. And it all starts with your database.

Upsell tactics

Many companies have similar products that are differentiated by price or quality. Automobile companies make compact cars and luxury sedans and everything in between. Airlines sell coach, business class, and first-class tickets. The butcher shop sells everything from ground chuck to filet mignon.

Naturally, you'd like to sell as many of your higher-end (more expensive) products as you can. If you recognize that a customer is interested in one of your products, you can often entice them to buy one that's a little higher grade. This is known as *upselling*.

Upselling works because you already have a willing purchaser. The customer has already become resigned to paying a given amount for a product. This allows you to focus the customer on the difference in price between one product and another. A customer may not initially be inclined to pay $16.99 a pound for filet mignon. But if that customer is already inclined to pay $12.99 a pound for a strip steak, you can focus on the relatively small $4 difference.

The automobile industry understands this concept very well. It's the reason that virtually every large auto manufacturer makes cars across a broad spectrum of price ranges. And the difference in price between one model and the next higher one is generally pretty small.

My wife is fanatical about taking care of her car. She takes it to the dealership religiously to have the scheduled service done. Every time, they give her a loaner car for the day, and that car is always a step or two higher in quality than the one she drives. They know she'll eventually by a new car, and they want the higher-end model on her mind when she does. They're grooming her for the eventual upsell.

By understanding the past purchase behavior of your customers, you put yourself in a position to know how far up the product scale you can move them. You're probably not going to move them from a two-door compact to a high-performance luxury sedan. But you may be able to move them from a two-door to a four-door. I discuss database marketing upsell tactics in more detail in Chapter 10.

Beyond Mass Mailings: More Sophisticated Campaigns

So far in this chapter, I've been discussing database marketing as if every campaign involves a simple mail drop. You actually have a great deal more flexibility in how you structure your campaign. A campaign can have several stages. It can use multiple channels. You can even set up a campaign to run continuously.

Communication streams

I've done a fair bit of college teaching over the years. It's been drilled into me by my mentors that students won't really absorb a concept until they've heard it several times. Three seems to be the magic number, I'm told. A similar idea applies in marketing. It may be necessary to communicate more than once with a customer to really get the message through. This is one reason why, with the exception of certain Super Bowl commercials, TV ads run more than once.

The idea is also valid in database marketing. It's sometimes helpful to follow up a message with a reminder. I frequently get direct mail from various retail stores announcing upcoming sales. Sometimes they send coupons or an offer of $50 toward my next purchase of $100 or more. These offers and sales are all limited in time. They all expire.

But the retailers don't just mail the offers and leave it at that. These database marketing campaigns have a second phase. I usually get one or more e-mails reminding me of the offer. And often I get an e-mail informing me when the offer is about to expire.

Each of these communications has a slightly different purpose. The first is meant to inform me and pique my interest. The reminder is meant to reinforce the first message. The final, expiration-related message is intended to impress on me a sense of urgency. In many cases, this last message is the one that actually pushes the customer into action.

This type of multiphase and multichannel campaign produces significantly better response rates than a simple one-time mail drop. The multichannel part is important. Because e-mail is so much less expensive than direct mail, the later phases don't add significant cost to the campaign.

Some industries have another reason for using multistage campaigns. Sometimes products have multiple components that need to be purchased over time. My wife and I recently took a Caribbean cruise. We actually responded to a direct mail offer that offered us a discount. When we called and booked the cruise, we were told we couldn't book many of the things we were interested in at that time.

Over the next few months, the cruise line sent us a series of e-mails. One told us we could now book fine dining reservations. Another told us that spa appointments were now being taken. Yet another told us that shore excursions could now be booked. And ultimately they sent us a personalized packet that included our luggage tags and all the details of our reservations and bookings.

This whole process really impressed us. And it served to reinforce our purchase. My wife and I both know from experience in the travel industry that cancellations are a big issue. The cruise line's multistage post-booking campaign confronted our potential cancellation head-on by continually reminding us of all the great things we were going to experience.

Event-triggered messages

One of your biggest advantages as a database marketer is that you can see what your individual customers are doing. You can also tell when something about the customer has changed. This puts you in a position to recognize and act on opportunities as they arise. Messages that are sent in response to a customer's behavior or status are known as *event-triggered* messages. Chapter 10 addressed this subject in detail.

Event-triggered campaigns are typically small. They tend to run continuously. Communications are sent every day or every week. Some sophisticated campaigns are executed in near real time as some customer event occurs.

Automobile leases provide a simple example of an event-triggered campaign. The dealership you leased your car from knows when you leased it, and they know when that lease is up. In other words, they know when you will be shopping for a new car. This allows them to send you a message about their latest models, offers, and rates at the time when it's most relevant to you.

A bank may recognize strange transactions on a credit card and take action to mitigate the risk of fraud. That's a near real-time event trigger. The bank may also communicate investment information to people as they near retirement.

Event triggers can take many forms. They can be based on transactions, product expirations, changes in age or income, birth of children, retirement, and more. Almost every customer trait that you track on your database changes over time. Using those changes to your advantage is what event-triggered marketing is all about. The power of event-triggered campaigns lies in their timing. Often the window of opportunity is fairly small. By striking when the iron is hot, you can address your customers' needs in a way that your competitors can't.

Chapter 3

The Forest for the Trees: Where Is the Customer in All That Data?

In This Chapter

▶ Understanding the basic structure of a marketing database

▶ Using independent service providers to clean up your data

▶ Grouping customers into households

▶ Complying with privacy laws and standards

Your success as a database marketer is closely tied to the quality of your marketing database. Marketing databases are strange creatures in the world of information technology. For one thing, they tend to evolve significantly over time. For another, they require a good deal of care and feeding. This means that database marketing is a team effort and requires support from a number of different departments in your company.

In this chapter, I lay out some basic concepts and terminology that will help you understand your database environment. This information will also help you communicate effectively with your partners across your organization. I also outline your key responsibilities in holding up your end of the database bargain.

A Marketing Database Is About Your Customers

Your ultimate goal as a database marketer is to increase revenues through direct communication with your customers. The more you know about your customers, the more effectively you can communicate.

No matter what business you're in, you're surrounded by data. Sales data, website data, financial data, product data — the list goes on. The systems that contain this data were designed to keep your business running. Cash registers, accounting systems, online booking engines, and movie ticket kiosks are all examples of such systems. You will hear them referred to as *transactional* or *operational systems.* The idea is that they are meant to efficiently manage the day-to-day operation of your business.

What makes a marketing database different

What your operational systems are *not* designed to do is answer the kind of questions that you, as a database marketer, are asking. Your accounting department, for example, could quickly tell you how many widgets your company sold between 3 and 5 o'clock on Monday. What they probably can't do is tell you much about who bought them. That's your job, in a nutshell.

The questions that naturally occur to you are not top of mind to the folks on the operational front lines. But even if they were, the data may simply not be available to them. Operational systems tend to operate in *data silos.* This means that they only store the data that is directly relevant to their specific function.

A movie ticket kiosk doesn't need to know how far a moviegoer lives from the theater. But if you were trying to decide how widely to mail a movie ticket offer, you would certainly care. You might also care how old they are and how many kids they have. These things could affect how you might communicate with them.

What you need is a database that's organized around the customer. And that means pulling together data from all (or maybe just some) of these *data silos* and organizing it in a way that serves your marketing needs. This is the basic notion behind a marketing database.

In your discussions with your IT partners, you will almost certainly hear someone refer to the *ETL process* (see Figure 3-1). ETL stands for *extract, transform, load* and is in reality three distinct sets of processes:

- ✔ **Extract:** Pulling data out of the operational data silos. The most important thing IT will want to know from you is how often extraction should be done. For example, do you need the data every night? Or is weekly enough?

- ✔ **Transform:** Anything that is done to clean up, standardize, consolidate, or otherwise make the data ready for prime time. Whenever a change is made to the database, you should be asked to approve what is done here.

- ✔ **Load:** The actual loading of the database.

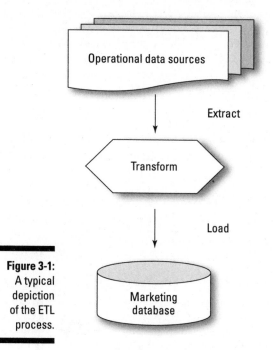

Figure 3-1:
A typical depiction of the ETL process.

Illustration by Wiley, Composition Services Graphics

What's in a marketing database

The specific data that best suits your needs is highly dependent on both your business and your systems environment. But there are some categories of data — referred to usually as *subject areas* — that are fairly universal in marketing databases. The following list gives a brief description of the most common subject areas:

- ✔ **Address data:** *Address* means more than just postal address. This category includes e-mail addresses, telephone numbers, cellphone numbers, and any other contact information that you might use. This category also includes customer contact preferences and records customer requests to opt out of communications.

- ✔ **Transaction data:** Includes what you know about what the customer has bought from you and when. It includes information about where and how each purchase was made — for example, online versus at a store. Because there tends to be a lot of it, transaction data almost always needs to be summarized to make it manageable. I address this topic in more detail in Chapter 8.

- ✔ **Demographics:** Age, income, and marital status are typical examples of demographic data. A staggering array of data is available from third-party vendors. These vendors are typically quite willing to work with you to identify the data that is most relevant to your business. I discuss the use of demographic data in detail in Chapter 7 and I also point out some companies that sell demographic data in Chapter 19.

- ✔ **Internet/mobile device data:** Virtual profiles are a valuable source of customer information. Because customers frequently create these profiles themselves, the profiles contain information that comes directly from the customer. This self-reported data can be some of the best quality data in your database.

- ✔ **Shopper data:** This category is similar to the transaction category. The difference is that these records didn't end in purchases. Browsing your website, requesting a catalog, and signing up for a newsletter are all considered shopping behaviors.

- ✔ **Campaign history:** An absolutely critical part of your database, this is a record of your marketing campaigns and who responded to them.

One thing to keep in mind is that data is being updated all the time. But not all data is updated on the same schedule. It's important to be aware of the "freshness" of your data. As I discuss later in this chapter, addresses can become outdated. In Chapter 16, I point out the importance of knowing how fresh your data is when you analyze marketing campaign results.

Your database needs to keep track of when data has been updated. This is standard operating procedure in database management. Virtually all database software provides the ability to "stamp" every piece of data with the date and time that it enters the database. These date and time stamps provide you with the ability to determine not just what's going on with your customers, but *when*. As I discuss in Chapter 10, timing your communications based on customer behavior is a powerful marketing technique.

How a marketing database is organized

Connecting all this data to a customer is not always easy. Sometimes it's impossible. Often, customer information isn't stored in your operational systems. If you work for a bank, this is not a big problem. At banks all transactions are tied to accounts, which are tied to customer records. The IRS, among others, cares very deeply that this is so. But if you work in retail — say, a grocery store — you don't have this luxury. I can walk in and pay cash for a gallon of milk, and you'll have no idea I was there.

Your ability to tie your company's data to individual customers is highly dependent on the nature of your business and the details of your information systems.

There are, however, some tricks of the trade that can help you make some of those connections. In the case of grocery stores, it has become commonplace to get customers to sign up for rewards cards. The grocery store I use gives me discounts on gasoline for every 50 dollars I spend. This makes me quite willing to let them scan my rewards card every time I shop there. Because they mailed me my rewards card when I signed up, the rewards card has the effect of tying all my purchases back to me. In Chapter 18, I divulge an assortment of tricks to help connect your data to your customers.

A marketing database is not typically limited to just data from within your company. Third-party marketing service providers can supply you with extremely useful data about your customers. I address the nature of this third-party data in greater detail in Chapter 7.

These providers are able to give you significant insight because they collect data from a wide array of sources across many industries. Definitely familiarize yourself with the major data providers and keep yourself up to date on new offerings. In Chapter 19, I point you to some of the big players in the demographic data arena.

The key to an effective marketing database is that everything revolves around the customer. The litmus test for whether to include some piece of data is this: "Can I connect the data to a customer?" You want to make the customer the star of the show. A very common and intuitive way to conceptualize this idea is illustrated in Figure 3-2. This figure, known as a *star schema,* shows the customer at the center of all the data. Data from various sources is connected to the customer like spokes in a wheel.

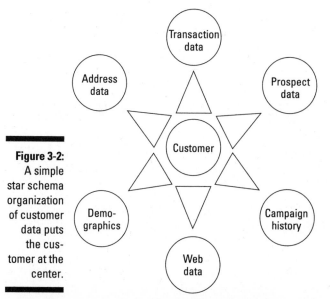

Figure 3-2:
A simple star schema organization of customer data puts the customer at the center.

Illustration by Wiley, Composition Services Graphics

Some Assembly Required: Building the Customer Record

So the customer is the star of the show. But it's not always easy to get the customer to center stage. At the most basic level, a customer is usually defined by a name and an address. Creating a *customer record* means matching names and addresses from different systems. You want to match the Elizabeth Smith of 123 Main St. who registered online to the Elizabeth Smith of 123 Main St. who signed up to receive your quarterly newsletter.

Sounds simple enough, right? The problem is that the data is rarely that clean.

Cleaning up addresses

Elizabeth may have registered as Elizabeth Smith online two years ago and mistyped her address as 123 Mane St. She may have more recently requested the newsletter be delivered to Elizabeth Smith at 123 Main Street.

It's no problem for you to recognize that *St.* and *Street* are a match. It's also fairly obvious that *Mane* is a typo and means *Main*. But you don't have the time to sort through all your address data. You need a computer to recognize this for you. And explaining the obvious to a computer is anything but simple.

Luckily this problem has been solved for you. Commercially available software packages will standardize your name and address data for you. They actually use the official U.S. Postal Service address database to identify invalid addresses. You can even purchase services that will perform these functions as data is being entered into your systems. For example, when a customer registers on your website, the software will not let them enter an invalid address.

The USPS website at www.usps.com lists software packages that it has evaluated and approved. Choosing the software that's best suited to your needs is more an IT function than a marketing function. The software is system specific. It depends on your database and operating system environment. But the good news is that you may be able to get your IT department to pick up the tab in its budget because software is essential to managing the marketing database.

Address standardization and validation are essential to building and maintaining a useful customer database. Software packages that perform these functions come with various bells and whistles for various prices. You may not need the high-performance sedan of software. But you can't afford not to have the basic model.

Updating addresses

Even after your name and address data have been standardized, you still have a potential problem: Customers move. The customer's address may not be current in all of your company's systems. In other words, you may have several different addresses that are associated with the same customer. If you're not careful, these different addresses can create the impression that you have several different customers.

I set up an online banking account a few years ago. I had just moved to Florida and had never done business with Bank XYZ — or so I thought. At some point, I had to enter my social security number, and the website immediately pre-filled my name and address data. I immediately realized it was the wrong address, but it looked vaguely familiar. Finally it dawned on me that I had lived at that address 15 years earlier while I was in college. Bank XYZ had bought the bank I used in college and were using the old bank's online banking system. That system had not heard from me since I left college.

Fortunately this problem is also easy to solve. The Postal Service maintains a database of address changes. This National Change of Address database is more commonly known by its acronym NCOA. Many of the companies that offer address standardization services also perform address updates using this database. Using an NCOA service is standard practice in database marketing.

Once you have your addresses standardized, validated, and current, you're in a position to create a central customer record. You have identified the star and are ready to get on with the show.

Marketing Is a Family Affair: Understanding the Household

Understanding a customer's household is a critical component of your database marketing efforts. Grouping customers together into "family units" is known as *householding*. In this section, I explain in general terms how this is done. More importantly, I examine some reasons why it is done.

What is a household?

In its most rudimentary (and naive) form, a *household* is a group of people with the same last name living at the same address. This definition is based on an outdated 1950s *Leave It To Beaver* view of the nuclear family. This view is clearly problematic in the real world. Many couples, both wed and unwed, do not share the same last name, for example.

What you're concerned with as a marketer is identifying domestic arrangements that involve some sort of mutual financial or budgetary decision making. Two college students sharing a dorm room do not have the same budgetary connection as a young married couple planning for their first child. Thus you would not generally be inclined to consider a dorm room a household. The young married couple's apartment, however, would be.

The nuts and bolts of householding are definitely not simple. If you don't use an outside service provider for anything else, hire one to do your householding for you. I list some of the larger providers of these services in Chapter 19. These service providers have access to data on virtually every household in the country from a wide variety of sources. They can see connections that you would never be able to spot in your own data.

Why the household is so important

One of the primary reasons for householding is to keep mail costs down. There is typically no reason to send separate marketing offers to every single person in a household. Especially when the offer involves something the household is only going to need once. For example, a family is typically only going to buy one local newspaper subscription. It would be senseless to keep offering everyone in the household the same subscription after one of them had bought it.

Generally, one communication per household is a good rule of thumb for your marketing campaigns. This rule is most important for more expensive campaigns, like first class direct mail. It's less critical for very inexpensive campaigns, such as those delivered by e-mail.

Because you're only mailing once to each household, you have a decision to make: Who gets the letter? You can sidestep this issue by simply mailing to *the Smith Family*. There are certainly cases where this makes sense. But it is also the case that such communications are more frequently discarded. Many marketers decide to flag one member of each household as the designated *head of household*. This is the person to whom marketing communications are addressed.

Contrary to common preconceptions, it has been fairly clear to marketers for a long time that more often than not, it is the wife, not the husband, who drives purchase decisions. For this reason, designating the eldest female as the head of household has become fairly common. Depending on your business, though, you may decide it makes more sense to communicate with a different member of the household.

Mailing just once to a household also reduces the risk of double counting responses. Say you mail multiple pieces to the same household, and the household actually makes a purchase. A common mistake is to count that purchase separately against each piece of mail that you sent to the household. In that case, you dramatically overstate the success of your campaign. I examine campaign evaluation in detail in Chapter 15.

The household is important for yet another reason. You are interested in understanding your customers as well as you can. A great deal of information that is available to you from outside vendors is actually household-level information. The famous Nielson TV ratings are gathered by household. Census data is gathered at the household level. Income data is generally reported at the household level.

You may decide to purchase household-level data about your customers. If so, it's important that you purchase data that's relevant to your business and your situation. The accuracy of each individual piece of purchased data varies greatly according to where it comes from. It's a good idea to compile the best data from multiple providers based on their ability to provide quality and accuracy for your unique customer base. You can do that by providing a sample of the database to several vendors and comparing the data that they provide.

Growing Your Customer Base: Prospective Customers

Your marketing database is about your customers — not just your current customers, but also your potential customers, otherwise known as *prospects*. It's not enough to keep your current customers happy and doing business with you. You need new customers to grow. You're always looking for prospective customers. Knowing who has shown some interest in your products gives you a head start in this search.

Online shoppers

Your website is a natural place to look. People do a lot of shopping online. By encouraging them to register while they're exploring your website, you can create an ongoing stream of prospective customers.

It's sometimes surprising how little incentive many people need to register on your website. You don't necessarily need to offer them special discounts. Sometimes it's as simple as offering them access to a planning tool or other convenience in exchange for the registration information. The idea is that you're trading information with your potential customer. The power of this approach is that you get more than the customer's contact information. You now know that the customer is interested in you.

My wife and I recently decided to replace our living room furniture. Because this represented a significant investment, we obviously wanted to put some thought into it. After shopping around on a few websites, we stumbled onto one that offered a really slick little application that allowed us to visualize the company's furniture in our living room.

It required us to register on their website to use it. But this registration actually served a purpose for us. It allowed us to store the dimensions of our living room on their site so that we could come back to it again and again. It also allowed us to store prospective furniture selections and layouts for comparison.

The company ultimately contacted us and set up a showroom appointment. We were already so pleased with their service that we were practically sold before we walked in. (If you're interested, check out the My Projects tab at www.ethanallan.com.)

Automobile companies employ a similar technique on their websites. They allow customers to select features and packages. Then, in exchange for their registration, they display a full color photo of the resulting car, complete with price and availability.

Many hotels and travel companies offer vacation-planning tools in exchange for registration. Maps, videos of the destination, and suggested itineraries are all examples of companies trading information with their potential customers.

In trying to generate website registrations, being reasonable about the amount of data you are trying to collect is important. Asking prospects to fill out an extensive form with their name, address, telephone number, and other personal information can be off-putting. At the very least, it takes away from whatever convenience you've told them could be gained by registering. Keep it simple. Sometimes just requesting the customer's e-mail address can be enough to get started. It's very easy to collect more detailed information when they decide to make a purchase. At that point, they need to provide that information to pay and receive shipment of their purchase anyway.

Call center data

If your company operates a call center, it can be another valuable source of information on customers' interests. Call centers are used for a variety of reasons. Customers call in to place orders, submit service requests, make payments, and complain about problems. Regardless of the reason, the call center agents are in a unique position to gather information about callers' interests and situations. They are actually talking directly with the customers.

Though it takes an investment in technology, much of this information can be captured and fed into your marketing database. It's become standard operating procedure for medium to large companies to implement call center systems designed to capture customer data. These systems also feed data to the call center agents from other sources, including marketing databases.

This type of call center system is often called *customer relationship management* (CRM) or sometimes *sales force automation.* Oracle/Siebel and SAP are two of the biggest players in this market. But there are literally hundreds of other companies that have products in the market across a broad spectrum of prices. Once again, the Direct Marketing Association's website, www. thedma.org, is a good place to start.

Some other sources of prospects

Newsletters are another useful tool in generating prospective customer lists. The principle is the same here as with web registrations. You give the customer something of value to them — namely, news about upcoming events and offers. The customer gives you their contact information along with an implicit acknowledgment that they have an interest in your product.

You may also have some opportunities to identify prospective customers in your internal source systems. The nature of these opportunities is highly dependent on your particular business and on your company's system infrastructure. But you should certainly explore these opportunities. At the very least, have some informal conversations with some of the folks who interact directly with your customers. I give some examples of how to get more useful data from your internal systems in Chapter 16.

When all else fails, you have another option: Buy a list. There are literally hundreds, perhaps thousands, of companies that are willing to sell you lists of prospective customers. Many of them will work with you to define a prospective customer profile and provide only names that meet this profile. In The Part of Tens, I point out the importance of belonging to the Direct Marketing Association (www.thedma.org). The website is a good place to find list providers.

The quality of purchased lists varies dramatically among list providers. It's important to understand where a list provider gets its data and how detailed it is. If you get vague answers to your questions on this subject, it's a red flag. Many providers brag about having very detailed age and income data, for example. But in some cases, this data is really only reflective of averages by neighborhood. All households in the neighborhood carry exactly the same description. I address this topic in more detail in Chapters 7 and 19.

One effective way to evaluate a list provider's data is to hand them a sample of names from your own database. Ask them to pick out those names that fit the customer profile you want to purchase. By comparing their results to the information you have in your database, you can get a good sense of how well they are doing.

Regardless of where you find them, converting prospects into customers is a core part of your job as a database marketer. I've found this aspect of the job to be quite fun. So much useful data can be found outside your company's operational systems. Going that route gives you the freedom to get creative about ways to engage your potential customers without needing to worry too much about impacting the core business systems. And given the pace of change in our world of electronic media, you will be continually coming up with new ideas.

No Trespassing! Respecting Your Customers' Privacy

Everyone is concerned to some extent about keeping their personal data personal. Identity theft is a potential nightmare lurking out there for all of us. You wouldn't think of storing your credit cards, social security card, birth certificate, or passport in the glove box of an unlocked car. If you're like me, most of those items are safely locked away.

Beyond your concerns about being fleeced by an identity thief, there are many things you simply don't care to share with the world. You don't publish your bank or investment records. You don't post your medical records on social media sites. Simply put, you value your privacy.

Your customers feel the same way that you do about their personal data. It's your responsibility to be your customer's advocate with respect to these concerns. You should treat your customer's personal data with the same respect that you treat your own.

Protecting customer data

Your customer data is a valuable corporate asset. You need to make sure that security measures are in place to protect that asset. Doing so is to some extent a technical exercise. But hacking into your computers system isn't the only, or even the most common, way for security to be breached.

Using technology to protect customer data

In part, data security means ensuring that technical measures are in place to prevent your customer data from unauthorized access. Your IT department will help a great deal in this effort. Network security, database encryption, and robust password standards are all necessary tools in the effort to safeguard data.

For starters, you need to store your data on secure servers that can only be accessed by authorized users. That access needs to be restricted using the full breadth of your network security system. Passwords need to meet security standards. An employee shouldn't be able to use their dog's name as a password, for example.

Your database itself needs to be password-protected as well. Virtually all database management systems offer the ability to do this. They also offer the ability to restrict access to individual variables in the database. This extra level of restriction should be considered for particularly sensitive information like credit-card numbers or social security numbers as well as names and addresses.

Beyond restricting access to sensitive personal data about individual customers, you should encrypt this data. Even if the data is somehow downloaded, encryption gives you another level of protection against the data being misused. Encrypting this sensitive information is not generally a problem for your analysis efforts. Beyond zip codes, you aren't going to be using addresses and credit-card numbers in your analysis and reporting efforts.

You also need to encrypt any data that you share with your marketing service providers. You'll need to send lists to your mail service providers, for example. Whether you're overnighting them on a CD-ROM or sending them electronically, they need to be encrypted. Vendors will typically have secure file transfer infrastructure already set up.

It's generally not a good idea to send sensitive customer data, encrypted or not, via e-mail. It's far too easy for e-mails to be intercepted or inadvertently forwarded. Using e-mail limits your security to a single layer of encryption, which can be more easily broken than the multiple layers provided by your servers and your secure file transfer channel on top of the file encryption.

Security isn't just about encryption

It is becoming increasingly common for advanced computer security systems to be thwarted by decidedly unsophisticated means. A laptop is left in the backseat of an unlocked car while the owner picks up their dry cleaning. A memory stick is left in the break room. A printout of passwords is thrown in the trash bin. All these situations provide an opening for opportunistic criminals.

Cellphone behavior in particular amazes me. First of all, I don't think I will ever get used to hands-free operation of cellphones. Every time I see someone walking down the street shouting into the air, my first impression is that they have lost their mind. And shout they do. Why is it that people's voices go up in volume the minute they answer a cellphone?

The really amazing thing is what people say. I have heard people giving out their credit-card numbers, complete with security code, while sitting in a hotel lobby. I once heard someone give out their computer password while sitting in a crowded coffee shop.

You have a responsibility to protect your customers' data. This means ensuring that security measures are in place in your organization. It also means being careful about what you say and do outside the office. Given the effectiveness of data security measures, sometimes the easiest way for someone to "hack" your system is to steal a laptop from your car in the grocery store parking lot.

As a general rule, you should not keep sensitive customer data on mobile drives or laptop computers that you carry around. You shouldn't share passwords. You even need to be careful about who is roaming around your office. Good old fashioned con games can be the biggest threat to your data security.

Sharing customer data

There are a variety of reasons why you may consider sharing customer data with third parties. When deciding what data to share with whom, you need to be aware that consumers are getting more and more sensitive about having their personal data used for marketing purposes. And as I point out in this section, you need to communicate clearly to your customers what you're doing with their personal data. There are several different scenarios related to data sharing.

For starters, you need to share your data with vendors that provide marketing services. The companies that provide address cleansing services, householding, demographic appends, and the mail houses that execute your campaigns all need access to your data. This is just standard operating procedure in database marketing.

In large companies — particularly companies that have a variety of different business units — customer data is often shared among these different subsidiaries. Because all these business units are technically part of the same company, this type of data sharing is not particularly problematic. But be aware that customers don't always recognize all of your brands as being part of the same company. For example, many consumers don't realize that the Italian restaurant Carrabba's and Outback Steakhouse are owned by the same company.

Companies may also decide to share data with corporate partners. An extremely common example is when a company partners with a bank to offer a cobranded credit card. Many of the airlines have such programs. Here data sharing is almost a necessity if the corporate relationship is to be successful.

Finally, companies sometimes choose to sell customer data. I'm not talking here about marketing service providers who aggregate data and sell it to marketers. They're not providing data on their customers. I'm talking about selling your customer lists to third parties. This is the sort of data sharing that consumers (and legislatures) are most sensitive about.

The decision to sell your customer data to third parties depends a great deal on your business model. In my experience, most companies decide not to do this. But a growing number of companies, particularly in the digital media arena, have a business model partly based on providing marketing services based on their customer data. If you do decide to sell customer data, you need to stay up to date on legislation related to consumer privacy, as discussed later in this chapter.

Keeping your customer informed

Respecting your customer's privacy is about more than just data security. It's also about transparency. You need to communicate with your customer about how you collect and secure their data. The customer also needs to understand how you're using their data. Many companies choose to sell or share their data with corporate partners, as mentioned in the preceding section. Whether and how you do this needs to be transparent to the customer as well.

All this information needs to be well documented. What you need is a *privacy policy*. This policy should be developed in conjunction with your legal department and senior management. It should be clearly communicated within your organization to ensure that it is followed. It should also be made easily available to your customers. At the very least, your website should contain a Privacy Policy link that allows users to review the complete policy.

Privacy policies are standard practice in virtually all medium to large companies. A simple web search can provide you with a host of examples that are specific to your industry. You probably get a privacy policy update letter from some company or other a couple of times a month.

Some legal considerations

Privacy policies are often not optional, but legally required. There are several industries whose data and data usage are governed by federal legislation. And new legislation continues to be proposed. It is critical that you understand your industry's legal environment.

Differences by industry

One industry that has come under broad scrutiny by the government is the financial services industry. The Gramm-Leach-Bliley Act puts significant restrictions on the sharing and use of customer data by banks and other companies involved in consumer finance.

Another industry that is highly regulated is the health care industry. The Health Insurance Portability and Accountability Act is a federal law governing data related to a person's health care. Data on children is highly sensitive as well. There are laws on the books and in the pipeline governing the gathering, storage, and sharing of information about young people.

In addition to federal legislation, some state governments have passed laws regarding the use of consumer data. Also, if your company does business outside the United States you'll need to understand the legal environments there as well. The United States is actually one of the least restrictive — anybody thinking about using their database for international marketing needs first to consult counsel and understand the regulations.

Differences by channel

In addition to being industry specific, both existing and proposed legislation regarding privacy differs by marketing channel. As I discuss in Chapter 4, you need to give your customers the opportunity to request that you *not* market to them. Your legal obligations regarding these *opt-outs* differ according to how you're communicating. Different legislation applies to telemarketing than to e-mail, for example.

But your obligations can also vary according to how data is collected. The widespread use of mobile devices has gotten the attention of federal and state legislatures throughout the U.S. The privacy issues related to mobile devices stem primarily from the real-time location data available from those devices.

One concern revolves around transparency. Many people simply don't realize what information they're broadcasting from their mobile devices. And because location is an essential part of many mobile apps, these broadcasts are often automatically turned on. Another concern relates to the privacy and safety of children. The Children's Online Privacy Protection Act (COPPA) was first passed in the late 1990s. This law aims to limit the data that websites collect from children under 13 years old. This law is actively enforced by the FTC and has resulted in a long list of companies that have been fined for breaching it. (For more information on COPPA, visit the FTC website at `www.business.ftc.gov/privacy-and-security/childrens-privacy`.)

More legislation is brewing around mobile device data. More and more children are carrying smartphones everywhere they go. As I write this, legislation is being considered in Washington to address concerns specifically related to mobile devices and location data. These concerns are legitimate. And the need to protect children is one of the few things Americans all agree on. I will be shocked if some sort of legislation isn't passed. Stay tuned.

Develop a relationship with the lawyer in your company who is responsible for privacy compliance. But also stay abreast of what is happening in your industry with regard to privacy legislation and especially how other companies are responding to it. You want to comply with relevant legislation, but you also don't want to unduly limit your ability to use your customer data.

Privacy compliance is not the most exciting aspect of your job as a database marketer. And it's certainly not the most convenient. But it is necessary. As time goes on, signs point to it becoming a larger, not smaller, part of your responsibilities. Privacy is also not the only aspect of your job that's guided by legislation. There is also legislation governing your need to allow customers to opt out of hearing from you. Chapter 4 addresses this in more detail.

Chapter 4

Using and Managing Your Customer Contact Information

*N*ame and address data as well as other contact information play a central role in your database. You cannot communicate with your customers without knowing how to reach them. This contact information also plays a key role in bringing customer data together. An e-mail address, for example, is what allows you to associate all of a user's browsing history with a single customer. In a loose sense, that e-mail address *is* the customer.

In this chapter, I discuss some pros and cons of communicating using different channels. I also discuss the basics of managing and maintaining customer contact information. Finally, I point out the importance of allowing customers to opt out of hearing from you.

Contacting Your Customers

The whole point behind database marketing is to enable you to contact your customers. But there are a variety of ways of doing this. Tradition mail using the USPS is always an option. But you have other options as well. E-mail, phone, and text messaging are among the more frequently used options. These are usually referred to as direct marketing *channels*.

This section explains some pros and cons of the most common channels.

Mailing physical media

There are certainly times when you want to communicate with your customers by mailing them a letter or postcard or an even more elaborate package. To do that efficiently, though, you need clean and current address data. I discuss the wider importance of clean address data in Chapter 2, along with some techniques and resources for managing this data.

There are some drawbacks to communicating via "snail mail." For one thing, it can be expensive. Creative development, envelopes, paper, printing, and postage all cost money. You have many decisions to make in managing these costs. Do you pay for first class postage? Do you mail a postcard or a letter? Do you use letter stock or glossy paper to improve photo quality? How much do you personalize the communication?

Unfortunately, with respect to traditional mail, the old adage that you get what you pay for is usually true. Letters tend to be more effective than postcards. Envelopes with first class stamps tend to be opened more often than bulk mail. Personalized communications with high production quality tend to better engage your customers. But these more effective options add cost to your marketing programs.

When it comes to communicating with your customers through the post, your fundamental trade-off is between the quality of the mail piece you're sending and the number of pieces you send. Higher mailing and production costs generally mean higher response rates, but they also mean fewer customers can be contacted.

Another potential drawback of traditional mail is timing. It takes time to physically print a mail piece, stuff it in an envelope, and get it delivered by the USPS. Also, the actual delivery of the mail will be spread out over several days, depending on the remoteness of the recipient. Many of your marketing messages are quite time sensitive and simply can't be effectively delivered by mail.

Firing off e-mails

The single biggest advantage of communicating with your customers via e-mail is that it is inexpensive. In fact it is dirt cheap. You will frequently need to pare back snail mail campaigns because your budget won't allow you to mail every customer that you would like to talk to. This just doesn't happen with e-mail campaigns. I'm only slightly exaggerating when I say that I would be shocked if this had ever happened in the history of e-mail marketing.

Beware abusing the e-mail channel

Given the ease and low cost of e-mail, it can be tempting to overuse it. Your customer has graciously allowed you to communicate with them via e-mail. Don't abuse the privilege. Overcommunication is the quickest way to lose the privilege.

It's extremely easy for your customers to start deleting your e-mails. If that's too much work, it's even easier for them to relegate everything from you to their spam folder. You don't want this to happen. Obviously, you lose contact with your customer, but you have another potential problem: You don't want to become known as a spammer.

Depending on how many of your customers flag your e-mails as spam, you could end up in hot water with your e-mail service provider. Your provider could ultimately drop you to avoid damage to their reputation or even potential legal problems.

E-mail is also fast — practically instantaneous. This allows you to get time-sensitive messages out while they are still relevant. E-mail can also be scheduled and automated. This makes e-mail a very attractive way for you to distribute regularly published newsletters.

Another significant benefit of using e-mail to communicate is that you can track it in great detail. Say you send out an e-mail containing a link to your website. You can tell if and even when the e-mail was opened. You can tell whether the viewer then clicked on the link to your website. None of this information is even remotely possible to get for a snail mail campaign.

Sending text messages

Though not quite as inexpensive as e-mail, text messaging shares the timing and quick turnaround advantages of e-mail. But the biggest advantage is that text messages tend to get read. Most people are closely attached to their cellphones. This means that text messages also get read very soon after they are sent.

The disadvantage compared to other methods of communication is that these messages need to be very short. Text messages are generally no more than a few sentences or a small graphic. They're limited by what can reasonably be presented on a smartphone screen. This disadvantage is shrinking, however, as mobile devices evolve.

One way text messages are commonly used is to give customers real-time updates. My wife travels frequently — so frequently, in fact, that I often joke that I have to call her secretary to find out where she is. I actually rely heavily on text messages from the airlines to keep me informed of her flight arrival and departure times as well as any delays.

These updates are not in themselves generating business for the airlines. They are, however, serving two other purposes: They give me a reason share my contact information with the airlines, which they might later use to contact me with offers, and they get me in the habit of viewing the airline as helpful. In other words, they're the beginning of a relationship that I feel good about.

Text messages can also be used to communicate very short-term offers. Cancelled reservations are a constant problem for restaurants, golf courses, and any business with limited capacity. Texting customers on a waiting list can effectively and quickly fill the opening created by a cancellation.

Think about text messaging like this: If your message is short and time sensitive, then consider sending a text. But make sure you're following the regulations regarding the use of text and mobile messaging.

Cellphone use is widespread among teenagers and even among younger children. Just as widespread are sensitivity and concern among parents and legislators about what messages children are getting as well as what information is being collected about children. I address the issue of privacy in general in Chapter 2.

Tread particularly carefully when it comes to text messages. This channel is more tightly regulated than any other. Unlike most other marketing regulations, this channel falls under the purvey of the Federal Communication Commission rather the Federal Trade Commission. Essentially, you're required to get a consumer's permission before you send them marketing messages via text. And the FCC does enforce these regulations. For more on the text message regulation visit `www.fcc.gov/guides/spam-unwanted-text-messages-and-email`.

Using other electronic media

This section merely scratches the surface of the potential of text messaging. A host of electronic and social media channels are also available to you. Facebook and Twitter are notable examples, but new ones are appearing all the time. In fact, there is a *For Dummies* book dedicated to this very subject. To explore this subject in a whole lot more detail, pick up a copy of *Social Media Marketing For Dummies* by Shiv Singh and Stephanie Diamond (Wiley, 2012).

Dialing the phone

The practice of making calls to potential customers is frequently called *outbound telemarketing*. This term is somewhat misleading. Call centers in most companies are not engaged in marketing at all. They are engaged in either sales or customer service or both.

What's the difference between marketing and sales, anyway? A simple example can help you understand. Say you work for an automobile dealership. Your database tells you that the lease on my car is expiring soon. So you send me a letter describing your newest cars and the latest and greatest lease terms. In this letter you invite me in to the dealership to take a look. This is *marketing*. Your goal as a marketer is to get me in the door. Once I show up at the dealership, the marketing role ends. I'm then greeted by a *salesperson* whose job it is to *seal the deal,* as the saying goes.

As a database marketer, you don't manage your company's telephone sales efforts. For one thing, outbound calling is generally prohibitively expensive as a marketing channel for large volume campaigns. It involves setting up call scripts, tracking the closing rates of the call center employees, and a host of other functions. *Telephone Sales For Dummies* by Dirk Zeller (Wiley, 2007) treats this subject at length.

You do have a role in telephone sales, though, because you're the one with the customer data. For this reason you may be asked to provide your call center with at least some of their call lists. You may also be involved in managing do-not-call lists.

There may also be times when it makes sense for you to contact a small number of customers by phone based on something you spot in your database. A mistake in an order, a cancelled transaction, or some other unusual circumstance may justify a customer service call to address some particular concern. These types of campaigns are sometimes called *event-triggered* campaigns (I talk in detail about them in Chapter 10).

Though phone calls are not widely used as a marketing tool, phone *numbers* still play an important role, of course. In managing your database, phone numbers can provide useful information that links guest data together into households (I discuss householding in more detail in Chapter 2).

Don't Waste Your Breath: Allowing Customers to Opt Out

Your customers have varying levels of tolerance for marketing communications. This tolerance may actually vary by communication channel. Some people can't stand sifting through junk mail. Others are profoundly annoyed by their e-mail inbox filling up with unwanted e-mails. You should give your customers the opportunity to tell you to stop contacting them. This is known as *opting out* of marketing communications.

Opt-outs are generally collected and stored separately by marketing channel. In other words, a customer may opt out of postal mailings but not from e-mails. Standard practice and even legal restrictions on contacting customers vary somewhat between channels. Phone and e-mail communications are much more tightly regulated than traditional mail.

Because it's the right thing to do

Allowing your customers to opt out benefits you by helping to control marketing costs. The idea is that if they don't want to hear from you, they aren't going to respond to your solicitations or offers anyway. There is some debate among database marketers as to how true that really is. But it is certainly the case that you're better served focusing on customers who are not negatively predisposed to hearing from you.

When it comes to traditional mail, there is a central repository of customers who have opted out. This repository is managed by the Direct Marketing Association, or DMA as it is commonly called (www.thedma.org). Database marketers are not required to honor these opt-outs, but it is widely accepted as a good idea. The mechanics of purging customers on this list from your mail files is generally done by the vendor who executes your mail campaign. Many, if not most, of these vendors require this purge to protect their own reputations.

The DMA also maintains an e-mail opt-out repository. This repository is not quite as universally used as the direct mail repository, probably because it hasn't been around as long.

There are also a variety of industry-specific opt-out registries. For example, the major credit bureaus offer a service to suppress credit-card solicitations. Because these mailings generally get run through the credit bureaus at the last minute to check credit-worthiness, the bureaus are in a convenient position to purge opt-outs from the mail lists.

Opting out through the credit bureaus can be done in writing or over the phone. The phone number is the same for all three bureaus, 1-888-5-OPT-OUT. If you prefer to do it in writing, you need to write directly to the bureaus. Here's a link to one of the bureau pages which explains the process: `www.experian.com/credit-education/opting-out.html`

Such services are not magic bullets. Customers will still try to contact you directly to opt out. You should have a straightforward way for them to do that. Just as importantly, you should have a convenient way to honor their requests. If a customer was annoyed at hearing from you before, imagine how annoying it would be to hear from you after they thought they had opted out.

Because sometimes it's the law

Chapter 2 discusses the legal environment surrounding customers' personal data. There are also laws regarding contacting customers for marketing purposes. These laws specifically address the ability of customers to opt out of such communications. There is not currently a wide-ranging legal mandate regarding direct mail. But there are laws that specifically address telephone and e-mail channels. In Chapter 19, I discuss several resources that can help you navigate the legal ins and outs of addresses.

The Federal Trade Commission (`www.ftc.gov`) manages a do-not-call registry. Consumers may enter their telephone numbers in this registry in order to avoid telephone solicitations. Companies are legally obligated to honor these opt-outs and can face penalties for not doing so.

There are some exceptions to this law. Nonprofits and politicians (what a surprise) are exempted. There are also some exemptions for communicating with your existing customers. The basic idea is that if you're communicating about an existing relationship, then it's not really a marketing communication. The FTC site (`www.fcc.gov/encyclopedia/do-not-call-list`) has a link labeled Industry that explains the regulations in detail.

As mentioned earlier, small telephone campaigns you may want to execute could fall under this exemption. But it is important that these campaigns are in compliance with the law. Consult your legal department, if you have one. Or familiarize yourself with the details of the FTC regulations. The broader telephones sales efforts in your call center are generally not exempted.

You also should be aware of the amusingly titled CAN-SPAM law. This law has nothing to do with potted meat products. Rather it deals with marketing via e-mail. (The acronym stands for *controlling the assault of non-solicited pornography and marketing*.)

The name aside, what the law essentially says is that you have to allow people to opt out of marketing messages sent by e-mail. In fact, you have to specify in all of your e-mail marketing messages how they can do this. Most often this means putting a link in your e-mail to an opt-out site.

CAN-SPAM also addresses some issues concerning misleading consumers as to who is actually sending the e-mail. It also deals with some of the more underhanded ways that e-mail addresses are sometimes collected. You should familiarize yourself with the basics of the law. But if you're running afoul of these provisions, you're probably already aware that you are doing something shady.

You should also be aware that regulations regarding opt-outs differ dramatically by country. The United States is actually one of the least regulated nations in this regard. Canada and especially the European Union have much more restrictive laws regarding marketing communications.

It's important to understand these regulations if you're communicating outside the U.S. Unfortunately, there's no global repository for marketing regulations. Each country needs to be researched separately. A starting point for understanding the European environment can be found at `ec.europa.eu/justice/data-protection/`.

Marketing to minors is also a touchy subject. Chapter 3 mentions the COPPA law (Children's Online Privacy Protection Act) which prohibits e-mail and text marketing to children under 13. But the FTC also retains broad powers to regulate marketing to children based on their interpretation of regulations regarding deceptive marketing practices. You can read this article about how this regulatory power is applied: `www.ftc.gov/speeches/starek/minnfin.shtm`.

In addition to government regulations, you should adhere to a number of self-imposed industry best practices. Start with the Direct Marketing Association website, `www.thedma.org`, for more information. Among other things, that website provides a template for generating a privacy policy specifically focused on data related to children.

The bottom line is that honoring customer opt-outs is just good business. It helps you manage costs and improve marketing campaign performance. It also keeps you from falling into an adversarial relationship with your customers. Happy customers are much more likely to continue to do business with you.

Different Strokes for Different Folks: Understanding Customer Preferences

The flip side of opting out is opting in. A customer who has told you not to talk to them is probably not the best person to communicate with. But a customer who has told you when and/or how to contact them is a great prospect. Many companies give customers a chance to do just this by setting up a web page where they can manage not just their contact info but their contact preferences. This is sometimes called a *preference center.*

The basic idea is that you want to get the customer's permission for you to contact them when you get their contact information. After they enter their e-mail address on your website, for example, you offer a check box for them to indicate whether they would like to receive special offers or promotions at this e-mail address. If the box is checked, they are considered opted in.

Opting in versus opting out

If your company has such a website or you plan to implement one, you'll discover yourself in the middle of an amusingly (or frustratingly) persistent debate. Every marketer seems to have a heartfelt opinion on whether the check box should be pre-checked on the website. At some level opinions on this matter are somewhat subjective, like whether or not you take cream in your coffee. But there are some points to be considered:

- ✔ **The case for pre-checking the box:** You will get more opt-ins. The customer has to actually take action to uncheck the box. They may not bother or they may not even notice the opt-in language.

- ✔ **The case against pre-checking the box:** If the customer has to take the trouble to check the box themselves, then they are truly interested in hearing from you. This makes them more explicitly opted in. By implication, these are higher-quality e-mail addresses from a marketing perspective.

The crux of the decision for me comes down to how you're going to treat the unchecked boxes. If the box is unchecked, do you treat that as an opt-out? Put another way, is opting out the same as not opting in? Regulations are ambiguous or silent on this issue, so it really is a judgment call for you and your team.

Regardless of where you land on this issue, it's important that you not keep changing your mind. Transparency is important in complying with regulations. It's also important in maintaining a positive relationship with your customer. If you're inconsistent in the way you treat the customers' preference data, you run the risk of looking foolish or even dishonest.

Other types of preferences

One reason having a preference center is useful is that it helps you prevent customers from giving you their contact information and then later opting out because you're contacting them with messages they don't want.

Newsletters provide a good example of what I mean. A customer may have signed up for your newsletter when it was a quarterly e-mail. But you've since decided to publish this letter on weekly basis. The customer was fine with quarterly but is tired of hearing from you every week.

Without a preference center, the customer may have no other option than to simply opt out of all e-mail communications from you. This effectively removes the customer from any future communication. But this may not even be what the customer wants. They may well still want to hear about special discounts.

A preference center allows the customer to opt out of specific communications without completely breaking contact. You can even ask them how often they would like to hear from you.

Many large companies have another reason for using a preference center. They share customer data, in particular mailing lists, across separate corporate divisions. Take, for example, a company which runs a variety of restaurant chains. These chains are very different from each other — one may serve Mexican food, one specializes in burgers, and another is a high-end seafood restaurant. It will not be at all obvious to customers that all these brands are run by the same company.

In cases like this, these three brands may all have separate marketing departments. They will certainly have separate websites. If you're in this type of environment, you may want to consider explicitly asking customers of one chain whether they want to receive offers from the others. This information tells you which e-mail addresses you should share among the different brands.

You can make your preference center as elaborate or as simple as you like. But don't ask for any preferences that you're not prepared to honor. If you can't control how often a customer is contacted, don't create the impression that you can.

Chapter 5

Getting Your Message Out: Marketing Campaign Basics

In This Chapter

▶ Preparing a bulk mail file for the U.S. Postal Service

▶ Honoring opt-out requests

▶ Ensuring a timely and high-quality mailing

▶ Keeping track of what you've done

▶ Limiting the number of campaigns you send to a customer

Database marketing campaigns cost money. In this chapter, I discuss some ways of managing that cost, particularly with respect to direct mail. In addition to cost-management this chapter is also about quality control. The techniques that I discuss here are standard procedure in the world of database marketing.

I also address another kind of cost: *Overcommunicating* with your customers can cause them to tune out. Whether you're communicating via direct mail, e-mail, or mobile messaging, customers can and will eventually say enough is enough. They can simply ignore you. Or they can go so far as to formally request that you stop communicating with them altogether. In either case, this degrades the value of your database by reducing the effectiveness of your campaigns.

Paying attention to how often you're communicating with your customers is an important part of protecting your investment in your database.

The guidelines I discuss in this chapter can help you manage the cost, quality, and effectiveness of your marketing communications. They can also help you preserve the value of your customer database by keeping your customers tuned in to your messages.

Measure Twice, Cut Once: Don't Skip These Steps

I've known a lot of database marketers over the years. Virtually every one of them has a story about learning the hard way how things can go wrong with a mailing. In one case, thousands of pieces of mail were returned as undeliverable. In another, a typo on a postcard offered an unintentionally deep discount. I've seen offers of credit mistakenly mailed to hospitalized children.

One reason for these mistakes is that the nuts and bolts of executing a mailing are usually done by a third-party mail house. And even the most competent mail house is not as familiar with your business as you are. Just because something is obvious to you, don't assume that it's obvious to your service provider. You need to have audit procedures in place before the mail hits the post office. This section outlines the audits that should be part of your standard operating procedure for every marketing communication.

Needless to say, mistakes can be costly and damaging to your company's reputation. The good news is that they're preventable. Even in the mad dash that usually occurs when your mailing is about to drop, there are a few things you should *never* overlook. That's what this section is about.

Cleaning up your mail file

In order to manage your mailing costs, you want to take advantage of bulk rates from the U.S. Postal Service. Whether you're paying first class or standard postage, you can still reduce your postage costs by performing some of the USPS's functions for them. In particular, standardizing and updating addresses using USPS-approved procedures can significantly reduce the cost of your marketing campaigns. Any credible mail vendor can perform this function for you.

Standardizing addresses

In addition to requiring updated addresses, the USPS also requires bulk mailings to conform to certain address formatting and accuracy standards. In particular, they want to make sure that all the addresses in your mail file match exactly to deliverable addresses in their database.

You normally won't perform this address standardization in house. It's something that's generally done by your mail house. There are literally hundreds of vendors and software packages out there that meet the postal service requirements. In fact, the USPS actively evaluates and approves software and service providers that meet its standards. This formal approval is known as *CASS certification*. This stands for *coding accuracy support system* but nobody ever remembers that. Just remember: Never use a mail vendor that isn't CASS certi-fied. A list of such vendors is at www.usps.com/business/certification-programs.htm.

In addition to ensuring that your mail can be delivered, CASS-certified soft-ware corrects address errors, recognizes business addresses, and adds the zip+4 codes (the additional four digits appended to your regular zip code) to your bulk mail. All of this reduces your mail costs and increases delivery rates.

Knowing who moved

Chapter 2 talks about the need to keep addresses current in your data-base. You do that, in part, by using the USPS's mover database. Updating addresses in this way is commonly referred to as *performing an NCOA* (which stands for *national change of address*).

You may be thinking, doesn't the post office forward the mail anyway? Yes and no. If you pay for first class postage, the mail will be forwarded. But stan-dard postage mail will not.

More importantly, the USPS does not like to forward mail. It's expensive for them to do. It will not offer you bulk rates, even on first class mail, without some assurance from you that it will not need to forward very many pieces.

One simple way to do this is to address all your mail pieces to *Occupant* or *Current Resident*. But although this guarantees that all mail will be delivered, it also guarantees that a lot of it will go straight into the recycling bin on the way from the mailbox to the front door.

The other — better — way to reassure the post office is to update your mail file using the USPS mover database.

Because people move so often, you should update the addresses on your mail file as close to the actual mailing date as is reasonably possible. You don't have to do it the same day. But if you do it two months in advance, you will likely be missing many movers.

In addition to providing tools to clean up and update your customer addresses, the USPS offers some other services that you may want to con-sider. In particular, there are a variety of methods for dealing with returned and undeliverable mail. (Chapter 19 describes some resources related to direct-mail services.)

Cleaning up your e-mail file

This section focuses on traditional mail only because the standards are so well defined. Some e-mail service providers provide similar e-mail address checks and updates for your e-mail. These services have advanced well beyond just checking to see that the e-mail address ends with .com. Though the cost benefits associated with cleaning up your e-mail files aren't as great as with bulk mail, you may want to explore these services. At very least, they'll improve your response rates by preventing undeliverable mail. You can search for vendors at www.thedirectmarketing search.com.

Picking the right e-mail service provider (ESP) is a really big deal. You should consider many things. You need to insure that your messages are being delivered. You want to stay out of spam folders and off "black lists" for over e-mailing. There are a variety of technical aspects to setting up Internet domains and links that need to be considered as well. Reporting capabilities are also important. Experience in your particular industry is a big plus for a service provider. Again, the DMA website is a useful place to find vendor candidates. But you should evaluate several formal proposals before settling on a service provider.

I discuss online and e-mail marketing in more detail in Chapter 13. I discuss reporting and measurement related to e-mail campaigns in Chapter 15.

Don't contact people who don't want to hear from you

As I discuss in Chapter 3, you must go to great lengths to give people the opportunity to opt out of hearing from you. A critical step in preparing a mail file is to honor those opt-out requests. This amounts to purging addresses that have opted out from your mail file.

You may think you already did this when you pulled the mail file from your database. It's standard practice to suppress known opt-outs at the time the initial mail file is pulled. But always have the mail house or e-mail vendor do another purge before mailing. Most vendors will insist on doing it anyway to protect their own reputations.

Last-minute purges prevent a couple of problems. First, your initial mail file may have been pulled significantly ahead of the actual mail drop. This means that your opt-outs were not completely up to date when you pulled your mail file. This is particularly important for e-mail addresses. Federal law gives you 30 days before you must honor an e-mail opt-out.

Second, and more importantly, you probably don't have (or want) direct access to the national opt-out databases I mention in Chapter 3. The national do-not-call registry and the direct mail opt-out registry are maintained independently by the FTC and the DMA, respectively. They're updated constantly. The only up-to-date opt-outs you have on your database relate to customers who have contacted you directly to opt out. Your mail vendor will have access to the national databases and can suppress those names.

Trust but verify: Proofing the mail piece

If you spend any time in the database marketing field, you will send out a mailing with some sort of mistake on the mail piece. There always seems to be a mad dash as the mailing date approaches: Pricing gets changed at the last minute, someone wants to tweak the verbiage on the mail piece, and so on. All this activity causes a multitude of versions to be sent back and forth between you and whomever is executing the mailing.

Don't just trust that the correct version of your file is the one that's being printed. Send someone over there to proof the actual physical mail piece *after* it has been printed. As a general rule, it's a good idea to send someone that can proof the copy with an eye toward the business strategy which underlies the campaign. The creative development team shouldn't be doing the last-minute proofing. This step is particularly important for large campaigns and brand new campaigns.

In the case of e-mail campaigns, you should have the e-mail vendor send you a test e-mail before they mail to your list. Most large e-mail firms have systems that allow you to proof the e-mail through a number of e-mail browser views — Gmail, Yahoo!, Outlook, and so on — and also allow you to get a preview of how the e-mail will "render" or look in those different e-mail browsers.

Planting a seed: How to spy on your mail vendor

Include yourself in the mail file. Also include several other people in your company. This allows you to verify that your communication was delivered on time, in high-quality fashion, and without errors. Include a list of company employees —called a seed list — in your marketing database is standard practice. The seed list is routinely embedded in mail files.

Don't let the mail vendor manage your seed list. And don't send the seed list separately to the mail vendor. It needs to be embedded in your mail file. Why? It's not unheard of for a mail vendor to get behind on a project and decide to pick out the seeds and get them mailed first. To be completely effective, it is also a good idea to make sure your seed list includes some people the mail vendor doesn't work with. The vendor can easily search a mail file for names of the people they work with all the time.

Obvious as it sounds, you also need to make sure the names on your seed list aren't opted out. You shouldn't have a problem finding such names. Many marketers don't register on opt-out databases because they have a professional curiosity about what other companies are doing. It's also easy to set up dedicated e-mail accounts specifically for seed purposes — just don't give them company e-mail addresses.

Remembering What You Did: The Importance of Promotion History

All the fussing around you did in the first section of this chapter will have inevitably eliminated some names from your list. That means you need a copy of the final mail file back from your mail vendor. Otherwise, you won't really know who was mailed.

If your database is well designed, this is typically a pretty easy process. The basic idea is that every customer has a unique customer number or customer ID in your database. Include these customer numbers in the initial file that you send to the mail vendor. The vendor can then simply send you back a list of customer numbers that made the final mail file.

It's about more than just who you mailed

The presence of customer IDs makes it extremely easy to integrate the final mail list back into your database. You don't need to do a complicated name and address match and take into account updated addresses. The customer ID is persistent, meaning it doesn't change as customer contact information is updated. You can perform a clean and simple match based on this ID.

Matching back to your database is important because you care about more than just who was mailed. You care about *what* was mailed, *when,* and *why.* This *promotion history* can be stored on your database at the individual customer level. Doing that allows you to evaluate and compare different offers, messages, and targeting strategies. It also lets you manage the frequency with which you contact your customers.

Recall the seed list mentioned in the previous section? As I mentioned, keeping track of which customers are seeds is not something you want the vendor to do — you don't want them to know. But you also want to be able to exclude these seed names when it comes time to evaluate campaign performance. Your promotion history file is a perfect place to flag these seeds.

Many database marketing campaigns use different messages or offers for different groups of customers. A cruise line, for example, might focus on different rate categories for different household income bands. Or it might use different imagery on pieces sent to families with young children versus retired couples. These offers and versions need to be part of your promotion history.

Timing is also important. In order to clearly define what constitutes a response to your campaign, you need to know when the mailing went out. If the mailing featured some sort of special offer, you also need to know when this offer was valid.

Your promotion history is basically your only record of whom you contacted, what you offered them, and when. When deciding what you should include in your promotion history file, it's better to err on the side of including too much information. It's better to have information that you don't end up using than to want information you can't find.

Documenting your mailing

In addition to promotion history, there are some other aspects of your mailings that you will want to refer back to. For one thing, it's a good idea to keep samples of your mail pieces on file. These samples can facilitate discussions about the "look and feel" of future campaigns. They can also prevent you from re-inventing the wheel with regard to creative development and copywriting. Most companies I have worked with have large catalogs of past campaign materials.

It is also important to document in detail how you chose which customers to contact. This information is central to understanding how to refine and improve your campaigns. It also makes it much easier to repeat successful campaigns.

Make sure that the technical details of how the mail list was created are documented and stored. You very likely gave instructions to a programmer like "I want to mail customers with teenage children who have bought a widget in the last six months." The details of how the programmer actually implemented that request might be a good bit more complicated. Those details — by which I mean the computer programs that were used — need to be documented and kept. Ideally, your technical team should maintain a library of computer code that is organized by campaign.

Knowing When to Shut Up: Contact Management

My wife and I took a cruise several years ago. When we returned home, we discovered a marketing packet from the cruise line in our mailbox. It was quite an expensive packet as marketing packets go. It included a high-quality color catalog listing some available itineraries.

Nothing really remarkable about that. Except that two days later we received another one, with slightly different itineraries and dates. The next day we received a postcard with a discounted offer. The day after, an offer to join their frequent cruiser program.

My wife and I had already decided that it was a nice enough cruise, but we weren't really interested in taking another. But being the curious marketers we are, we wanted to see how long this communication deluge would go on. So we didn't even attempt to get off of the cruise line's mailing list.

That was five years ago. Since then, we've had four different addresses in three different states. The cruise line keeps finding us, so they're managing their addresses quite well. But in those five years, I don't believe we've ever gone more than three days without receiving something in the mail from said cruise line. I'm not exaggerating. Most of these are glossy, full-color pamphlets or catalogs, and almost all of them are sent first class.

It's become a running joke in our house. "Hi honey, I'm home. Where's the cruise line going today?" And I'm pretty sure that any profit they made from our one cruise has pretty much been spent on marketing by now. From the looks of things, these mail pieces must be costing the cruise line at least a buck apiece for production and postage on average. At two or three per week for five years, that works out to somewhere between $500 and $750. I don't know what their margins are, but that's a lot of money to spend fishing for a rebooking.

You can use your promotion history to prevent this type of over-communication with your customers. You don't want to become annoying. How much communication is the right amount? Unfortunately, there are no hard-and-fast rules for deciding that. A lot depends on your business and the types of communications you're doing. But surely it's less than twice a week for five years with no positive response from the recipient.

Make it a priority to develop an explicit policy regarding the frequency of your marketing communications. Such a policy, usually called a *contact management strategy,* should be a core part of your standard operating procedure. You can certainly review and refine your strategy over time. But it starts with actively paying attention to how often you are contacting your customers — and more importantly, whether or not they are responding.

There are no hard-and-fast rules for what constitutes a good contact management strategy. Your strategy is highly dependent on your industry. It also varies by channel. But there are a couple of things to keep in mind.

First, you don't need a one-size-fits-all policy. Different customer segments will have different levels of tolerance for your marketing communications. For example, you'll find that you have a segment of high affinity customers. These are customers who are very loyal to your brand. They will tolerate a much higher level of marketing communication than other segments before they tune you out.

Second, your policy can be different for different channels. Direct mail is to some extent self-regulating because of its cost (my cruise line experience excepted). But it's very easy to fall into the trap of overcommunicating via e-mail. E-mails are extremely cheap to send. And e-mail campaigns can be developed and executed quickly. But e-mails also provide a great deal of hard data on which to base your decisions regarding how frequently you contact your customers. In Chapter 15, I talk about a variety of metrics that are tracked by your e-mail service provider. These metrics track which e-mails are opened and which customers click the links in the e-mails, among many other things. This information is extremely useful in gauging the interest level of your customers.

Getting agreement on a contact management strategy can sometimes be a challenge. It is particularly challenging for large companies with separate business units that have separate marketing goals and even separate marketing departments. But if everyone is communicating with the same customers, marketing overload will cause those customers to tune everyone out.

Part II
Digging Deeper into Your Data: Analytics

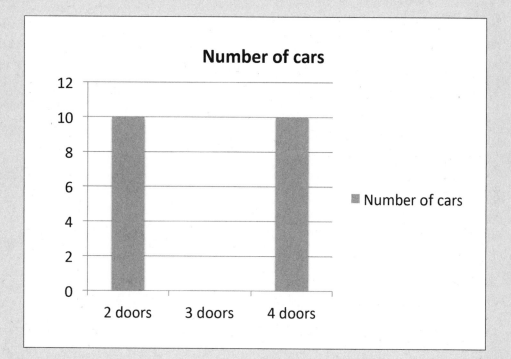

Number of cars

Find out ways data driven marketers deal with common data quality issues in a free online article at www.dummies.com/extras/datadrivenmarketing.

In this part . . .

- ✔ Get familiar with some basic ideas from statistics and data analysis and ways to use them in your marketing.

- ✔ Learn how and why marketers group customers together into segments.

- ✔ Find out how to use transactional data effectively in your business.

- ✔ Understand how to calculate and use customer-level profitability to more efficiently invest your business dollars.

Chapter 6

You're Going to Need a Geek: Introduction to Analyzing Data

....

In This Chapter

▶ Using statistics to analyze data

▶ Recognizing how your data varies among customers

▶ Understanding connections between customer traits

▶ Designing effective tests

▶ Using data to predict customer behavior

....

*T*he world of database marketing revolves around customer data. Lots of data. But data is just raw material. What you're truly after is insight into your customers' preferences, needs, attitudes, and behavior. In short, you're after *information*. Information is the result of analyzing and organizing your raw data in the context of a particular business problem or opportunity. It's information, not data, that drives decision making.

Customer data is messy. It's often incomplete. Sometimes the accuracy of the data varies from customer to customer. Data for some customers may be old and outdated.

Analyzing data and teasing information from it can be a complicated and technical exercise. It requires some expertise in the field of statistics and data analysis to do it carefully and effectively. In other words, you will need the assistance of a geek. Being a full-fledged geek myself, I use this term endearingly.

In this chapter, I do not make any attempt to dive into the technical details of statistical geekdom. For that I refer you to *Statistics For Dummies,* 2nd Edition (Wiley, 2011). I only have space to attempt to introduce you to some key concepts that will help you to communicate effectively with your technical team. These concepts will help you be clear in how you ask for analytic assistance. They will also help you understand and critically evaluate the results of that analysis.

What Are Statistics, Anyway?

Turning raw data into meaningful and useful insights is what the field of statistics is all about. A *statistic* is essentially a measurement of something. More specifically, it's a summary of several measurements. Some examples: A batting average is a statistic that purports to summarize how well a player hits. Intelligence quotients summarize the scores from a test. Political poll results summarize how a group of people answered certain questions. Stock market indices summarize the performance of a group of stocks.

The field of statistics is, to some extent, the black sheep of the mathematical sciences. A popular saying lists the degrees of dishonesty as "lies, damn lies, and statistics." I once had a statistics student nickname the course "Sadistics." She was responding to my introduction of the term *mean*, which is the technical name for a certain kind of average.

The fact is, in many cases, the conclusions reached by performing statistical analysis are just downright counterintuitive. Numerous studies show that even people who are well trained in statistics can be really bad at applying that training to real-world situations. In other words, when people try to intuitively interpret data, they are pretty bad at guessing.

The counter-intuitive nature of statistics leads inevitably to its misuse. I've heard people half-jokingly (or maybe not) claim that, given any set of data, they can make it say whatever they want it to. This is known as *fudging* the data. In its simplest form, fudging involves ignoring or excluding data that doesn't support the desired conclusion.

People have a innate tendency to fudge data when it comes to their past experiences. Horoscopes, for example, are popular for precisely this reason. People look for and remember situations when their horoscopes was right on target.

The same sort of thing happens when people report their lottery winnings. People never forget the $1,000 prize they won two years ago and will tell the story over and over again. But they leave out the fact that they've spent $20 a week for 5 years on buying lottery tickets, which works out to more than 5 times their winnings.

Fudged data is the enemy of good database marketing. It prevents you from learning what is and isn't working. When you decide to analyze data regarding your marketing campaigns, you need to analyze all of it. You can't pick and choose the results you want to see.

Despite having a somewhat spotty reputation, the science of statistics really is a science. Proper use of statistical techniques can bring some order to what at first appears to be a chaotic mass of data. Careful analysis can provide you with useful insights into your customers.

An example of the power of statistics when it's properly used can be found in the gaming industry. Casinos are associated with gambling. But the casinos themselves are doing no such thing. They understand the statistics — the odds — associated with every game they operate. And they set the payouts.

If you've ever been to Vegas, you've seen countless advertisements about slot machine payouts. They entice you with claims that they pay out something close to 99 percent of what they take in. True enough. But that means the casino keeps 1 percent. And literally millions of silver dollars are dropped into those machines.

The business of database marketing uses statistics in a similar way. The idea is that you want to stack the odds in your favor when you choose whom to communicate with. The majority of the people who receive your offer may not respond. But you use the power of statistical methods to guarantee that enough *will* respond to cover the cost of your marketing efforts and provide a healthy profit to boot.

The results of data analysis are often open to interpretation. Often the results are inconclusive. But respect whatever the data is or isn't telling you. Don't respond to disappointing results by asking that the data be analyzed differently. Trying to find what you expected to see in the data will not help you learn. And it won't improve the effectiveness of your marketing efforts. Unless you have specific concerns about the way an analysis was done, trust what your analyst is telling you.

The Average Customer Doesn't Exist: Understanding Variation

You encounter averages on a daily basis. You can watch the Dow Jones average bounce around on the ticker to your heart's content. Athletes are judged on their batting averages, average points per game, or first-serve percentage. Endless studies report that Americans eat an average of so many pounds of beef, potato chips, or broccoli per year. But what do these averages actually tell us?

By themselves, they don't really tell us a lot. As a database marketer, you're much more concerned with understanding how certain traits vary from customer to customer. Statisticians call these traits *variables*. (This is one of those rare occasions when a technical term actually reflects what it means, so enjoy the moment.) Customer age, household income, number of children, and date of last purchase are examples of variables you frequently encounter.

Variables can *vary* in several different ways. In this section, I discuss some scenarios you're likely to see in your attempts to understand your customer data. In comparing these scenarios, you'll come to appreciate how little an average, taken by itself, is really worth.

Growing or shrinking: Variation over time

Suppose you've saved up $1,000 and you're considering an investment in the stock market. Do you really care whether the Dow Jones average is at 15,000 or 1,500? The simple answer is no. What you really care about is whether it's going up or down. I'm oversimplifying your decision, but you see the point.

Trends are sometimes more important than the actual value of an average. A *trend* represents the general direction that something is moving. Trends discount small fluctuations along the way. For example, I-95 extends from south Florida all the way up through Maine. You can find places along the way where the highway travels east, west, north, and everything in between. But the general trend is northeast.

Part of your job as a database marketer is to spot trends in your customer data. Detecting a potentially negative trend early on gives you the opportunity to intervene. Recognizing a positive trend allows you to encourage it and "ride the wave."

A few years ago I was doing some work for a bank. We began looking through several years' worth of customer data. One observation that popped out was that the average age of their customers was increasing steadily. This became deeply concerning when they realized that the customer base was aging quite a bit faster than was the nation as a whole.

There were a number of alarming factors here. Obviously, mortality being what it is, it meant a shrinking customer base. But this trend also explained why deposits and loans weren't growing. As the customer base aged, more customers were on fixed incomes. And older customers also tend not to take out loans or carry balances on their credit cards. All bad news for the bank's bottom line.

This discovery lead the bank to begin actively pursuing younger customers. They targeted college students and young professionals with marketing programs. This is a case where the marketing database yielded insights that changed the entire corporate marketing strategy.

By continually tracking key customer traits over time, you can respond to trends as they are happening. Develop tracking reports and run them on a regular basis. Even just taking a monthly or quarterly look at the state of your customer base can help you spot potential problems or opportunities in time to act.

The average car has 3 doors: Variation in groups

Imagine there are 20 vehicles in a parking lot. You decide to count the passenger doors on each vehicle. You find there are seven pickups with two doors, three two-door coupes, and ten four-door sedans. Adding all that up gives you 60 doors. Divided by 20 means a mean of 3 doors per car. Clearly, this average is not reflective of the vehicles in the parking lot — in fact, not a single vehicle has three doors.

A more useful way of looking at that data is to graph it. Figure 6-1 is a graph showing how many cars have two, three, and four doors. This graph is much more informative and useful than the average. It clearly shows that the cars fall into two distinct groups.

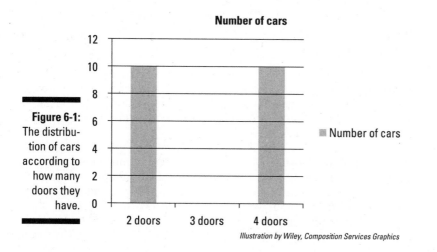

Figure 6-1: The distribution of cars according to how many doors they have.

Illustration by Wiley, Composition Services Graphics

Figure 6-1 is an example of a histogram. A *histogram* is a type of graph that shows you the *distribution* of a variable across its various values. It gives you a much better sense of what's really going on in your data than a mean does.

In your explorations of your customer data, you won't find a variable whose values are grouped symmetrically around the mean. The famous *bell curve* is a fundamental part of statistical theory, but you will never run across one in your marketing database. Always look at how the data is actually distributed.

My car door example is completely made up. But it's typical of a pattern that you'll frequently see in your data. Your geek may refer to this pattern as a bi-modal distribution. *Bi-modal* means there are two bumps in the distribution where the data is congregated. Distributions can sometimes have more than two such bumps.

Bi-modal distributions are often signals that you're dealing with two distinct customer behaviors or motivations. You may find that customers buying a particular product are largely grouped in the 20-something and 60-something age groups. In this case, you clearly don't want to be targeting the average — that is, 40-somethings. But you can develop separate marketing strategies for the two groups that reflect their differences.

Misleading averages: Wide variation

You will run across situations where your data distribution seems to go on forever. Income data is like this. The vast majority of households have incomes in a fairly narrow range. Certainly, the percentage of households making less than a million dollars accounts for almost everyone. But no matter how high you go, $10 million, $100 million, even $500 million, you will still not have accounted for every single household. This situation is commonly called a *long-tailed* distribution. These distributions make averages extremely misleading. The reason is that data way out yonder in the distribution contributes a lot more to the average than data at the bottom.

A simple calculation will illustrate my point. Suppose you have 100 people making $50K and 1 person making $10 million. This gives a total of $15 million. That comes out to an average income of just over $148,500. This is three times what anyone really makes. And this misrepresentation is being caused by one data point.

A long-tailed distribution is one instance where ignoring data is a good idea. When performing analysis on these types of distributions, it's all right to throw out the extreme data points, called *outliers*. If you don't want to throw them out completely, then at least cap them at some reasonable level so they don't muddy up the works.

You'll find that very wide distributions arise frequently in looking at behavioral data. I recently looked at some annual pass data for an entertainment company. Some people used the pass only once. The vast majority used it less than ten times. But I found passes that were used well over 200 times.

In situations like that, it's impossible to graph the whole distribution in a meaningful way. If you group the data into wide ranges, you don't see the meaningful variation at the bottom. I illustrate this in Figure 6-2.

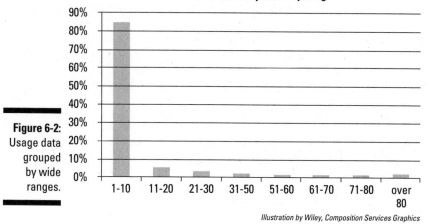

Distribution of annual passes by usage

Figure 6-2: Usage data grouped by wide ranges.

Illustration by Wiley, Composition Services Graphics

The better alternative is to cap the distribution at some fairly early value and create a create a bar for "everything else" (see Figure 6-3).

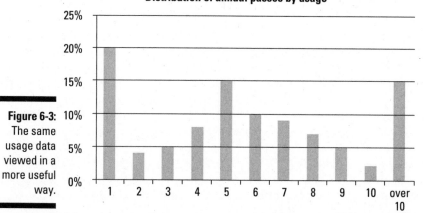

Distribution of annual passes by usage

Figure 6-3: The same usage data viewed in a more useful way.

Illustration by Wiley, Composition Services Graphics

Now you can see that there is actually a bi-modal distribution at the lower end. Lots of customers use their pass only once, and there's another spike centered around five uses.

The bubble on the right isn't really a bubble. If I actually continued to graph out the entire distribution it would go on for several pages and no page would have more than a handful of customers represented on it. But this not-really-a-bubble does give you a sense of how many customers are using their passes a lot.

This distribution suggests that, if you were this entertainment company, you'd have two different marketing opportunities. First, you'd want to get the single-use customers to come back. You'd need to figure out why these folks aren't returning and try to overcome those barriers. Second, you'd want to maximize your revenues from the second group. You might do this by communicating special events or keeping them informed of what's new. The high-use customers probably don't need a lot of additional database marketing attention.

My point here is that, in this example, you've identified three distinct groups of customers. And you've done that by looking at only one variable. Now you can dig deeper into the data about each group separately and develop marketing campaigns to address each one.

Understanding the way data varies among your customers or over time helps you to identify marketing opportunities. It allows you to group your customers together in meaningful ways.

I explain some more advanced approaches to grouping customers in Chapter 7. But first I want to look at some other aspects of basic data analysis.

Looking for Relationships in Your Data

Customer data is interrelated. It may seem at first glance that age and income represent two completely different aspects of a customer. But a relationship emerges when you look across your database as a whole. You'll find that as customers age, their incomes tend to go up as well.

Connections between customer traits

This tendency for two traits to share a common tendency is known as *correlation*. Such tendencies may be strong or weak or nonexistent. People's heights might be very strongly correlated with their mothers'. But they probably aren't quite so strongly correlated with their great-grandmothers'. They probably have nothing at all to do with what day of the year they were born on.

These tendencies may also be positive or negative. People's total debt tends to go down as they get older and pay off mortgages and other loans. This is an example of a *negative correlation*.

Understanding cause and effect

The existence of a statistical tendency does not, by itself, imply that one thing in any way causes another. I'm quite sure that there is a correlation between the number of cigarette lighters that a person buys and their risk of lung cancer. But it's the cigarettes they also buy, not the lighters, that explains this tendency. The connection between lighters and lung cancer is known as a *spurious correlation*.

An example from my banking days involves a marketing program that was designed to increase deposits in CD accounts. We started to analyze the results of that program after it had been in market for a while. Initially, we noted that the number of CDs sold since the program was in market had jumped significantly. Great news! The campaign was working.

But when we tried to calculate the profit that had been generated by this wonderful campaign, we ran into a problem. Despite the fact that we were opening all these new accounts, the overall dollar volume hadn't changed much.

After digging around a bit, we discovered that in order to support the CD campaign, the branch network had put an incentive program in place for tellers. This program, not surprisingly, rewarded them for opening CD accounts. But the rewards were based on the number of accounts they opened.

Armed with this little piece of information, we went back through the data and looked at the customers who were opening new CD accounts. It turns out that this wasn't new business at all. Rather, the volume was due to expiring CDs that were being rolled over into new accounts. The tellers were simply rolling them over into multiple new accounts. A $20,000 CD was being rolled over into four $5,000 accounts.

Our initial excitement over the success of our marketing program turned out to be unjustified. We had mistaken the spurious correlation between our marketing campaign and the new accounts for cause and effect. The actual cause was the teller incentive program.

You need to be careful about attributing cause and effect to correlations. This is especially true when you're evaluating the success of your marketing campaigns. The best way to do this is to design your marketing campaigns in the same way that scientific experiments are designed. (I touch on this subject in the next section and I address measurement in detail in Chapters 14 and 15.)

Sometimes even spurious correlations can be useful

Spurious or not, you can take advantage of statistical tendencies to enhance the power of your marketing database. You will run into situations where you know or suspect that a particular customer trait is central to understanding customer behavior. The problem is that you don't carry that trait in your database.

Here's where correlations come in. You may very well have a variable in your database that *is* correlated with the trait you are interested in, called a proxy variable. Survey research often uncovers these kinds of correlations. There is also a great deal of demographic research in the public domain — census data, for example — that analyzes connections between variables. Chapter 19 talks about some resources that may be helpful in this regard.

By replacing one variable with a different, correlated variable — called a *proxy variable* — you can essentially make use of information that you don't actually have. The proxy variable certainly won't be the same as actually having the information you want. But finding a proxy variable that's highly correlated with the trait you're interested in is the next best thing.

In the lighter versus cigarette example, it's clear that attempting to reduce lung cancer rates by targeting the sale of lighters is misguided. The lighters aren't the source of the problem. But if all you want is to *identify* people who are at risk of lung cancer, then lighter purchases would make a reasonable proxy.

Campaigns Are Experiments: Using the Scientific Approach

Measuring results is a fundamental part of database marketing. You are in a unique position to be quite precise in quantifying the effectiveness of your campaigns. You know exactly whom you contacted, when, and how. And you know who responded. This allows you to conduct your campaigns the same way a scientist would conduct an experiment.

Designing a measurable campaign: Control groups

When a drug company wants to test the effectiveness of a new drug, they don't just give it to a bunch of people and see if they respond. They design an experiment where some people get the drug and some people get a benign, neutral substance that has no effect, called a *placebo.* This placebo group is known as a *control group.*

They basic idea is that they want to isolate and measure the effects of the drug and only the drug. It might happen that 5 percent of those taking the drug develop a rash. If 5 percent of the people taking the placebo also develop a rash, then it is not likely that the experimental drug was the cause.

Control groups play a central role in your measurement process. The idea is the same as in the drug experiment. Once you have identified your target audience for a particular campaign, you need to send some of them a "placebo." Actually, you need to send some of them nothing at all. You just need to flag them in your database as members of the control group for this campaign.

When it comes time to analyze responses, you check to see how many customers from the control group responded without being contacted. This may sound silly. How would they respond if you didn't even send them the offer? But remember that your company has other marketing initiatives out there designed to drive sales. I have personally never seen a control group that didn't have at least a few responders.

You then compare the response rate of the control group with that of the group you actually mailed. This allows you to calculate how many of the responses can reasonably be attributed to your campaign.

I talk about measuring marketing campaigns in detail in Chapters 14–17. In this section, I simply introduce a couple of basic ideas related to campaigns as experiments.

Taking a sample: Selecting customers at random

After starting a new job as a database marketing analyst years ago, one of my first assignments was to do a response analysis on a fairly large marketing campaign. Taking everything they told me at face value, I compared response rates between the mail and control groups. Much to my surprise, the control group outperformed the mail group. And by a large margin.

I scratched my head and rooted around in the data for a couple of days. One thing I discovered was that response rates varied significantly by geography. Our brand was more established in some places than others. So I started asking about the control group selection. Who did it? How was it done?

Turns out, the company had recently hired a new vendor to execute its mailings. The previous vendor had always pulled its control groups for them, so they asked the new vendor to do so as well. But the new vendor didn't really understand control groups. It was asked to hold out 20,000 names in a control group, so they simply peeled the first 20,000 names off the list.

Now, one thing that mail vendors do is prepare mail for bulk rates from the USPS. This involves, among other things, sorting the mail file by zip code. Our entire control group came from the top of a sorted list. Everyone in it lived in a small number of zip codes in a region that had an unusually high response rate. This made meaningful measurement of the campaign's success impossible.

Your control group needs to accurately reflect your target audience. If it doesn't, then your experiment is flawed, and your measurements will be suspect or meaningless. The best way to ensure that your control group is representative of your target audience is to select its members randomly.

Selecting a group of customers at random is called *random sampling*. Creating random samples is a job for your technical team. Every list that's pulled out of a database is sorted by some customer trait or other. That sorting can render your measurement plan completely ineffective.

It's a good idea to have at least a general sense of how your technical team is selecting your control group. Database and analytic software, even spreadsheets for that matter, have the ability to generate random numbers. These numbers typically range from 0 to 1. To split the file in half, you simply generate a random number for each record. If the number is less than .5, you put it in the target audience. If it's greater than .5, you put it in the control group. In Chapters 14–16, I talk in much more detail about creating and using random samples.

Looking for Significant Results

Every election year we are inundated with poll results. It seems like every day there is a new poll out. Each poll is followed by a debate about how to interpret the results. Part of this debate is spin doctoring. But part of it is rooted in statistics.

The results of each poll are accompanied by an estimate of the *margin of error* associated with that poll. Essentially, this margin of error measures how significant the results really are. Fifty-one percent of respondents might say they will vote for a particular candidate. But this doesn't really mean much if the margin of error is 3 percent. Such a result is not *statistically significant*. What these results are actually saying is that somewhere between 48–54 percent of respondents will vote for that candidate. Not conclusive.

Being confident in your measurements

The error margins that are reported along with political polls are due to the fact that the polls are based on random samples. There's certainly room to question the way these polls define an eligible respondent. But the error margins are related only to the size of those samples. These samples are quite small compared with the overall population. But large or small, whenever you estimate based on a random sample, you introduce the possibility of errors.

If you flip a fair coin ten times in a row, you don't expect it to come up heads all ten times. This almost never happens. The key phrase here is *almost never*. If you flip a coin enough times, it's eventually going to come up heads ten times in a row. That's just the nature of random variation.

What does this have to do with marketing, you ask? When you run a campaign, you randomly hold out a control group. This allows you to measure how many campaign responses were directly due to your communication. You compare your response rate to the number of responses in the control group.

Because the control group was selected randomly, it is possible that by pure chance it isn't really representative of the overall audience. Luckily, you can, or rather your geek can, calculate exactly how likely it is for this to happen.

That calculation results in a *confidence level* for your response results. This is a measurement of how likely it is that your results are due purely to chance. In the coin flip example, it's a measure of how often you would expect to get ten heads in a row. Results that have sufficiently high confidence levels are considered *statistically significant*.

In the worlds of statistics and science, results need to have a confidence level in excess of 95 percent to be considered significant. This means that there is only a 5 percent chance, or 1 in 20, that the results are due to purely to chance. But because you're doing marketing, not medical research, it's reasonable for you to treat 90 percent confidence as significant. But anything lower than 90 percent should be treated as inconclusive.

Paying attention to confidence levels keeps you focused on what actually is working. It also makes your financial calculations extremely credible. You can literally say with 95 percent confidence that your campaign made money for your company.

Sizing your control group

Getting significant results is not a crap shoot. You can stack the deck in your favor from the beginning. The size of your control group is, in a sense, the determining factor in whether you can report high confidence in your response rates.

Essentially, larger control groups lead to higher confidence levels.

There is a trade-off here, though. Control groups also represent lost opportunities. Sometimes control groups need to be quite large. To the extent that your campaign is successful, not mailing to the control group costs you responses.

Your geek can help you to determine the appropriate number of customers to hold out in the control group. You will need to provide two pieces of information:

- ✔ The response rate you expect.
- ✔ How much you think your campaign will increase responses.

Clearly, both these estimates are guesses on your part. Campaign history is a good place to get a sense of what to expect. Experience — yours or someone who has executed campaigns in your industry — is really your only guide to estimating campaign response rates before the fact. Over the years, I've seen campaigns with response rates that range from a fraction of a percent to above 50 percent.

If you're reasonably close in your estimates, a control group can be sized that will greatly increase your chances of seeing significant results. I talk more about predicting in a later section.

Developing measurement plans for your campaigns is a core part of your job as a database marketer. Good measurement leads to learning, which in turn leads to better results. I talk in detail about campaign measurement in Chapters 14 and 15.

Multitasking: Combining Customer Traits

Earlier in this chapter I talk about understanding the variation in your customer data. That section focuses on looking at one customer trait, or *variable,* at a time. But the heavy duty power of data analysis really comes into play when you start looking at multiple traits at once. This is known as *multivariate analysis.*

Finding useful groupings of customers

Looking across multiple customer traits at once is not easy. For one thing, it gets complicated quickly. And the number of customers that share several traits in common gets small quickly.

You may have a lot of customers in their 20s, a lot who have kids, a lot who are married, and a lot with incomes between $40–50K. But if you search your database for customers who have *all* of these traits, you'll be shocked at how few you find.

This is a universal problem in dealing with customer data, or almost any data for that matter. When you focus on grouping customers together based on the values of particular variables, you end up with a huge number of very small groups.

In marketing, you want to identify groups, or *segments,* of customers with an eye toward their common needs and preferences. Dividing your customers into groups in this way is known as *segmentation.* Because your segments are focused on customer needs, they don't necessarily need to be completely uniform. The customers in a segment don't need to be cookie cutter copies of each other.

Chapter 7 is all about developing useful customer segments. I discuss various types of data that can be used in these efforts. I also talk about some common schemes that are used frequently in marketing.

 Because customer segments are the result of some pretty advanced analytics, it often isn't clear how the segments are defined. It may in fact be a rather complicated process to decide which segment a customer belongs in. Leave this to your technical folks. Concentrate instead on what the segments actually look like. In other words, focus on describing these customer groups. What do they have in common and how do the groups differ from one another?

One customer segment that's common to almost all companies is the high-affinity customer. These are customers who are very loyal to your brand. This high-affinity segment is identified through analysis of past purchase data. But this segment is generally far from uniform with respect to age, life-stage, and other demographic data. The high-affinity audience for children's toys includes both parents and grandparents, for example.

The crystal ball: Making predictions

Ultimately you want to know who is likely to respond to a given marketing campaign. Many statistical techniques can help you with this goal. Again, these techniques require some advance knowledge of data analysis, which should be left to your geek. But a couple of things are worth noting.

A statistically derived prediction is known as a *predictive model*. In database marketing, such models are generally used to predict responses to a campaign and are therefore called *response models*. To develop such a model, you need to have response data from previous campaigns.

As with the customer segments I discuss in the previous section, it is frequently not obvious why or how the model is making its prediction. This mysteriousness is typical of predictive models.

At some point in your life you have probably received a letter from your credit card company telling you that your interest rate has gone up or you need to start paying an annual fee. Beyond the bad news, these letters can be annoying for a different reason. It's that sentence that says, "This action may be due to one of the following...." It then goes on to list a bunch of things like late payments or high balances, many or all of which don't apply to you.

What's going on here is that the credit card company is required to tell you not only that they are taking "adverse action," but why. The problem is that the real reason they are taking adverse action is due to a statistical model, such as a credit score. And it isn't easy to sort out exactly why such a model's score went up or down.

You can certainly understand which variables the model is using. You can usually understand which ones are most important. But once everything gets thrown together, it's best to just let the model tell you what it thinks. I talk in more detail about response models in Chapter 15.

Chapter 7

Birds of a Feather Buy Together: Segmenting Your Customers

*Y*our fundamental goal as a database marketer is to take advantage of information you have on your customers and use it to your benefit. You want to understand who is likely to buy and how to entice them to do so. You want to speak to them in a relevant way. You want to show them that you understand their particular needs and are able to meet them.

But your customers are not all the same. You will find substantial variation in virtually every customer trait that you track on your database. You will, however, be able to find pockets of customers who share similar traits. These pockets are frequently referred to as *segments*.

By grouping your customers into segments, you can focus separately on how best to serve each segment. Understanding the common traits of each segment will help you to define your offer, your message, your marketing channel, and even the timing of your message.

This chapter looks at some common types of customer groupings. The mechanics of coming up with useful segments usually requires some technical and statistical knowledge, which I don't have room to address. I focus instead on the underlying data and how you might use different types of segmentation schemes.

Understanding Demographic Data

Demographics refers broadly to the statistical study of a population. What is the birth rate? How many people are married? What's the average age of the population?

In marketing, understanding the demographic traits of a particular audience is crucial. For example, the whole art of purchasing television advertising revolves around understanding the demographic makeup of the audience. TV stations have a very good sense of who is watching and when. Providing that data is precisely the purpose of the famous Nielson ratings.

You may occasionally be asked to provide customer profiles to assist your advertising department with its media strategies. Remember, it's not just about TV. Radio stations, magazines, and even billboards all have audiences who share particular traits. Your customer database can help in getting advertising in front of the right people.

The success of your database marketing campaigns also depends on your having a pretty good sense of whom you're communicating with. Demographic data is central to all aspects of a marketing campaign. Whether you're selecting a target audience or trying to customize your message, chances are good you'll be using demographic data.

Common types of demographic data

The demographic data commonly found in marketing databases falls into a few general categories.

- ✔ **Financial data:** Household income is probably the most widely used piece of financial data. In the financial services sector, sometimes net worth is more useful, although it's typically much harder to get at. Home value is another common trait.

- ✔ **Gender:** Certain products are gender specific. Gender is also used in selecting the so called *head of household.* This is the person who receives your marketing communication and is considered to be the primary decision maker. The world of marketing is not the world of Beaver Cleaver, however. The head of household is usually female.

- ✔ **Lifestage data:** Age, marital status, and presence of children are all examples of lifestage data. The number and ages of children can also be important.

> ✔ **Lifestyle data:** Lifestyle data revolves around consumption. Does the customer own or rent their residence? How many cars, boats, TVs, or motorcycles do they own?
>
> ✔ **Geographic data:** This essentially amounts to the customer's address. But there are some standard ways of grouping addresses together, which I discuss later in this chapter.

Where does demographic data come from?

You can get some demographic data directly from your customer. This is known as *self-reported data* and is generally considered to be the best and most accurate source. But in many cases, you can't get it.

That's when you turn to a third-party data provider. A number of companies will take your customer list and attach a wide array of demographic data to it, generally at the individual household level. Several of these companies have demographic information on virtually every household in the country.

At various times in my career I've done business with three of the largest marketing service providers. Acxiom, Epsilon, and Merkle can all provide customized segmentation schemes. The major credit bureaus, Equifax, Experian, and TransUnion also provide segmentation services.

These third-party databases are assembled from a variety of sources. The USPS, the U.S. Census Bureau, and other public records all provide valuable demographic information. This data is all public record data and so doesn't generally raise privacy concerns.

Tread carefully with census data. Even though this data can be attached to individual households, it does not really reflect the individual household. It actually represents the average of a relatively small group of households that are geographically close together — a neighborhood, for example. The data for a given household is the same as for their next door neighbor.

These averages can compromise the quality of your targeting criteria, especially in densely populated areas. The residents of a large apartment building on the West Side of Manhattan may have, on average, two kids and a household income above $100K. But that doesn't mean that everybody in the building meets those criteria. In general, it's best to have data that relates to specific households if you're using it to define target audiences.

Data providers also get information from their corporate partners. Product warranty information, credit-card transactions, Internet activity, and a host of other industry-specific data is combined to form a comprehensive picture of consumers. Chapter 3 discusses the notion of consumer privacy. Privacy comes into play here as well. For legal, ethical, and practical reasons, these vendors will not share the actual customer data that they have collected from their corporate partnerships. At least, they won't share it at the individual customer level. Instead they use the data to analyze your customer base. They will produce a customized set of segments specific to your particular needs. In essence, they say things like, "I can't tell you how I know, but I know that these customers are young affluent couples without children."

Some of these third-party customer segmentation schemes are quite elaborate. They break your customer base up into hundreds of small segments. Each of these segments is quite uniform with respect to its demographic makeup. The best way to understand what segmentation is all about is to look at an example.

One segmentation scheme that's quite famous among marketers was developed by Claritas PRIZM, which is now owned by the Nielson company (of TV ratings fame). One of the endearing things about this particular scheme is that the company spent a lot of time naming these segments in a clever and informative way. You find segments with names like Money and Brains and White Picket Fences. My personal favorite has always been Shotguns and Pickups. You can check out these segments along with a brief description of each at www.claritas.com/MyBestSegments/Default.jsp#. Wikipedia lists them as well in its article "Claritas Prizm."

Third-party data does cost money. Over the years, though, it's become cheaper and cheaper. It has also become more and more accurate and comprehensive. Good demographic data does contribute significantly to the effectiveness of your marketing campaigns. It's worth your time to explore what's available.

If You Have to Ask, You Can't Afford It: Grouping Customers Using Income Data

Your marketing campaigns are intended to convince people to buy a product or service. Because that involves a financial transaction, understanding your customer's financial situation is useful. Having some financial information, most commonly household income, helps you match your offers and messages with the means and needs of your customers.

Fish where the fish are: Understanding affordability

You have some products that are more expensive than others. It won't do you much good to target middle-income families with information on a $200,000 Italian sports car. As you try to identify who might buy a particular product, it's natural to ask a simple question: Who can afford it? If you have household income data in your marketing database, you can answer this question fairly easily.

A simple approach is just to look at who has bought the product in the past. Is there an income level below which very few customers bought?

Income data is normally reported in ranges rather than actual dollars. In other words, you won't see a household with an income of $37,512. You'll see that the household has an income in the $35K–40K range. This actually makes it quite convenient to look at how purchase behavior differs from one income band to the next.

If you find an income threshold below which purchases drop off, you can focus only on customers with incomes above the threshold. Marketers call this *income qualifying an audience.* It's an extremely common approach to targeting, particularly when it comes to expensive or luxury items. You need to consider a couple things when establishing an income threshold.

Often the number of purchasers drops off a little at a time as you move down through the lower income bands. This means that your response rates drop as you include lower bands. You may eventually pass a break-even point where a few additional responses won't pay for the additional mail costs. I talk more about evaluating campaign costs in Chapter 14.

For some low-cost channels, particularly e-mail, this break-even point isn't an issue. But there is another kind of cost to consider: Mailing to people who can't afford a particular product annoys them. You only get so many chances to talk to a customer before they tune you out. You're far better off talking to these customers about a different product or approaching them with some sort of discount.

Speaking of discounts, there is a flip side to income qualification. You don't want to be discounting your products unnecessarily. When marketing a discounted offer, you may want to keep high-income households out of the target audience. This is sort of a reverse income qualification. If they can afford full price, why start the conversation with a discount?

Champagne taste or beer budget: Price-sensitive customers

As I just said, when it comes to higher-income households, you may not want to lead off with a discount. But in some cases you may end up there. Some people just will not pay the initial asking price for anything ... ever. For some people, being frugal is a matter of necessity. For others, it's a matter of principle. For still others, it's almost a matter of sport.

Just last week I saw a woman load up her purse with free cookies that were put out for kids on her way out of the grocery store. Judging from the luxury sedan that she climbed into, I was pretty sure she could have afforded to buy a box of cookies.

Whatever the reasons, there is a difference between a customer's ability to afford full price and their willingness to pay it. Marketers often refer to price-sensitive customers as *value oriented.* These are customers who will wait for sales, discounts, or other deals before buying. The Black Friday people, who are in line at 3 a.m. on the morning after Thanksgiving, are classic value-oriented customers.

On the other end of the spectrum are customers who enjoy luxury goods and high service levels. They buy higher-end cars. They pay for first-class tickets. These consumers are variously referred to as *service oriented* or *experience oriented.*

When communicating with these experience-oriented customers, you don't need to entice them with discounted offers. Often, you can actually entice them to pay extra for added services. Focusing your message on exclusivity, special treatment, or enhanced features of your higher-end products may actually resonate more with this group.

When trying to distinguish your value-oriented from your experience-oriented customers, household income certainly comes into play. The higher-end consumer does need to be able to afford the higher price tags. But past customer behavior is also important. Almost anyone will take a discount if one is offered. But looking for people who bought without a discount will help you to increase your profit margins.

Generation Gap: Grouping Customers by Age

You've heard of the Baby Boomers, Generation X, and the Greatest Generation. These are all examples of what sociologists call *age cohorts* or *generational cohorts. Cohort* is just a fancy word for group. These groups have been studied extensively by both academics and marketers. That research can be very useful to you in developing your marketing campaigns.

Understanding generational differences

The basic idea is that we are all influenced by the society we grew up in. Major events and cultural shifts help shape our attitudes. The Great Depression, World War II, the Cold War, and the Vietnam War are all examples of events that define generational cohorts.

People who grew up during the Great Depression tend to have attitudes toward frugality and self-reliance that reflect the scarcity of the times. Generation Xers' attitudes toward authority are reflective of the tumultuous 60s and 70s. Their attitudes toward technology reflect the fact that they were around when the computer age took off.

There is a classic generation gap between my parents and me when it comes to banking. I don't believe my parents have ever used an ATM machine. They go into a branch when they want to get cash or make a deposit. I, on the other hand, don't believe I have been inside a bank branch in ten years.

Understanding this type of generational difference can help you communicate effectively with different audiences. For starters, it can help you to pick an effective marketing channel. Older and younger generations have very different attitudes toward and experience with technology. So called "new media" campaigns using text messaging or social media are probably not going to resonate (or even reach) older generations. But they are indispensable for younger ones.

You can tailor your marketing message toward different generations as well. Being relevant requires understanding the popular culture of each generation. If you own a music store, you aren't going to help your business by pushing Lawrence Welk CDs to 20-somethings. And you aren't going sell many gansta rap MP3s to baby boomers. Your communications need to match your inventory to the generations for whom it is relevant.

The generation gap and digital media

Generational differences are particularly critical when it comes to marketing through digital channels. When I was in junior high school, my family still had a party line phone that we shared with the neighbors. My first computer stored data on a cassette tape. Now a large and growing percentage of the population has never seen a cassette tape or a roto-dial phone. Not only have CDs replaced vinyl records, but CDs are now being replaced by smartphones as the primary medium for music.

One of the most important reasons to understand these differences is to gauge where consumers fall on the digital technology spectrum. In general, younger consumers have grown up in a highly advanced technological environment. When it comes to operating a smartphone, I'll admit I'm totally out-classed by most ten-year-olds.

In order to communicate with younger consumers, using the so-called *new media* is critical. Having a robust web presence isn't enough. Smartphones, tablets, and other mobile device are where young people are focused. Getting your marketing messages across depends on integrating with those devices. It also depends on making use of social media outlets like Facebook, Twitter, and Instagram.

In many ways, the process of buying ad placement in new media mirrors the way it's done in traditional media like TV. You identify target audiences and place your advertisements on websites, search engines, and social media sites according to who's viewing those sites. Communicating in the digital space is generally much less expensive than TV advertising. And there's a whole lot of customer information available for these channels. This information enables you to target specific audiences very effectively.

There's a wealth of information describing in great detail the common traits of various generations available on the web. Countless studies have been done, and many of those publications are available for free or simply by registering on a website. I've found the Pew Research center to be a useful resource. Pew continues to research the characteristics associated with difference generational cohorts. You can find a wealth of articles on the subject at www.pew research.org/topics/generations-and-age/.

Grandkids? I Don't Even Have Kids! Grouping Customers by Lifestage

Though useful, age groupings only tell you about broad similarities among your customers. Even within age groups, there is wide variation in people's preferences and needs. Age is often combined with other variables to classify customers by their *lifestage*. In marketing, the notion of lifestage revolves around traditional rites of passage in our society. People grow up, go to college or straight to work, get married, have kids, send their kids to college, retire, and so on.

The simplest and most common lifestage groupings make use of age data combined with marital status and information about the presence and number of children in the household. Clearly, any particular age group will vary with respect to these other two factors — it will contain both single and married people as well as large families and childless couples.

Young newlyweds, families with young children, empty nesters, and grandparents are all examples of traditional lifestage segments. But you also have unmarried couples, single parents, and countless other variations that comprise a significant portion of your customer base.

The value of lifestage groupings to you as a marketer is largely, though not exclusively, related to the unique product needs of different segments. Young single mothers are probably not going to be your primary audience for a golf-club membership campaign, for example. But empty nesters might finally have the time to play golf regularly.

When you try to define a target audience for a particular product, look at the way previous purchases are distributed across lifestage segments. Don't prejudge the groups that you think might be interested. Often you'll find surprising niche groups that are buying a particular product more often than you would have expected. As I mention several times throughout this book, surprises lead to insights. It may not occur to you to market pacifiers and baby blankets to single women in their 30s without children. But after a look at your data, you may realize that this group of women gets invited to a lot of baby showers.

On the other hand, you may find lifestage segments that do not perform as well as you would have expected. Knowing that allows you to investigate why these segments are underpenetrated and take corrective action.

When developing or customizing a lifestage segmentation that fits your particular business, work with your advertising group. Lifestage segments are a fundamental part of how TV, radio, and other media are categorized. A particular cable station may be popular with young single women. A radio station may appeal mostly to retired men. Keeping your lifestage segments somewhat consistent with the way your advertising group buys its media lets you more easily integrate your campaigns with your company's advertising.

What Would 1 Do With a Parka? Grouping Customers by Geography

Geographic data can be used in a surprising number of ways to enhance database marketing campaigns. As the title of this section suggests, some products are just not needed in certain regions. But you can also use geography to customize messages and determine appropriate campaign timing. Geography is also correlated with many demographic traits, which can be both helpful and potentially risky.

Geographic groupings

There are a variety of ways to group addresses together. The USPS uses zip codes to do just that. But the federal government also groups addresses together in a couple other ways. These groupings are related to government reporting and the census.

One common grouping is the *Metropolitan Statistical Area,* or MSA for short. An MSA is essentially a population center. They generally contain one or more fairly large cities. By fairly large, I mean at least 50,000 people. Pittsburgh and Minneapolis-St. Paul are examples of MSAs.

There is also a lower-level grouping called Micropolitan Statistical Areas that's used for government reporting. These areas are smaller than Metro areas — less than 50K but at least 10K in population. The delineations of both Metro and Micro areas is available on the U.S. Census website at www. census.gov/population/metro/.

Closely related to the Metropolitan Statistical Areas is the notion of a *Designated Market Area* or *DMA.* Be careful not to confuse this with the Direct Marketing Association. Unfortunately, the acronym DMA is used liberally to refer to both things.

Census results, economic conditions, and practically everything else that's tracked by the federal government is reported by MSA. This data is all publicly available. This means that you have at your disposal a fairly detailed demographic profile of each MSA. Because MSAs are closely aligned with TV and radio markets, these profiles are naturally of interest to marketers. The Census Bureau provides an array of data exploration tools at `http://www.census.gov/main/www/access.html`.

Census results are actually reported at a much lower-level grouping as well. They actually get reported at the *census block* level. You can think of this as a city block. It gets a little more subtle in rural areas. But these are quite small groups. There are more than 8 million census blocks in the U.S. This means that these groups typically only contain a few dozen households.

Because there is so much demographic data available on these geographic groups, many database marketers choose to have census group and MSA codes appended to their customer addresses. These codes also allow you to select audiences based on the market they live in. A variety of software packages do this. Melissadata provides geocoding services. If you're using SAS software for analytics, it also offers geocoding capabilities. Or it may be simplest for you to have the vendor that's doing your householding add geocodes to your file.

In the context of geography, a DMA is essentially a television market. These market definitions are managed (and trademarked) by Nielson. Because Nielson is the ultimate authority on TV viewership, television advertising purchases are broken up by DMA. Nielson will license data to you for a fee. To get started, visit `www.nielsen.com/us/en/campaigns/dma-maps.html`.

Knowing where to focus

Some products have regional appeal. This appeal can be related to a number of factors. Culture is a big one. A lot more grits are sold in the South than in the rest of the country.

That's not to say that you can't expand regional products to a wider audience. But the approach you take to marketing those products will definitely be different outside your core market. Expanding your market requires you to overcome an awareness gap. Everybody in the South knows what grits are. But in the Midwest, you need to answer the question "What's a grit?" You need to be more informative about what grits are and how they should be served.

Regional appeal of a product can also be related to weather. Parkas aren't going to sell in south Florida. After having lived in the South for many years, my wife and I recently spent a couple of years in Maine. Much to our surprise, none of the houses we looked at had central air conditioning. We quickly discovered why and are now happy to be Southerners again.

Geography itself can be a factor as well. Boats are not going to sell as well in the Great Plains as they are on the Gulf Coast, for example. Nor are surfboards going to be popular in the mountains of West Virginia.

It is important for you to let your data tell you where your products are selling. You may find unexpected geographic pockets where your products do quite well. This is especially true in cases where a product is associated with travel. Ski equipment is a good example. My wife has a closet full of ski equipment and she's never lived anywhere near a mountain. And a product may have an unanticipated use. I associate moth balls with storing wool sweaters. But many people in warm climates use them to keep snakes out of their yards.

Sending your customers to the right place

Customizing your messages is another application of geographic data. It's one thing to refer in your communication to "a location near you." It's quite another to actually tell your customer where that location is. The latter is far more helpful and consequently more effective.

Customizing is absolutely crucial if your business is adding new locations. Getting the word out about a new store is fundamentally about geographic targeting. By looking at your current customer base, you can come up with a profile of your typical customer. You then look for customers who meet that profile in the vicinity of the new store. In fact, the new location was probably chosen, at least in part, based on a similar analysis.

Geocoding software has gotten quite sophisticated over the years. It's now quite easy to identify households that live within a given distance of a store location. This ability is apparent on many websites. Pizza delivery chains make good use of it in directing users to the store that serves their area. Many retailers make use of it to dynamically find which store may have a searched-for item in stock.

For businesses that don't have the option of doing business purely online, it's important to understand the geographic range of their customer base. Theme parks and restaurants are examples of businesses that require the customer to actually visit their location. To market these businesses effectively, you need to know how far people are willing to travel to do business with you.

Travel destinations typically group their customers according to how far away they live. A distinction is made between customers that are close enough to drive and those that need to fly. Understanding this distinction is important because of the significant cost difference between the two modes of travel. Customers in fly markets may need to have higher incomes in order to afford the trip. The drive-market customers may be close enough to visit frequently. The marketing messages that are most effective differ between the two groups.

Timing your communications

The lives of families with children revolve around school schedules. Winter break, spring break, prom, summer vacation, back-to-school time, and graduation come and go like clockwork. This calendar dictates the timing of vacations and purchases of everything from prom dresses to school supplies.

What does this have to do with geography, you ask? Quite a bit, as it turns out. I had a colleague a number of years ago who was quite knowledgeable about geography. We were working for a travel-related business that was quite dependent on vacation schedules. He pointed out to me that school calendars are not all the same. Depending on where people lived, school could begin anywhere from early August to mid-September.

This variation has a pattern — a geographic pattern. He essentially showed me that as you move from New England down the Eastern Seaboard, the first day of school gets earlier and earlier.

This actually turned out to be a very useful insight. By timing campaigns differently for different states, we were able to hit the sweet spot in our customers' planning cycles and improve our response rates. We were also able to spread out the revenue. We started looking at spring break as five weeks long instead of one.

Many seasonal events vary by geography. Like school schedules, the arrival of winter varies geographically. And also like school schedules, winter's arrival drives the demand for a specific set of products. By analyzing the timing of the demand for your products geographically, you can position your messages to be in market when they are most relevant.

Staying Out of Trouble: Some Legal Considerations

Customer groupings, or segments, are an indispensable tool in database marketing. But they sometimes require careful handling. Income and especially geographic data can prove problematic in some instances. The seriousness of the problems is heavily dependent on your industry. It's important that you understand clearly which regulations apply to you.

Consult your attorney: Knowing your industry's legal environment

The financial-services industry is heavily regulated with respect to data collection and usage. Several federal statutes related to credit reporting and fair lending apply not only to banks but to other lenders as well. It's far beyond the scope of this book to address these regulations in any detail. It's important for you to understand, however, that these regulations don't just apply to banks.

Even if you don't work for a bank, fair lending regulations apply to you whenever you extend an offer of credit. When you're communicating to customers about payment plans, deferred payments, or co-branded credit cards, be sure to consult your attorney to ensure that your offers are compliant with federal regulations. The health care industry is also highly regulated. Consumer privacy with respect to medical records is jealously guarded by legislation and audit oversight. Practically any use of consumer data for marketing purposes in this industry should be run past your legal team.

There is also growing concern among consumers and legislators about the collection of geographic data from mobile devices like cellphones and tablets. The concerns stem partly from the fact that so many children are using these devices. As I'm writing this chapter, no legislation has been passed on this subject. But it has been proposed.

The regulatory environment related to database marketing in the U.S. is dynamic. You need to stay informed about and adapt to new legislation. In Chapter 19, I provide some resources that will help you do this. But you do need to get a legal opinion from your corporate counsel on these issues.

Watching where you tread: Potential data landmines

Chapter 6 talks about the notion of customer traits being related to one another. The technical term I used was *correlation*. Two traits are correlated if they tend to appear together. A simple example would be the presence of children and minivan ownership.

The customer groupings I talk about in this chapter are useful precisely to the extent that they correlate with customer purchase behavior. You target a specific lifestage segment with a message about your product because people in that segment tend to buy your product.

 Some groups, particularly geographic groups, can be highly correlated with income and with race and ethnicity. By simply using an income level cutoff to target an audience, you may inadvertently be introducing a racially discriminatory selection criterion. Similarly, targeting specific geographies can lead to the same result. The smaller the geographic grouping, the more correlated it is with race. In other words, individual zip codes are more correlated with race than greater metropolitan areas are. Banks are very careful about this issue because of legislation surrounding fair lending practices.

 It's important to be familiar with the entire demographic profile of your audience to avoid introducing racial bias into your campaign. Even the appearance of racial discrimination, intended or not, can lead to legal problems.

Chapter 8

Getting the Most from Your Transaction Data

*Y*ou can learn a great deal about your customers by paying attention to what they're doing. Your company's transaction systems contain a wealth of data about how customers are behaving. In this chapter, I use the word *transaction* in a much broader sense than just sales transactions. In essence, I consider any customer interaction with your business to be a transaction.

Certainly purchases are transactions. But so are returns. A phone call to your call center, registering and logging on to your website, and searching for a particular product on your website all count as transactions. When trying to make use of transaction data, you typically run into three obstacles:

✔ **Not all your transaction data is tied to individual customers.** I address a number of approaches to solving this problem in Chapter 18. Basically, these tricks of the trade amount to giving your customers a reason to identify themselves at various points in their purchase cycle.

✔ **Sheer volume.** Individual transactions tend to be fairly simple from a data perspective. A purchase transaction contains data about the product, the price, and the date, time, and place where the transaction occurred. But there are a lot of them.

✔ **Transactional systems are generally busy running day-to-day business operation.** That means the data is changing all the time. It also means your operations folks don't want you poking around their systems and slowing down the works. They typically want to restrict access to off-peak hours, which usually means nights and weekends.

This chapter covers some ways to wrangle your transaction data into a useful form. It then goes on to talk about some common ways of using transaction data in your marketing programs.

They Bought How Many? Simplifying Transaction Data

A number of years ago I was working for a regional bank. This was before the online revolution, when automated telephone banking was the shiny new technology. The grand idea was to try to move as many transactions as possible out of the branches into lower-cost channels like ATMs and telephone banking. When we actually looked at the data, though, we found branch transactions weren't going down, despite the fact that we were seeing a great many transactions coming through the telephone banking system.

On closer inspection, we found that the vast majority of these transactions were balance inquiries and inquiries about recent account activity. Not too surprising, given the limited functionality of the telephone banking system.

What *was* a little surprising was that the vast majority of these transactions were done by a very small number of customers. We expected people to check their balances once in a while. And we found several thousand customers doing just that. They were calling into the banking center once or twice a month. But we also found a much smaller group of customers who were using the system hundreds of times a month. Some of this behavior was remarkably strange. We found one customer who had checked his balance every three or four minutes from 11 o'clock one evening until 2 o'clock in the morning.

The preceding example is typical of transaction data in general. When you make yourself more accessible to customers, they will take advantage of that accessibility — sometimes to extremes. When you begin looking at your transaction data, you'll often find a small group of customers who account for a disproportionate volume of transactions. These *outliers* should be ignored when you calculate means and other statistics. If you include them in your calculations they'll distort your understanding of what's really going on with the vast majority of customers.

Chapter 6 talks about how to approach such wide variation in data. The next section discusses some ways to summarize high-volume transaction data. There are times when you will need to go back to the detailed transaction data to answer specific questions. But for the purpose of profiling your customers, summarized data is more manageable and can be quite informative.

The latest big idea: Big data

Thomas Watson was the chairman and CEO of IBM corporation at the dawn of the computer age. He's been widely quoted as saying in 1958, "I think there is a world market for about five computers." Whether he actually said this isn't clear. But the statement reflects the utter disbelief that we all tend to feel when we see the latest advances in technology. For the last 30 years, I've asked myself dozens of times, "How much further can they take this?"

IBM is currently running a series of ads touting its efforts to use data to "build a smarter planet." And it doesn't mean just any data. We're talking *big data*. How big? Imagine, for example, trying to integrate and analyze real-time measurements of temperature, rainfall, humidity, barometric pressure, and every other piece of data available from every weather station on the planet. The challenges involved don't end with just the collection and storage of this data. Trying to perform statistical analysis with this data would bring even a powerful mainframe computer to its knees.

Data is created all the time. Websites generate huge logs of browsing behavior. Photos are uploaded to websites constantly. Billions of text messages are sent daily. IBM estimates 90 percent of the digital data that currently exists has been created in the last two years.

It's no surprise that the technology and techniques used to wrestle this data into submission are being applied in the marketing space. Virtually every vendor that calls on you offering analytic services will address the issue of big data. And you should listen. There's a wealth of useful marketing information buried in those web logs. And it's impossible to hire enough people to sit down and read all the social media posts that reference your brand or products. Big data is here to stay. But you're going to need professional help to exploit it.

Just count 'em: Summarizing transactions at the customer level

Raw transaction data can be difficult to deal with. It's time consuming and complex to go back to lists of individual transactions every time you want to answer a question. What you really need is summarized transaction data.

It's certainly important for your company to understand overall sales numbers. Knowing how many widgets were sold at what price and when is central to running your business. These metrics are essentially summaries of transaction data. Your job involves understanding customer behavior. This requires a lower-level summary of your transaction data than is generally provided in accounting and financial reporting. You want to get a sense of what individual customers are doing.

One simple way of knowing what customers are doing is to keep a running tabulation on your customer record of how many transactions they performed in a given time period. If you're summarizing purchase transactions, you may also want to keep track of how much they spent.

Your monthly bank statement is a classic example of such a summary. You can certainly flip through your statement and view every individual transaction. But the front page tells you your balance, the number and total value of your deposits, the number and total value of your withdrawals, and the interest you earned.

Or consider the grocery store. I have one of those loyalty cards that earns me discounts on gas based on how much I spend each week on groceries. Every time the cashier hands me my receipt, she tells me how much of a discount I've earned. This is essentially a summary of my recent grocery purchases.

Another approach to summarization is to restrict your focus to recent transactions. Consumer auto purchases don't typically happen 200 times a year. A customer's most recent transactions are often the most informative. What web pages did the customer view *this week*, for example? In these cases, it's perfectly reasonable to store transaction details for a few recent transactions on your customer record.

Bucketing transactions into categories

Many companies sell a large number of different products. In the case of consumer goods retailers, they sell many different brands of each product. Grocery stores, department stores, and retail stores in general have thousands or even tens of thousands of distinct products in inventory at any given time. And these inventories change all the time.

Though not as extreme, this product diversity exists in other industries as well. Banks and other financial institutions have a fairly significant range of products. Six-month, one-year, and five-year CDs are all different products with different yields. Automobiles differ not only by make and model, but by color and optional accessories as well.

Making sense of product diversity requires you to simplify your view of the product world. Think product types. Most companies have different levels of summarization for their products, called *product hierarchies*. These hierarchies resemble the classification system in biology — order, family, genus, species, and so on. Using such classifications you can generate a picture of your customer's product needs that's manageable and actionable.

Banking products fall into a fairly natural hierarchy. At the highest level, banks offer deposit products and loan products. At the next level, a distinction is made between demand deposits like checking accounts and time deposits like CDs, which have a maturity date. On the loan side, installment loans that have a defined payment schedule are distinguished from revolving lines of credit such as credit cards.

At still another level down, products are grouped by product type. Checking accounts, savings accounts, CDs, IRAs, mutual funds, and so on. At this level, there are somewhere around 15 or 20 product types. That's still a manageable number of buckets. There's enough detail to get a pretty good picture of the customer relationship.

Grocery stores have a similar set of product types. When you wander through, you pass the produce department, the meat counter, the bakery, and so on. These departments form the basis for a useful product grouping. Again, there are a relatively small number of product types based on these departments.

When summarizing your products into groups at the customer level, you need to balance simplicity and completeness. You want to have a manageable number of buckets, but you also want to capture the full breadth of your business. There is no hard and fast rule for the right number of groups other than you'll know it when you see it. But typically if you get much over 20, you'll be sacrificing the simplicity you were after.

Deriving customer attributes from transaction data

In Chapter 7, I talk about the need to distinguish price-sensitive customers from those that are more focused on premium benefits. I focus on the connection between price sensitivity and income. I point out that people that buy top-of-the-line products need to be able to afford them. But I also point out that income is not the whole story. Certainly lower-income households tend to be quite sensitive to price. But there are high-income households that display a high degree of price sensitivity as well.

Determining which customers are price sensitive requires you to look at detailed transaction data. Does the customer only buy your products at your spring clearance sale? Do most of their transactions involve coupons or other discounted offers? Answering these questions takes effort and data crunching.

You'll use price sensitivity a lot in developing target audiences, offers, and messages. You don't want to have to send your geek back to the detailed transaction data every time you want to take this trait into account. So don't. Perform the analysis once and then store price sensitivity as a customer trait. In other words, create a variable that indicates whether a customer is price sensitive and store it on your customer record. This makes the information readily available, without bothering your technical team.

It's often possible to summarize transaction data into customer traits that are meaningful. If *Customers that do X* are a core focus, there is no need to re-invent the wheel every time you want to focus on that group. Treat *doing X* as a customer trait in itself and store that information on your customer record.

This way of summarizing transaction data gets you what you really need while insulating you from large transaction files.

Transaction Data from the Web

When a customer interacts with you online, it gives you access to a wide variety of information that can be useful in your marketing efforts. You obviously have access to customer purchases. But beyond that, virtually every click, search, and page view can be recorded and accessed. Furthermore, because you control your web content, you can react to many customer interactions instantaneously. In Chapter 13, I talk in more detail about how to use this data online. In this section, I want to touch on a couple of types of data that are available to you.

Data related to e-mail campaigns

When you send a marketing e-mail, you almost always include a link to your website in the e-mail. Your call to action often involves directing the customer to your website to register, shop, purchase, or go for a discounted offer. Your customer's response to these campaigns can be measured.

Your e-mail service provider will typically provide you with daily or even more frequent reports that include two key metrics for these campaigns:

- ✔ **How many customers actually looked at your e-mail.** That is, how many people actually opened the e-mail and presumably read it.

- ✔ **How many customers clicked on the link in your e-mail and proceeded to your site.** This is the more important metric. The *click-through rate* often forms the basis for judging the success of an e-mail campaign in getting the attention of its audience.

Your e-mail service provider (ESP) can provide you with a good deal more as well. To really understand the success of your campaign, however, you need to know who purchased. Click-through data can actually be tracked to the individual customer. More precisely, it can be tracked to the individual e-mail address. Your ESP can provide you with this *e-mail disposition data* so that you can load it into your marketing database for analysis purposes.

The customer may click through to your website but not purchase immediately. They may come back to your website later by clicking on the browsing history button in their browser. If they make a purchase during that session, you may want to attribute that purchase to your e-mail campaign. This can be done by tying the e-mail address associated with the purchase transaction back to the e-mail address on the mail file.

Page-use data

Another useful type of data pertains to how your customers use your website. Most websites have a large number of different pages full of various kinds of content. Your web-hosting system can keep track of every one of the pages a user views and even the order in which they view them.

Later in this chapter (and in Chapter 10), I talk about market-basket analysis and groups of products that are frequently bought together — suits and ties, for example. Much of this kind of analysis is based on purchase data. But page-view data can also tell you a lot about the groups of products that customers are interested in.

Websites frequently make suggestions while customers are shopping on the site. "Customers who bought that often bought this too," for example. The page-view data is critical to understanding how well these recommendations are performing. If no one ever clicks on the recommendation, then you know you'd better find a different recommendation.

You also have access to data about how your customer got to your site. You can know, for example, whether they came to your site from a competitor's site or from a search engine or sponsored link. You also have access to information about where they went afterwards. Many websites allow their users to perform keyword searches of their websites, and you can analyze that data — in context. In other words, you know what page the user was looking at when they searched for a particular keyword.

 Much of the page-use data from your site is anonymous. You may not recognize many of the customers viewing your page. But this data is still incredibly valuable in understanding how customers are using your website and how they shop for, and ultimately buy, your products.

Grouping Customers Using Transaction Data

Chapter 7 talks at length about grouping customers based on a variety of types of data. In that chapter, I explore the basic idea of finding pockets of customers with similar attitudes and needs. The similarities within these pockets, or *segments*, allow you to identify opportunities that are specifically relevant to customers in a particular segment. They also let you construct offers and messages that will resonate with those customers.

Your customer-level transaction summaries are useful in identifying a different type of customer segment. Transaction data can be used to develop *behavior-based* customer segments. In what follows, I give a couple simple examples of behavior-based segmentation schemes.

Finding and keeping your loyal customers

In the movie *Up in the Air*, George Clooney plays a business traveler. One of the ongoing themes in the movie has to do with how he deals with his frequent air travel. Among other things, he had set a goal of reaching 10 million frequent flyer miles. This is an extreme case. But there are customers who are extremely loyal to particular brands and companies. No matter what business you're in, you will find that you have a core segment of loyal customers, often call *high-affinity* customers.

Finding these high-affinity customers is a matter of looking at purchase patterns in your transaction data. Affinity is not just a measure of how much business they throw your way. You can combine information from your transaction data with survey research about your customers' overall spending habits. This gives you a sense of how much of their business you're getting and how much is going to your competitors. This *share of wallet*, as it's called, is a simple measure of affinity.

High-affinity customers tend to contribute disproportionately to your bottom line. For that reason, it's extremely important to keep them happy. By recognizing who they are and acknowledging their loyalty, you can protect and strengthen the relationship.

A customer my show high affinity for many reasons. Maybe they simply like your brand. There really are Coke people and Pepsi people. But the affinity may be born of necessity or convenience as well. Location and availability may play a large role in driving the customer to your business. You can't take your best customers for granted. If they're doing business with you out of convenience, then inconveniencing them may push them elsewhere.

Grocery stores have reward cards to encourage customer loyalty. Mine gives me discounts on gas based on how much I spend. I do the vast majority of my shopping at the store that's closest to my house. But, all things being equal, I'd rather shop at a different chain. The rewards card does just enough to keep me from driving the extra 8 minutes or so to my preferred store.

Airline frequent flyer programs are designed to do the same thing. Credit cards often offer cash or other rewards based on purchase volume. Almost every large retail business, from department stores to coffee shops, offer some sort of reward program.

You don't need to offer discounts and financial rewards to reinforce your relationship with your loyal customers. Simply acknowledging that loyalty in your communications is a start. Several companies that I do business with actually send me birthday or Christmas cards every year. I've always thought that this was pretty clever, given the connection to buying presents.

Another way to reward loyal customers is to offer them special access to your products or stores. You can allow them to pre-order the latest model.

I've seen department stores open their doors early to loyal customers "by invitation only." Some theme parks offer early entry to guests who stay at their hotels so the guests can avoid long lines.

An example from the credit-card industry

The credit-card industry is one that's awash in transaction data. Marketing and customer profiling in this industry depend heavily on summarized transaction data. One simple but incredibly useful way that credit card companies segment their customers depends fundamentally on only a couple pieces of information.

Everybody knows credit card companies charge interest if you don't pay them off every month. They also charge a variety of fees for late payments and various other offenses. But credit cards also generate revenue in another way. When you use your credit card to buy something, the merchant you bought it from pays a small percentage of the purchase to the card company.

Leaving fees aside, this two-source revenue stream leads to an important distinction between credit-card customers. Customers who carry balances and pay interest every month are profitable. Customers who pay off their balances ever month can also be quite profitable if they make a lot of purchases. But they are profitable in a very different way.

The "industry terms" for these segments are *revolvers* and *transactors*. Customers who *revolve*, or carry a balance forward, pay interest every month. Transactors, with a lot of purchases, generate income from merchants. If you throw in a third group comprised of inactive cards, you have a simple behavior-based segmentation.

This segmentation is really based on only a couple of pieces of information. How much interest does the customer pay each month, and how much do they spend on purchases each month? If you put yourself in the card companies' shoes, you'll arrive at very different marketing strategies for these segments.

In the case of the transactors, you probably won't have a whole lot of success with balance-transfer offers. If they're paying off your credit card every month, they're probably paying off their other cards as well. The more effective strategy is to encourage them to keep spending. This is exactly what "cash back" offers and rewards programs are designed to do.

On the other hand, revolvers may be very good candidates for balance-transfer offers. Again, the way they do business with you is a pretty good indication of the way they do business with your competitors. You can entice some of them away by offering low rates on transferred balances.

In the case of the inactive credit cards, you would probably take a hybrid approach. For these customers, the marketing challenge is to get them to use the card. Since you don't know how they would be likely to use the card, you might use both purchase and balance-transfer incentives.

Timing Is Everything: Understanding When Customers Purchase

It's important for you to understand the timing of your customers transactions. Certain products are seasonal, some products are bought impulsively, and others require time and careful consideration. Some transactions may be signals to you that you need to take action. In all these cases, knowing when the customer did something will help you to communicate appropriately with your customer.

The Christmas rush: Seasonal purchase patterns

Many retail businesses live and die according to their performance in December. When I worked for a credit-card company years ago, I was absolutely astounded at the large percentage of purchase volume that occurred late in the year. December was bigger than any three-month period combined.

But even in the consumer goods industry, seasonal patterns need to be taken into account. As I mention in Chapter 7, school schedules dictate the timing of many purchases for families with children. Back-to-school sales are a staple of the late summer, for example. Prom dresses are a staple of spring.

This dependence on school schedules extends far beyond consumer goods. Summer vacation, spring break, and other holidays are busy times in the travel industry. Test-preparation services revolve around standardized test dates. Limousine rentals and hair stylists are in high demand at prom time.

Don't forget the actual seasons. Weather affects the demand for many goods. Snow shovels, air conditioners, and bathing suits all have seasonal appeal.

When you recognize a seasonal pattern, you need to understand what's driving it. Your database marketing campaigns begin by identifying your target audience. It's not enough to recognize that limousine rentals spike in May. You need to get to the fact that it's families with high school children that are driving the demand. From there you can craft offers and messages that will help you to take advantage of the seasonal opportunity.

Transactions and seasonal patterns

Many, if not most, of the examples I just gave may seem intuitively obvious. But obvious or not, you still need to examine your transaction data to be precise about exactly when and for how long a particular window of opportunity may be open.

In Chapter 7, I talk about the relationship between school schedules and geography. It turns out that these schedules vary quite a bit from state to state. The back-to-school time window is actually four to five weeks long, depending on geography. Careful examination of your transaction data can inform the timing of your back-to-school campaigns.

You may also find some surprises when you look at your transaction data. As I point out throughout this book, in database marketing, surprises mean insights. Last summer, my wife came home one day complaining that the air conditioning in her office was freezing her half to death. I suggested that she get a space heater to put under her desk and volunteered to go buy one for her. Little did I know what I'd signed up for. Seven stores later I finally found one lonely space heater at the back of an empty shelf.

Apparently, space heaters are considered a seasonal item. Who needs a space heater in July? Well, I'm certain that my wife is not the only person on the planet who has a dislike of air conditioning. I suspect that an industrious data analyst could discover an untapped opportunity in transaction data related to small appliances.

Responding to customer behavior

In Chapter 2, I mention that some campaigns are based on event triggers. Essentially this means that a particular customer behavior triggers a marketing communication or a series of communications. Often these triggers are based on customer transaction data.

I get regular service reminders from the auto dealership where I bought my car. This is a simple example of an event-triggered campaign. The trigger is actually the date of my last service appointment, along with the mileage at that time. The dealership lets the appropriate amount of time go by and then reminds me that I'm due for an oil change or my 50,000-mile service. The timing and the content of this communication depend on the details of my last service transaction.

This sort of communication is useful in cases where the relationship between you and your customer does not end with their purchasing a product. Even after I drive my car off the lot, I still need maintenance. Vacation planning is like this as well. I often don't buy airline tickets, make hotel reservations, and arrange for a rental car at the same time, even though I may use the same website to do all of this.

Some events may trigger real-time messages. Fraud alert calls from your credit-card company happen within minutes of a transaction. Confirmation e-mails for online transactions are sent almost instantaneously.

Your customer's transactions are full of information that can inform your communications. From service calls to targeted offers, understanding what your customer is doing allows you to be in the right place at the right time with the right message.

In Chapter 10, I talk about triggered-event marketing in much greater detail.

History Has a Way of Repeating Itself: RFM Models

When database marketing was first coming into prominence, analysts developed a relatively simple targeting technique that is still widely used today. The technique was first developed for the catalog sales business. The motivation was that catalogs are expensive to print and ship, so it's important to mail them to people who might actually use them.

Recency, frequency, and monetary value: The RFM framework

The technique, known as *RFM modeling*, is based on looking at three facts about customer transactions.

- ✔ **R is for recency.** How long ago did the customer last buy from you?
- ✔ **F is for frequency.** How often or how many products did the customer buy?
- ✔ **M is for money.** Well, actually it's for *monetary value* but it means money. How much did the customer spend?

The basic idea is that each one of these factors individually is somewhat predictive of response rates. Combining them makes those predictions even better.

RFM models are developed using the summarized transaction data discussed earlier in this chapter. Transaction counts, purchase totals, and recent transaction dates are grouped into ranges. A simple RFM model might only distinguish high, medium, and low transaction volumes, for instance.

Each customer is ranked on each of the three attributes. Customers are then segmented based on their combined ranking. For example, one segment is made up of customers who fall into the low category on all three attributes. There is another segment for very recent, low volume, and high monetary value. And so on.

The number of segments gets big fast. If each attribute is split into three ranges, you end up with 27 distinct RFM groups. If you split them ten ways, you end up with 1,000 segments.

Building the model

The real insight comes when you apply these segments to customers who have received marketing campaigns from you in the past. You look at the response rates for each of the RFM segments. Typically, some segments dramatically outperform others.

Like all models, you should test RFM models before using them in defining target audiences. The standard way of testing a model involves splitting up the customers you're analyzing into two randomly defined groups.

You might be analyzing the response rates of 100,000 customers who received your spring campaign. You want to randomly split that group in half. You use the first half to do your analysis and define your high-performing segments. Then you use the second half to confirm (or not) that those segments really do perform better than the others.

You can accomplish this random split with a random number generator. Database software, analytic software, and even spreadsheets have functions that will produce random numbers between 0 and 1. The idea is that you generate a random number for each customer record. If the number is less than .5, you put the record in your analysis file. The rest of the records go into your confirmation or *test file.*

By focusing future campaigns on the high-performing segments, you can achieve higher response rates while reducing campaign costs. You should consider some technical issues when implementing any type of analytic model. For one thing, you don't want to assume that your segments will perform as well in the future as they did in the past. I address these issues, as well as the notion of testing models, in Chapter 16.

Beer and Diapers: Market-Basket Analysis

Another strategy that has been around for a while involves trying to understand what products are purchased in bundles. There are obvious product bundles. You need paper when you buy a new printer, for example. But there are sometimes not so obvious bundles. Increasingly sophisticated analysis techniques are being used to cull through large amounts of transaction data to find those less obvious bundles. This type of analysis is known as *market-basket analysis.*

Whenever the subject of market baskets comes up, you're likely to hear someone bring up a famous story on the subject. In the early days of this sort of analysis, a grocery store chain began analyzing its data to look for products that were purchased together. Much to their surprise, so the story goes, they found that when men bought baby diapers very frequently also bought beer.

I'm pretty sure this story is more urban legend than truth. I've never seen a diaper display next to the beer cooler in a grocery store. But it does illustrate the potential element of surprise inherent in data analysis. Unexpected patterns do exist and can be used to your advantage.

But grocery stores do tend to be pretty good at this sort of analysis. When I do my shopping for Thanksgiving dinner, I rarely have to actually walk down an aisle. The supplies for various traditional side dishes are all laid out at the ends of the aisles. One display has the green beans, mushroom soup, and fried onions for the green bean casserole. Another has the canned pumpkin, brown sugar, and condensed milk for pumpkin pie.

You often see the results of market-basket analysis when you shop online. Whether it's books, clothes, or appliances, you frequently get prompted with a message about what other customers bought along with a particular item. "People who bought this also bought these things..."

Chapter 9

The Good, the Bad, and the Ugly: Understanding Customer Profitability

*Y*our customers vary widely with respect to how much they contribute to your bottom line. In Chapter 9, I talk about the importance of keeping your loyal customers happy. You generally find that your most valuable customers are among your most loyal ones — but not always. You may find that you have apparently loyal customers who aren't contributing a great deal of revenue.

In trying to understand customer profitability, it's not enough to just look at their total spending. You need to take into account costs and discounts. Revenue is not the same as profit. This means that customers who buy a lot of products from you may not always be your most profitable customers.

Revenue Isn't Profit: Accounting for Costs

There's an old joke about a businessman who was so focused on generating sales that he kept discounting his products. He finally reached a point where he was selling his products at a loss. When his accountant pointed this out, he replied, "I know, but I'll make it up on volume."

You might be surprised: The 80/20 rule

Early in the 20th century, an Italian economist named Vilfredo Pareto was studying the distribution of wealth and income in society. He once famously observed that 80 percent of the land in Italy was owned by 20 percent of the population. Pareto wasn't actually claiming that this was a universally applicable split. He had developed a generally applicable formula relating income levels to the number of people above those levels. But this 80/20 split is commonly called the *Pareto principle,* or even more commonly, the *80/20 rule*.

The 80/20 rule has spread like wildfire. It's widely assumed to apply to a variety of situations. It's been linked to resource allocation: 80 percent of your time is used to do 20 percent of your work. And profitability: 80 percent of your profit comes from 20 percent of your customers.

Don't take the 80/20 rule too literally. There's nothing magical about it. The rule is an oversimplified and somewhat arbitrary formulation. You often do see a large proportion of assets being attributed to a small percentage of sources. But it isn't always going to be 80/20.

Years ago, I was helping a group of analysts at a bank dig into their profitability data. We found something like the 80/20 rule applied. But it was even more extreme. We actually discovered that the most profitable 20 percent of customers were actually generating 110 percent of the profits. This may sound absurd at first glance. But the situation arose because the bottom third or so of our customers were simply unprofitable. And not just unprofitable, they were *negatively* profitable. They were costing us more to maintain their accounts than we were earning in revenue.

When setting up a customer-profitability framework, the revenue side is relatively simple. You know what products you've sold and at what price. As long as this information is attached to individual customers, you're golden. Even in industries like banking, which have a more complicated revenue stream, the revenue side isn't that hard to get your arms around. Fees and interest paid as well as the balances that drive interest income all appear on the customer's monthly statement. The harder part is taking costs into account. You have to work closely with your finance and accounting folks to do this in a way that accurately differentiates the costs associated with servicing different types of customers.

Your accounting folks have a pretty good idea of the profit margins on each of your products. But these margins often don't take customer behavior into account. How the customer bought the product, online versus from a store, can affect the costs related to that particular customer.

To take customer behavior into account, you need to allocate many costs at the individual customer level. Finance professionals can help you determine an approach that fits your particular business model. Often they employ things like *activity-based costing* (*ABC*) and *economic value added* (*EVA*) techniques to address this issue. ABC involves distributing costs based on the extent to which various resources are used. A checking account puts a larger burden on a teller than a CD, for example. So checking accounts are assigned a larger share of the branch network cost. EVA is a technique for calculating profit that takes into account the cost of capital. In the context of product and customer profitability, *capital* means infrastructure like office buildings, computer systems, and so forth.

Allocating customer-specific costs

Many costs can be directly associated with particular customers. The cost of a database marketing campaign can be directly linked to the customers who received it. Shipping costs for an item purchased online can be linked to a particular customer. The fees you pay to credit-card companies when a customer puts a purchase on a card can also be tied back to the customer.

I recently had an alarm system installed at my house. The installation was free, as was most of the equipment. The guy who installed it for me was a chatty sort of fellow, and we got to talking about profit margins in his business. He told me that the company wouldn't break even on my purchase until sometime in the second year of my contract.

Many business face similar setup costs. Phone and cable service providers make an investment in equipment when they initiate service. Many cellphone service providers offer free or steeply discounted phones. All these costs can be tied back to individual customers.

Customers also require different levels of service. Catalog retailers often offer free shipping on returns. Customer A may buy a given product and love it. Customer B may try one or even several products and return them before settling on the same product purchased by customer A at the same price. But the extra shipping costs may make the second purchase unprofitable.

There are also costs related to the failure of customers to pay their bills. People default on credit cards, mortgages, and auto payments. But even outside the financial services industry, payment can sometimes be a problem. People write bad checks. They refuse to pay for services after they have been rendered. These payment (or more accurately nonpayment) related costs are tied to individual customer behavior.

Combined with their spending levels, transaction-related costs are key to understanding customer profitability. Transaction-related behavior varies widely from one customer to the next, as does spending. These two variables help you usefully differentiate profitability among customer segments.

Allocating infrastructure costs based on usage

You know that you gave your customer a free phone to sign up for your company's cellphone service. But how do you allocate the cost of building and maintaining your cellphone towers to individual customers? And what about the cost of the home office, the call center, and even your own salary?

These questions about infrastructure and other fixed costs, in my experience, are the questions that cause the most headaches in developing a customer-profitability framework. They simply don't have clear-cut answers. Before you even start these discussions, get explicit agreement from everyone involved about the purpose of your customer-profitability calculation. Knowing in advance what you do and don't want to do with it makes answering these sticky allocation questions much easier.

When I was doing customer-level profitability analysis in the banking industry, there was a great deal of discussion surrounding how to allocate the cost of brick-and-mortar branches to individual customers. It somehow didn't seem fair to burden customers who only used online banking and ATM machines with the same costs as customers who went to the branch three times a week. Why should bank teller payroll count against the profitability of customers who never see them?

And it's not just a matter of fairness. Different channels have different costs. That ATM network and the online banking infrastructure are far less expensive to maintain than the branch network. At that time, a key corporate initiative was to move customers into lower-cost channels. We wanted to reward our profitable customers for being profitable.

The approach we took was to allocate costs based on usage. We did this not at the individual customer level, but by grouping customers together. We defined low-, medium-, and high-volume customers in each channel and then allocated those channel costs differently for each group.

Tying cost back to the product

Sometimes it's not a matter of how much a customer uses your infrastructure, but *whether* they use it. It doesn't make sense to allocate executive salaries in the mortgage company to customers who only have a credit card, for example.

Manufacturing costs for consumer goods belong at the product level. Some products are more expensive to produce than others. In the case of retailers, wholesale costs — the price that the retailer pays for a particular product — also depend on the particular product.

In both cases, it's relatively straightforward to assign cost to individual products. It's then a simple matter to subtract this cost from the sales price to get a net profit for each product. These profits can then be assigned to customers based on what products they buy.

Not Rocket Science: Keeping It Simple

Your customer profitability calculations aren't intended to be used as a basis for your company's annual report and SEC filings. Those are essentially legal documents and follow very strict accounting standards. The main purpose of customer-level profitability is to differentiate more profitable customers from less profitable ones. Doing so gives you some freedom to make simplifying assumptions. Simplicity yields stability and consistency over time.

One decision you have to make has to do with the time period you include in a profitability calculation. It doesn't make any sense to try to calculate customer profitability based on short time periods. Daily or weekly calculations would bounce around from negative to positive based on what the customer is doing, or more likely not doing, on any given day.

The time period you settle on depends a great deal on the nature of your business and your data. In the case of banks, a monthly calculation based on information from monthly statements might be the shortest time period that is even practical for a profitability calculation. But even monthly calculations could turn out to bounce around quite a bit.

As I discuss later in this chapter, you want to track customer profitability over time. In order for profitability measures to be meaningful from one time period to the next, they need to be consistent. You want changes in customer profitability over time to reflect changes in customer behavior. You don't want those changes to be artifacts of changes in cost allocations.

In many cases, the most useful profitability calculation reflects a whole calendar or fiscal year. One advantage of using a whole year is that it you eliminate fluctuations due to seasonal purchase patterns. Another is that it simplifies cost allocations that may fluctuate throughout the year as well. Perhaps the biggest advantage is that you won't be bouncing customers around from one marketing strategy to another based on short-term changes in profitability. A year lets you be consistent in your messages.

My wife and I typically take an annual vacation to the island where we got married. And we typically spend a lot of money to rent the honeymoon suite where we originally stayed. Suppose that resort were to focus on our quarterly profitability. They'd view us as unprofitable in the quarter before our visit. But that's just when they need to be marketing to us to plan our annual trip.

Understanding Household-Level Profitability

Back in my banking days, I was involved in analyzing customer profitability. This was a relatively new topic at the time, and certainly new to the bank. The focus had always been around product profitability. Customer profitability started with product profitability. We calculated the value of each individual checking account, savings account, and so on. We then added up the profit from all of the accounts owned by each customer.

Management was already well aware that, at the individual product level, they had a whole lot of unprofitable accounts out there. (See the earlier sidebar on the 80/20 rule.) The vast majority of the bank's profit was coming from a small number of accounts. And this was true in almost every product category. The same thing was true at the customer level. Most of the profit was tied to a relatively small number of customers. This led to much discussion about raising fees on checking accounts that were unprofitable. Trying to drive unprofitable customers away was discussed.

This discussion was somewhat tempered by the results of an analysis I did on household-level profitability. At first blush, it was more of the same. A small number of households accounted for a large portion of revenue, but they also accounted for a large proportion of the accounts. Unprofitable households averaged one or two accounts with the bank. Profitable households averaged many more. Some had a dozen or more accounts. This wasn't really a surprise. The more widgets you sell, the more you make, right?

But what we found was that these high-value households contained a substantial number of very unprofitable accounts. They had unused credit cards, accounts with small balances, and high transaction volume.

This example points up the benefit of understanding the whole household. It would be potentially problematic to be raising fees on the husband's checking account while waving them for his wife. That's the sort of thing that will drive customers to a competitor.

Retaining Your Profitable Customers

Because your most profitable customers generate a large portion of your revenues, it's important to keep them happy. By identifying those customers, you can focus some of your marketing investment on retaining them.

I've talked about customer reward cards before. Businesses from grocery stores to coffee shops have customer rewards programs. These programs tend to involve issuing a card that accumulates points toward discounts or free products. Often these cards let those businesses to track purchases at the customer level. What would otherwise be an anonymous cash purchase is tracked back to the customer via a swipe of the loyalty card.

You don't necessarily need to give stuff away or provide discounts. Sometimes pampering your best customers is very effective. Loyalty programs that provide differentiated service to your best customers can be just as effective, if not more so, than financial rewards. Some theme parks offer early entry to season pass holders, for example. Department stores open their doors early to customers in their loyalty programs.

These so called *surprise and delight* strategies differentiate service and other benefits without discounting. This approach is quickly becoming a popular and effective way for marketers to reward loyal customers without cutting into already narrow profit margins. It's also an effective customer retention strategy since it gives new customers an incentive to become more loyal.

My wife travels a great deal on business. She goes out of her way to use the same airline every time. She's trying to accumulate frequent flyer points. The reason has nothing to do with flight discounts. It has to do with getting differentiated service. Early boarding privileges prevent her from having to check her luggage when the overhead bins get full. She frequently gets upgraded to first class which gives her more room to work while in flight.

Using Profitability to Find New Customers

You're always looking for new customers. More precisely, you're always looking for new *profitable* customers. Understanding what makes your current customers tick can help your acquisition and advertising campaigns. The basic idea is to profile your current profitable customers. Using all the data at your disposal, you want to find patterns that are associated with profitable customers. Ask questions like these:

- Do they tend to come from a specific age group or set of age groups?
- Do they tend to have incomes above a certain level?
- Do they tend to have young children?
- Are they concentrated in rural, suburban, or urban environments?
- Are they mostly single or married?
- Do they tend to buy certain products in particular?

Once you have a profile of your most profitable customers, you can target acquisition campaigns at people who fit it. You can use this profile to help your advertising team choose the best media for its messages.

You can also use this profile to buy lists for mail or e-mail campaigns. Many list brokers have a large amount of demographic data at their disposal. If you provide them with a specific customer profile, they can create a list of prospects that closely resemble that profile.

Dealing with Unprofitable Customers

Some businesses talk about "firing" their unprofitable customers. They may choose to raise prices or reduce service levels to drive these customers either into profitable territory or drive them away altogether. This is a somewhat risky strategy. Bad publicity is one potential negative consequence. But another is cutting off a potential future revenue stream. In some businesses, it takes time to move a customer into profitable territory. You may need to get customers in the door and then expand the relationship until it's profitable.

Actively trying to drive customers away should be an approach of last resort. A more passive strategy is to just not spend a lot of time and effort marketing to unprofitable customers. If a customer isn't profitable, it doesn't make much sense to keep sending them discounted offers, for example.

It may also be possible to turn unprofitable customers into profitable ones by expanding the relationship. As discussed earlier in this chapter, the profitability of customers in the banking industry is at least partly related to the number of different products they have purchased. You may find a group of unprofitable customers who only have a checking account. It may be possible to turn them profitable by selling them a credit card and driving some of their transactions from the checking account to the credit card.

In developing a strategy to deal with unprofitable customers, it's important to understand what's behind the situation. Is it the product the customer buys? Or is it the way the customer is interacting with you? You might be far more likely to "fire" a customer who returns a large number of purchases than fire one who just doesn't buy that much.

It Takes a Lifetime: Understanding Changes in Customer Profitability

A customer's profitability is not a static measurement. People's means and needs change over the course of their lives. As a consequence, their behaviors and buying habits change as well.

People move in and out of your business footprint. My wife and I have lived in three different states in the last three years. (We're officially sick of moving.) This means we've changed everything from doctors to grocery stores. We've gone from profitable to unprofitable as we moved out of each area. The companies that don't recognize these shifts are at a disadvantage. They waste money continuing to market to us once we've left their footprint. Or they miss an opportunity to connect with us at our new location.

Recognizing movements in customer profitability

Your customer base, as a whole, may appear fairly stable when it comes to profitability. Year over year, you may see about the same percentage of your customers in the ranges of high, medium, and low profitability. But upon closer examination, you will see that some customers are moving up and down among those ranges. By examining these migrations from one profitability range to another, you can begin to identify challenges and opportunities in your customer base. You can build profiles that help you identify customers who may be ready to move up the profitability scale.

Of particular concern to you is understanding *customer attrition*. That is, understanding how many customers are leaving. The percentage of customers you lose in a given time period is frequently referred to as your *churn rate*. You need to take a two-pronged approach to dealing with this churn:

- ✔ Reduce your churn rate through customer-retention programs.
- ✔ Replace the lost business through customer-acquisition programs.

You can approach customer acquisition through a combination of advertising and purchased lists. Acquisition also depends on recognizing people who are shopping for your products, particularly online. (I talk about customer retention in Chapter 10 and address aspects of customer acquisition related to converting shoppers into buyers in Chapter 12.)

Calculating Customer Lifetime Value

It's quite helpful to understand the contribution your customer base will produce over the lifetime of your relationship. A common calculation in this vein is known as *customer lifetime value* or CLV. Giving a detailed explanation of the math behind this calculation is far beyond the scope of this book. It involves some degree of advanced knowledge of finance. But the basic idea is worth understanding.

Essentially, CLV takes into account two factors related to time:

- **The change in the value of money over time:** This is done via the finance equivalent of *a bird in the hand is worth two in the bush*. Because money earns interest if you save it, a dollar in hand today is worth more than the promise of a dollar in the future. If the interest rate were 4.2 percent, I could deposit only 96 cents today and have a dollar a year from now. In that case, you'd discount every dollar of revenue you expect to get next year to 96 cents to make it equivalent to today's dollar. Understanding the nuts and bolts of this calculation requires some advanced knowledge of finance. In particular, determining the interest rate to use in applying this principle depends heavily on what sort of revenue stream is being analyzed.

- **The churn rate:** This is a measure of how many customers you expect to lose over the course of the year. If your churn rate is 5 percent annually, for example, you would only include 95 percent of next year's expected revenue in your CLV calculation.

You (or your finance partner) perform these discount and churn calculations for each year going forward. You'll have to choose a reasonable time period that represents the expected lifetime of your customer relationship. Once you do, you add up all the yearly contributions to get the customer lifetime value.

You can do this calculation at the individual customer level. But it doesn't really represent what you can expect from an individual customer. The churn rate is what you expect to see across a particular profitability segment. It doesn't tell you which customers are actually going to leave. CLV calculations should only help draw conclusions about customer segments.

One useful application of CLV is in budgeting. By knowing what you can expect to earn from a given segment over the entire lifetime of the relationship, you can make an informed decision about how much you want to invest in acquiring or servicing that segment.

Part III
Putting Your Data to Work

Five Tactical Marketing Goals

- ✔ **Goal 1:** Retain your existing customers.
- ✔ **Goal 2:** Upsell recent purchasers.
- ✔ **Goal 3:** Cross-sell recent purchasers.
- ✔ **Goal 4:** Convert prospects and shoppers into purchasers.
- ✔ **Goal 5:** Increase customer profitability.

Check out all the customer information you can harvest through web analytics in an online article at www.dummies.com/extras/datadrivenmarketing.

In this part . . .

✔ Discover how to use data to cross-sell, upsell, and retain your existing customers.

✔ Understand the importance of keeping prospects in your pipeline and discover methods of converting them into customers.

✔ Check out the basics of developing marketing messages to maximize their power and efficiency.

✔ Find out how to take advantage of online and mobile device data in your data driven marketing efforts.

Chapter 10

The Tactical Advantage: Designing Data Driven Marketing Campaigns

As the old saw goes, the only constant in life is change. This is as true of your customers as it is for your business. People grow up, go to college, get married, buy their first house and car, retire, and do many things in between. With every change comes changes in their needs, preferences, and means.

Your products have a life-cycle as well. Retail consumer goods wear out or are used up and need to be replaced. Loans are paid off. Annual passes expire. These events all create opportunities for you to make new sales.

By recognizing and even anticipating changes in both your business and your customers, you can design communications and offers that are relevant to your customers' new situations. With relevance comes revenue. In this chapter, I examine a number of ways that you can be proactive in turning change to your advantage.

Event-Triggered Campaigns: Understanding the Basics

Timing is everything, as another saying goes. It's one thing to know how many widgets you sold last year. It's quite another to know who bought how many widgets and when. And it's worth even more to know about these events immediately — at the time they happened.

This chapter introduces you to some strategies and tactics that database marketers use to take advantage of time-sensitive customer information. This information might be related to their recent purchases. But it may also be related to a move, the birth of a child, or any number of life events that affect their needs and attitudes. In Chapter 7, I talk about the identification of lifestage segments. The life events I mention here essentially signal that a customer has moved from one lifestage segment to another.

Changes in your data about customers may signal marketing opportunities. Campaigns that are designed to address these opportunities are known as *event-triggered* campaigns. Because you're responding directly to a customer's changing situation, your message will be powerfully relevant to your customer's current needs.

As I've mentioned, my wife and I have moved several times over the years. Each time we do, we get a note or a postcard from several national retail chains, home improvement stores, computer retailers, and so on. These are simple event-triggered campaigns.

These communications are all designed to guide us to the closest store in our new community. They're triggered by the change-of-address forms we filled out at the post office. The database marketers at these retailers subscribe to change-of-address services from the USPS and they send these communications accordingly.

In many cases, these communications are quite helpful. Not only do they help us to learn our way around our new environment, they often contain special offers for exactly the kind of stuff that new homeowners need. I don't think we've ever paid full price for shelf liner.

Event-triggered campaigns versus mass mailings

Event-triggered marketing campaigns differ in a couple important ways from more traditional mass mailings. The power of event-triggered campaigns comes from recognizing when an individual customer has experienced or caused some event.

In order to do take advantage of this information, you must run these campaigns continuously, rather than in one large mail drop. The communications are literally *triggered* at the time when you recognize that some event has occurred. Depending on the situation, these campaigns can be executed monthly, weekly, daily, or even in real time.

An important distinction between event-triggered campaigns and mass mailings has to do with the size of the target audience. Your customers are typically not all doing the same thing at the same time. You don't have half of your customer base moving every month, for example. Because event-triggered campaigns are run continuously, the target audiences for these campaigns tend to be much smaller than the audiences for mass mailings.

There are seasonal fluctuations that cause demand to spike throughout your whole customer base at once. Think Black Friday after Thanksgiving, for example. In these cases, event triggers don't really make any sense. You would take a more traditional mass-mailing approach to reach your target audience when you expect a seasonal spike in demand.

Because of the continuous nature of event-triggered campaigns, they provide an ideal laboratory for learning which messages and offers work and which don't. In mass-mail drops, you have to wait awhile to apply what you learn to the next campaign. What you learn from your Christmas mailing can't be applied until next Christmas.

With event-triggered campaigns, if you run the campaign for a month and it isn't working to your satisfaction, you can tweak your messages and offers on the fly until you see the desired results. This adaptability, along with the inherent relevance of your timing, makes event-triggered campaigns an extremely effective way to generate revenue.

In Chapters 14–17, I talk at length about measuring and learning from your marketing campaigns.

Choosing a marketing channel

The success of an event-triggered campaign depends on its timing. You don't want to be closing the barn door after the horses are out. When you're deciding whether to communicate via mail, e-mail, or some other channel, it's extremely important to understand your window of opportunity. It isn't open forever.

Suppose you own a busy restaurant. How do you deal with last-minute cancellations? You don't have time to send a postcard to a customer on your waiting list. That table is a perishable asset, and you will lose revenue if it sits empty tonight. So, to respond effectively to the cancellation trigger, you need to communicate quickly. A text message or phone call would be your only viable options.

This points up an advantage of event-triggered tactics as opposed to mass communications. Because of the relatively small audience size, you open the door to more expensive marketing channels. It might be financially unthinkable to call everyone that lived within 20 miles to tell them you're opening a new restaurant. But calling a handful of customers on your waiting list to fill a cancelled reservation is perfectly reasonable. It's also extremely effective.

The same idea applies to event-triggered campaigns that you execute through the mail. You may not want to pay first class postage for a large mailing. But if you're only mailing a few pieces each week, you may choose to pay the extra postage. This would get the mail into the customer's mailbox a little faster as well as make it more likely that they actually read it. (In Chapter 4, I talk more about the relative costs and advantages of different marketing channels.)

Campaign timing depends on data timing

Because event-triggered campaigns have such a quick turnaround and high effectiveness, they can be very useful marketing tools. But their effectiveness comes with a cost.

In database marketing, everything starts with the data. For an event-triggered campaign to be effective, it needs to be based on fresh data. Your window of opportunity might last only 1 or 2 days after a particular customer event occurs. If data about that type of event is only loaded to your database weekly, you're powerless to take advantage of the information.

The freshness of your data is commonly called *data latency*. In simplest terms, this means the time it takes to be able to act on that data. The data in your marketing database has varying degrees of latency, depending on its source.

For example, you might only purchase third-party data on your customers monthly or semiannually. On the other hand, you may load transaction data weekly or even daily. Unfortunately, it's a pretty general rule that your infrastructure costs go up with the frequency of your updates.

I don't have room in this book to get into the technical architecture of your data systems. But as a general rule, you don't want to be updating your marketing database on a real-time basis. For one thing, your reports will never come out with same results twice. For another, doing so would put an unwelcome burden on your transaction systems.

Two strategies can help you to get around the cost implications of frequent database updates:

- ✔ **Focus only on the small number of transactions that display the event trigger you're interested in.** Rather than trying to convince your IT department to invest in daily, rather than weekly, updates from your transaction systems, you could ask for a daily feed containing only the relatively small number of transactions that you're actually interested in.

- ✔ **Execute the campaign from the transaction system itself.** Most real-time, or near real-time, campaigns are executed through electronic media. E-mail confirmations or follow-up offers are typically triggered by an online purchase. You can execute these communications based on information available from your Internet service provider. There is no need to download the online data and integrate it into your customer database before this communication is sent.

An Ounce of Retention Is Worth a Pound of Lure: Holding on to Your Customers

It's a generally accepted fact among marketers that it's far less expensive to keep an existing customer than to acquire a new one. Cost estimates vary, but acquiring a new customer can cost several times more than retaining an existing one does. It's not unusual for companies to find that acquisition is ten times more expensive than retention. For this reason, even relatively modest improvements in customer retention rates can pay big dividends.

No matter what business you're in, customer retention is important. Event triggers are not a replacement for a broader retention strategy, but they can be a useful tactic. Ask yourself what you know or can learn about when and why customers stop doing business with you. Knowing beforehand gives you the chance to do something about it.

Sometimes *you* create the customer-retention risk. You sometimes need to increase prices for example. Or you may have oversold services to your customer — services they don't really need. The key is to recognize when a customer is at risk and intervene before they leave you. How you do this is obviously highly dependent on what business you're in.

Take it to the bank

The financial-services industry, particularly retail banking, provides a good context for a discussion of event triggers. For one thing, bankers have the luxury of having a large amount of data on their customers. The very nature of banking requires that they keep track of everything. For another thing, bankers have been aware of the value of their customer data for a very long time — the banking industry was one of the first to really embrace the use of customer databases in marketing.

The basic idea of banking is to take in deposits at a low rate of interest (don't you just love the three cents a month you get on your checking account?). These deposits are then loaned out at a significantly higher rate of interest. For this reason, among others, keeping deposit customers is very important.

The approach that banks might take is to monitor the average balances in large deposit accounts. For example, they may keep an eye on customers who keep at least $10,000 in a savings account. What they look for is a sudden drop in the size of the account.

A customer can have any number of reasons for withdrawing money from such an account. They may be making a large purchase — a house or car, for example. They may be paying off a debt. They may be moving the money to a higher-yielding investment like a CD or a mutual fund.

Here's where having a large amount of guest data can come in handy. The bank knows what other accounts the customer has. So the bank can check to see if this withdrawal was immediately deposited in another account. The analytics here can get very advanced, but the basic idea is to predict what the customer has in mind for the money.

If the money went from savings into a checking account then the customer is probably getting ready to spend it. Because this was a significant amount of money, they may be getting ready to spend it on something big. But large purchases are often partially financed. The money from the savings account might be intended to cover a down payment. In that case, this would be a good time to communicate with the customer about the various loans offered by the bank. This gives the bank a chance to replace the lost deposit with a loan and not only keep the customer but actually deepen the relationship.

Another simple train of thought might revolve around how the money left the savings account. If the money was transferred out via a wire transfer, it becomes more likely that it may have gone into some sort of investment account. In this case, it might be a very good time to have an investment advisor contact the customer to talk about the bank's products in that area. This may seem futile if the customer has already invested the money elsewhere. But remember, even a small percentage recovered is very valuable.

These examples all relate to banking, but similar thought processes can be applied to any number of different businesses. Resort hotels have customers that come back every year. They can be on the lookout for folks who haven't made their usual reservation. Automobile dealers know how long people usually drive their cars before buying a new one. They can contact them proactively; extolling the virtues of this year's new model.

Experience matters: Dealing with customer problems

Every business wants happy customers. Every business strives to create a smooth and satisfying customer experience. But nobody is perfect. Mistakes will be made, and problems will occur. The way you deal with your customers' problems is central to keeping them as customers.

It has been said that no marriage is perfect. The measure of a good marriage is how well a couple resolves conflict. The same is true of your relationship with your customers. Research suggests that your most loyal customers are not those that have never had a problem with you. They are the ones for whom you have resolved an issue in a satisfactory way.

Saving Christmas: A customer service story

Last Christmas, I ordered some CDs from Amazon for my wife, intended as gifts. Getting them delivered in time for Christmas wasn't an issue according to the website. Amazon estimated I would have them at least a week ahead of time.

Given the hectic nature of the holidays, this purchase had slipped my mind. Two days before Christmas, I got a phone call from Amazon. We had moved that year and they had shipped them to our previous address. The CDs had been returned to the retailer as undeliverable. The customer-service person apologized and volunteered to re-send the package overnight at no charge to me.

Now, I honestly have no idea whether the address mix up was my fault or theirs. Nonetheless, I was floored. Not so much by their willingness to fix the problem, but by the fact that a company of that size knew it before I did. They had picked up on a problematic transaction among the tens of millions (or more) transactions that they process every day. And more importantly, they did something about it. Needless to say, they now have a loyal customer.

Being proactive: Identifying customer problems

You almost certainly have a credit card. And you've probably experienced a very effective event-triggered communication related to that card. I'm talking about the fraud prevention call. Someone from the credit-card company calls you and asks if you actually made a certain transaction.

So what's going on here? They bank is trying to protect you, and itself, against credit-card theft. Their computers are constantly sifting through credit-card transactions looking for suspicious patterns. Again, there are some pretty heavy-duty analytics going on here. But the basic idea is that thieves do some predictably unique things. For example, a thief does not typically steal a card and proceed directly to the mall to buy a flat-screen TV. More often they buy a small item or two first to make sure the card works and hasn't been reported stolen.

By checking with the credit card holder when suspicious transaction patterns are observed, the bank is able to significantly reduce its losses. They have also spared the customer a great deal of hassle. This makes it far more likely that the customer will not throw up their hands and bolt to another credit-card company. The bank can issue a new card and retain a valuable customer.

Anticipating problems: Optimizing service levels

I got a call from my cellphone provider recently in which they pointed out that I wasn't using anywhere near the minutes that I had purchased. They asked me a few questions about whether my low usage level was likely to continue. They then proceeded to adjust my plan to better reflect my actual usage. And not surprisingly, my monthly bill went down.

This may sound counterintuitive. Why reduce their revenue stream? But in fact, this was a classic, data-driven customer-retention initiative. The cellphone provider realizes that because competition is so fierce, cost is a big driver of customer attrition. They also realize that they need to keep customers on the books for a long time before they recoup the cost of free phones and introductory offers that they use to acquire customers.

The company didn't wait for me to initiate the conversation. And they didn't wait until my contract was about to expire to start the conversation. By proactively reducing my bill, they made themselves more competitive should I start shopping around when my contract does expire.

They get the additional benefit of my positive experience with them. They've instilled some trust in me that they are interested in serving my particular needs. This positive attitude may actually be more important to my continuing to do business with them than the monthly bill.

Buyer's remorse is real. When you push a customer into buying a product or service that they really don't need, you create bad blood between you and your customer. This in turn creates a customer-retention problem. By recognizing how a customer is, or isn't, using your product, you can take action to get your relationship with your customer better aligned with their needs.

Expiration date: Keeping the relationship alive

Many industries sell products with an explicitly defined lifetime. Your automobile lease is a two-year contract. Your auto insurance card needs to be renewed every six months. Your season ticket is only good for one season. Cellular service contracts, golf club memberships — the list goes on. Customer retention in these industries comes down largely to getting the customer to renew or re-affirm their relationship.

Easy does it: Making it convenient

The good news for marketers in these types of industries is that these "defined lifetime" products come with built-in triggers. There is no mystery here about which customers are potential flight risks or when they are most likely to disappear. You know when their contract is up. The basic database marketing strategy here is obvious: *Don't wait until customers become ex-customers before contacting them.* If you do, then someone else probably has their business.

On the other hand, competition in these industries can be fierce. The media, both broadcast and digital, is full of advertising for car companies, insurance policies, and cellular phone services. Such media presence requires a significant marketing investment, which makes it all the more important for these industries to keep their customers in the fold.

One approach is to remind the customer and streamline the process. In many states, the DMV sends out a notification that your driver's license is about to expire. In many cases, you can renew it via mail or online. Any business that's dependent on annual memberships could do something similar. Theme parks, museums, and golf courses could all benefit. This approach takes advantage of the fact that a customer's membership information is already on file. In other words, a renewal is much simpler than signing up a new customer. The customer can verify and update their information without having to leave the house.

The timing of a renewal reminder is important. It may be tempting to trigger the communication based on an upcoming expiration. But sometimes it's far more effective to trigger the reminder based on the customer's usage. A customer may have had a recent, presumably positive experience at your theme park. You want this experience to be fresh in the customer's mind when they consider renewing their annual pass. Of course, that also means it's not a really good idea to pitch them an annual pass renewal if they've just called in to complain about poor service.

Automatic renewals

Another common strategy is to provide automatic renewals. This happens at the time of the initial purchase. The customer essentially gives permission for the annual renewals to be charged to a credit card or other account. The renewals then happen automatically until the customer says to stop. This is a popular approach with software companies who offer annual licenses.

Automatic renewals appeal to both the seller and the buyer because of their convenience. But there is some risk for the consumer. Convenience can sometimes become forgetfulness. Consumers sometimes fail to cancel the renewal when they no longer want or need the product. If they're not carefully watching their bank statements, they may not discover this for quite a while.

You need to protect your brand and your company's reputation. Your customers can be quite sensitive to, and even angered by, automatic renewals if they aren't done in a straightforward way. Relying on confusing offers to mask the fact that an automatic payment has been established is a sure way to annoy your customers. Equally annoying is a confusing and difficult cancellation process. Be clear with your customers when you sign them up for automatic renewals.

Because of this sensitivity, it's preferable to put some safeguards in place. Checking to make sure the consumer is getting software updates may indicate they're still using your product, for example. Another, very inexpensive safeguard is to simply send out an e-mail confirmation of the automatic payment. In any case, setting up an automatic renewal doesn't mean you should just ignore the customer.

Knowing when it's time

Many products have a fairly predictable lifetime. Some products wear out. My wife and I know we need to stain our deck every three years or so. Our air filters need to be replaced every three months. The cars need to be serviced every few months. (And as I write this, I realize mine is overdue.)

The lifetime of other products has more to do with their becoming obsolete, at least from the customer's perspective. Many people like to have the latest and greatest. This is true of cars. In fact, it's one reason why auto leases are so popular. They tend to be fairly short — only two or three years. A lease allows the consumer to get more car for a lower monthly payment than a purchase. And the best part for some people is that they get a new car every couple of years.

This shiny-new-toy mentality is especially true in the technology sector. I've been calling my wife Gadget Girl for years because she jumps on the latest device as soon as it's out. She hasn't kept the same cellphone for more than two years since we've been married. I, however, am still using the same flip phone I bought ten years ago.

Or I should say I was still using the flip phone. For years Gadget Girl has been feigning embarrassment over the antenna on my phone (at least I think she was kidding.) Finally, just last weekend, she took matters into her own hands. While I was home working on this book, she disappeared to the Verizon store. When she returned, she presented me with a brand new iPhone 5. And she had actually synced it up with my iPad so it was ready to go. I had to admit that I had definitely been missing out.

My point is this: Cars and computers and cellphones don't come with the same kind of explicit expiration dates as an annual pass or an auto insurance policy. But they have an implicit lifetime. That lifetime depends on the customer. But you have a great deal of data in your purchase history that can tell you which customers are replacing products and how often.

Armed with an understanding of your customer's purchase cycle, you can design communications that talk about the latest shiny new toy. You can base your communication timing on the amount of time that has elapsed since they last bought the product. And you can get these communications in front of customers at the time they're beginning to bet bored with their now not-so-shiny old toy.

Sticker shock: Don't just send them a bill

Prices do go up, sometimes significantly. But trying to sweep the increases under the rug is a risky strategy. Businesses don't hesitate to sing loudly and often about price decreases. When prices go up, it's worth telling your customers your side of the story. They might just understand.

The examples in this section are not, strictly speaking, related to event triggers. They do however relate directly to customer retention. How and when you communicate rate or fee increases to your customers can make a big difference in their willingness to pay them.

Explaining yourself

A number of years ago, I had a membership at a local golf course. The membership dues were collected annually on the anniversary of my joining. Every year they would send me an invoice for the next year's dues. Predictably, the dues increased every year. But the size of the increase was not predictable. Some years it was nominal, and others it was huge. In either case, no one knew how much it was until they saw the bill.

Since I actually lived on the course, many of my neighbors and friends also had memberships. In our collective observations and conversations with the golf course staff, we were all pretty well aware of the improvements and alterations that were happening. In other words, we were able to figure out why some years had such large increases. It usually meant some significant money was being spent on improving the course.

Over time, membership shrank. The problem was sticker shock. Some members were so annoyed at the large increases that they never bothered to find out what they were for. Even had they known, their annoyance might well have clouded their judgment about whether they were worth it. The members that weren't neighborhood insiders were particularly at risk. Many just never came back to find out why their bill was so high.

The point of this story is that people really do shoot the messenger. I heard countless neighbors make comments like, "Did those idiots think I wouldn't notice?"

Now suppose a couple walked into the clubhouse around the time the dues increase went into effect to inquire about joining the club. The marketing director would give them a tour of the facilities. She would explain that some work was being done on the golf course and why. She would treat the course improvements as a selling point. And you can bet she would quote them the new higher membership rate.

Why not give the current members the same treatment? Instead of just sending them the bill, why not give the same sales pitch as a prospective member would get? You could even organize a tour for the members to explain the planned upgrades. For the members, the improvements would be readily understood because they're familiar with the course.

The golf course missed an opportunity to anticipate the negative reactions to their price increase. Simply acknowledging and explaining the increase would have gone a long way toward softening the sticker shock. "We're finally getting around to solving that drainage problem on the 14th fairway. Unfortunately, this is going to cost a little bit to do." That's a far better message than an invoice.

When you increase prices, you're going to have to convince new customers to pay those prices. You generally do this by highlighting the quality and value of your product. You need to convince your current customers as well. But with your current customers, the discussion needs to be about the added value related to the price increase.

Giving your customers an alternative

I have a love/hate relationship with my cable/Internet provider. Over the years, I've been somewhat trapped by the lack of alternatives and have often resented the fact that my provider seemed to behave as if it knew this. As the market has gotten a little more competitive, that provider has actually adapted fairly well. The quality of its service and my opinion of it have both increased significantly.

Recently I got a notification that the cable modem which they provided upon installation was no longer going to free. They were going to institute an additional monthly fee to rent it to me. When I saw the amount of the rate increase, my initial reaction was "Just when I was starting to like you! I could buy a modem online for the price of six monthly rental fees!"

Now, five years ago, this company would have just included a note on the back of my bill and applied the increase. But as I read this fee increase notification further, they actually addressed my frustration directly. They gave me an alternative.

They had anticipated precisely my reaction and acknowledged it. They explicitly told me that I could avoid this fee increase by purchasing my own modem. And they were careful to point out that I didn't need to purchase it from them.

The cable company obviously lost a potential revenue stream when I did purchase my own modem. But that revenue stream is small. It pales in comparison to the monthly bill I'm already paying.

The strategy of offering alternatives to fee increases is especially important in industries where there is significant competition. It's almost essential if the industry also suffers from a generally negative public perception. If customers are already primed to take their business elsewhere, then any fee increase could be the straw that breaks the camel's back. Banks, for example, are well aware of the need to waive fees to protect profitable relationships with their customers.

We miss you: Reactivation

Sometimes, despite your best retention efforts, customers do leave you. They may decide to try a competitor's product. They may no longer have need of your product. They may have had a bad experience with you. But these *lapsed customers* have a history with you, and you have some knowledge about them. That means that you may be able to recover their business. It certainly makes them more likely prospects than people who have never done business with you.

When identifying which customers are active and which are lapsed, you need to be careful about the time period you look at. Different businesses have different purchase cycles. A credit-card company might consider a customer to be lapsed if they haven't done any transactions for six months. But an auto dealer wouldn't flag a customer as lapsed a year after they signed a two-year lease.

When designing a reactivation campaign, it's important to try to understand why a customer has lapsed. If it's a service or quality issue, you may communicate to them about improvements that have been made in that regard. Automobile companies often take this approach after recalls, for example.

It's also important to understand what your lapsed customers were doing before they lapsed. Clues to why they stopped doing business with you may be found in their previous purchase history.

In Chapter 8, I describe a simple approach that credit-card issuers use to group their customers based on their behavior. Some customers, called *transactors,* do a lot of transactions and pay off their balances every month. Other customers, called *revolvers,* carry large balances over every month. Still others don't do much at all.

This last group of inactive cardholders can be divided into two subgroups. First you have the truly inactive cardholders — those who have never used their cards at all. The other subgroup is your lapsed cardholders. These customers have used their card in the past but have since stopped.

Now, suppose you're asked to design a reactivation campaign targeted at these lapsed cardholders. A critical piece of information for you is which category these cardholders fell into when they *were* active. In other words, you need to know which ones were transactors and which ones were revolvers.

Their previous behavior offers strong clues about why they left. The transactor didn't leave you to take advantage of a low-interest balance transfer. He didn't have a balance. But the revolver may well have done just that.

This line of thought leads to two different reactivation strategies. You focus on usage with one group and balances with the other. You offer cash back or other rewards to the lapsed transactors, for example. And you offer low-interest balance transfers to the lapsed revolvers.

The success of your reactivation campaigns depends heavily on your understanding of why your customers lapsed in the first place. As the preceding example illustrates, previous purchase history can sometimes tell you quite a bit. But understanding why customers lapse is also a popular subject for survey research. You can gain a lot of insight by just asking some of these customers where they went and why.

If You Like That, You're Going to Love This: Upselling to Your Customers

You probably have a spectrum of products that vary in price and quality. New cars vary widely in price depending on the class of the vehicle, for example. This variation is largely due to the fact that your customers vary widely in what they can afford or are willing to pay.

Generally, you would like your customers to buy as far up the price scale as is reasonable or possible. Once they've purchased or are committed to purchase a certain product, it's sometimes quite effective to try to push them just a little bit higher up the scale. This technique is known as *upselling*.

Why upselling works

The psychology behind upselling is fairly simple. Once the customer has decided to pay the asking price for a particular product, they're resigned to spending that money. At this point, getting them to buy a slightly more expensive product is all about focusing them on the incremental cost of upgrading their purchase. If this cost is small relative to the cost of the product they want to buy, you have a chance to convince them that it's worth it.

My wife has become an expert at upselling me when it comes to everything, from home improvements to automobiles. She and I both know I'm unreasonably miserly when it comes to making large purchases. So she has perfected the strategy of getting me to agree to something that costs significantly less than what she actually has in mind. Over the course of the next few days or weeks, I'll get up sold a couple hundred dollars at a time into what she really wants. Generally, these conversations start with the phrase "As long as we're doing this, we may as well . . ."

There are two keys to successful upselling:

✔ **Do it in manageable bites.** You're typically not going to sell someone a car that is twice the price of the one they're initially interest in.

✔ **Upsell them into something that fits their tastes and needs.** Strong-arming them into something they'll regret buying creates bad blood and ultimately a customer-retention problem.

Upselling service levels

Many companies are in the business of providing services. Your cellphone, tablet, computer, and TV all require a service provider to make them work. Those service providers are not one-size-fits-all operations. They offer a variety of different service levels with varying costs.

In all these cases, your service provider has some sense of how you're using their products. Your Internet service provider knows how much data moves across your connection. Your cellphone company knows about your data use as well as how many minutes you use and how many text messages you send. Your cable provider knows when you make a pay-per-view purchase.

I have a bundled cable, Internet, and phone package. When I first signed up for it, I suffered a bit of sticker shock, and my miserliness kicked in. I bought the package that gave me the smallest bill I could manage while still giving me the service that I need.

Over the next six months, the company proceeded to upsell me into a number of upgraded services. Both my wife and I do a great deal of work from home, much of which requires us to move large amounts of data across our Internet connection.

After letting us stew for about a month over the time we were wasting on both successful and aborted file transfers, our service provider sent us an offer in the mail related to upgrading our Internet data plan. The price of this upgrade was a few dollars a month and represented a small fraction of our overall bill. So we bit.

A month or two later, I got another offer related to adding a sports package to my basic channel lineup. Again, it was a nominal increase in cost per month. Both my wife and I are avid sports fans. In fact, I'd estimate that upwards of two-thirds of the time we spend in front of the television is spent watching sports. So the offer resonated, and we bit again.

Now, according to the cable company's privacy policy, they don't track what shows or channels people are watching. They didn't know how much sports we watch. At the time I got the sports package offer, I was thinking that the company was doing some pretty good segmentation to identify us as targets for the sports package. But then a while later I got another offer.

This one was related to baseball. They were offering me coverage of every major league game for the entire season. Again, this turned out to hit home. From a baseball perspective, I live in the Atlanta Braves market. I've been routing for the Detroit Tigers since I was a kid. Between the National League focus in the south and the distance from here to Detroit, I only get to see a handful of Tigers games during the season, at least through the regular broadcast channels.

The timing of this offer, a month after the season had started, got me thinking that my service provider was not just pretty good at database marketing but *very* good at it. I don't know for sure, but I suspect that the offer for the baseball package was related to my searches for baseball games on the company's website. For the first month of the season, I had logged in and checked their listings almost daily.

In any case, the upsell worked again. And my current monthly bill is now actually higher than the initial package that caused me to go into sticker shock. The offers had been extremely relevant to my tastes and needs. Had the offers been for movie channels, they never would have worked. The offers had also been made one at a time, gently moving me up the price scale.

Using bounce-back offers

A common approach to upselling is to re-contact your customer soon after a purchase is made. An offer related to a recent purchase is often called a *bounce-back* offer. You're trying to get the customer to "bounce back" to do more business with you.

This is particularly easy to do when their purchase is made online because online purchases generally require an e-mail address. Also, the communication you send is related to an established relationship — namely, their recent purchase. This releases you from some of the burdens of the opt-out compliance discussed in Chapter 4.

Any venue that sells tickets can benefit from a simple bounce-back tactic. Sports teams, museums, theme parks, and zoos all offer one-day tickets as well as season tickets or passes. Clearly, selling a season pass is the ideal sale. It generates revenue from the pass, and the more times customers come back, the more they spend on food, drinks, and souvenirs.

Once the customer has bought the ticket, wait for them to use it. Then, once they've used it, immediately send them an e-mail offering them a deal on an annual pass. You might even allow them to apply the price of the ticket to the annual pass price, for example.

You want to instill a sense of urgency with this offer. Give the customer a fairly short window of time to take advantage of the offer. You're banking on the fact that they enjoyed their recent experience. Having that experience fresh in their mind will be what gets them to upgrade.

Batteries Not Included: Cross-Selling to Your Customers

Closely related to upselling is the tactic of cross-selling. Upselling is about getting the customer to buy *better* stuff. Cross-selling is about getting the customer to buy *more* stuff.

Chapter 8 talks a little bit about market-basket analysis. As you may recall, this is an analytic technique designed to identify groups of products that are typically purchased together. It forms the basis for many cross-sell campaigns.

Whenever I visit the grocery store, for example, the cash register prints out a handful of coupons with my receipt. These coupons are generated based on my purchases. If I buy a particular brand of tortilla chips, for example, I might get a coupon for that same brand's salsa. The coupon is an attempt to cross-sell me products based on my current purchases.

Cross-selling online

Like upselling, cross-selling can be particularly effective online. You can design your online sales engine to offer additional products at the time a customer makes a purchase. These offers are based on what other customers have typically done.

Virtually every e-commerce site follows the grocery store model. They all use a shopping cart metaphor that allows the user to shop for and select multiple items before checking out. Data about the items in past shopping carts forms the basis for cross-sell recommendations that appear while the customer is still shopping.

Whenever I buy a book online, other books by the same author appear as suggested additional purchases. For me, that isn't terribly helpful. If I like a book, I typically go search for other books by the author anyway. But what is helpful is that I also get a list of books by other, similar authors who write in the same genre. These suggestions often lead me to discover good books that I might not have stumbled onto otherwise.

Websites that sell clothing do a lot of cross-selling. I recently bought a new pair of golf shoes and was offered a deal on golf shirts. When I buy slacks, I typically get offered dress shirts. A scarf purchase leads to an offer on gloves.

In addition to exposing the consumer to related products, another technique is commonly used to get them to buy more stuff. The technique is to offer some incentive for purchases that are above some dollar value. That incentive could involve free shipping or a free upgrade to overnight shipping. It could involve a discount on a future purchase.

When implementing an offer based on a purchase threshold, do some analysis on how much your customers typically spend. If most of your products cost between $30 and $45, then a threshold of $50 won't strike the customer as unreasonable. And if they continue to shop, they'll probably buy another $40 or so item that will get them significantly over the threshold.

Back to bounce-backs

A bounce-back offer can be an effective cross-sell tool as well. They idea is that you want to generate repeat business. If a customer has recently bought a product from you and liked it, they may be willing to give you more of their business.

In Chapter 8, I explain the use of recency, frequency, monetary (RFM) models in marketing. These models, which are popular in the catalog and retail consumer goods industries, focus on three measures of the customer's purchase patterns: how recent, how frequent and how much.

Ideally you'd like to have customers that score high on all three measures. Bounce-back offers are born of this view. You've got the recency part down. Now you want to address the frequency and monetary part. By giving the customer an offer that incents them to make another purchase, you're inching them along the path to loyalty.

I experience a simple example of a bounce-back offer almost every time I buy clothes online. Shortly after my purchase, I get an e-mail or direct mail message that I've earned a discount off my next purchase. Typically this involves some code that I can enter online when I decide to buy.

As I say frequently throughout this book, creating a sense of urgency is important. If your bounce-back offer doesn't come with an expiration date, it's more likely to be put in a drawer for later consideration. And for most people, *for later consideration* generally means *to be forgotten about.*

Chapter 15 goes into detail on measuring the success of your marketing campaigns. I do want to point out here, however, that the offer code you include with your bounce-back message serves two distinct purposes:

- ✔ **The code facilitates the transaction.** It allows your e-commerce site to process the discounted transaction.

- ✔ **It allows you to measure your campaign's success.** You can count the number of transaction that were made with that offer code, and that count forms the basis for understanding your response rate.

Welcome (Back) to the Neighborhood: Using Address Changes

People are moving around all the time. Your customers move into and out of your markets. They also move around within your footprint. Chapter 3 emphasizes the need to keep your customer address book up to date. Part of the reason for this is to avoid wasting money on postage. But recognizing address changes when they happen can also expose marketing opportunities related to a customer's relocation.

Having moved many times over the years, I've come to appreciate the fact that many of the national companies that I do business with recognize the fact that I've moved without my needing to tell them. Moving is hectic, and things fall through the cracks. Communications from these companies help me to find them and sometimes remind me that I need to modify my service.

Just getting a postcard telling me the closest location of a store is helpful. But equally helpful is the note from my investment advisor giving me the contact information for my new local representative. Some companies send me e-mails saying, "We notice you've moved," and asking me to confirm the change.

If your business doesn't have a national presence, you'll find that customers do leave your footprint. Clearly, it doesn't make much sense for you to keep marketing to them. But don't just relegate those customer records to the dust heap. Continue to update their addresses. Sometimes people move back.

My wife and I are a case in point. We have returned, after several years of wandering around, back to the place where we lived when we first got married. Clearly it was good to be back among familiar faces, friends, and family. But we were also pleasantly surprised to see that many businesses remembered us as well.

Our surprise actually began when we went to the DMV to get new driver's licenses. We, like almost everyone, dread this experience. But when we walked up to the counter, the attendant said our old driver's licenses were still in the system and she could issue replacement licenses for a nominal fee. She didn't even take our pictures. Now, this example has more to do with databases than it does with marketing, but it was only the beginning.

My favorite gourmet grocery store sent me a "welcome back" letter complete with a new loyalty card. Our alarm system company, Internet provider, and gas company all proactively re-established contact with us. In many cases, we were offered service renewals at a discount below the fees paid by new customers.

By welcoming previous customers when they return to your area, you gain a big leg up on your competition. Businesses, including yours, can buy lists of customers that are new to the area. Recognizing your previous customers as such strongly differentiates you from your competitors. "Welcome back!" is a much more powerful message than "Welcome."

Chapter 11

From the Window to the Counter: Getting Shoppers to Buy

Chapter 10 discusses ways you can protect and grow your relationship with your current customers. But you also need to find new customers. You can't grow your business — in fact, you can't even keep your business from shrinking — without a steady stream of new customers.

Many of your company's marketing and advertising efforts are directed at increasing awareness of your brand and interest in your products. This means there's a group of potential customers out there who are ready to begin a relationship with you. Many have gone so far as to actively investigate your product offerings. These are your hottest leads.

In this chapter, I use the term *shopper* to mean anyone who has shown an interest in your product. I talk about some ways to identify these potential customers. I also address some basic strategies for moving them from interested consumers to customers.

Identifying Shoppers

To execute database marketing campaigns targeted at shoppers, you need to know who they are. At a bare minimum, you need to have some sort of contact information — an e-mail address, phone number, or physical address, for example. You may know in great detail what potential customers are looking at on your website, but until you get them to identify themselves, you can't communicate with them.

In this section, I explain a few approaches for getting anonymous shoppers to "raise their hands" and provide you with their contact information. In some cases, you can get customers to give you a great deal more information than that.

The information you can get from your shoppers ranges from just a simple e-mail address to a detailed description of their needs and interests. All the approaches I mention here boil down to one simple strategy: quid pro quo. Something for something. You need to give your shoppers something in return for the information you seek. That something doesn't need to be financial. In fact, frequently an exchange of information is sufficient.

But you should be aware that even if a customer isn't registered and logged into your website, you can still re-contact them. In Chapter 13, I talk in much more detail about marketing on the web. In particular, I discuss the notion of *cookies* — small files placed on a user's machine to enable customization and tracking.

A common marketing technique is to place a tracking cookie on a user's machine when they visit your website. When you buy advertising on other websites, you can ask those websites to look for that cookie and use it to serve up advertising content based on what the user was looking at on your website. This technique is called *display re-targeting*.

Put me on your mailing list: Getting customers to raise their hands

Suppose you're in charge of customer acquisition for a catalog retailer. You have a limited marketing budget, which means you can only send a limited number of catalogs to prospects. One of your options is to buy prospect lists that match your typical customer profile.

But what if you have a group of potential customers that have actually requested a catalog? Being the savvy marketer you are, you'd recognize these as hot prospects. They have proactively shown an interest in your products. You wouldn't think of spending money on a prospect list until you knew you could fulfill every single one of the catalog requests.

Allowing people to request information about your products is a simple way of identifying shoppers. In order to receive the requested information, the potential customer must at least give you some sort of contact information. Whether you fulfill the request via e-mail or traditional mail, you need some sort of address. Getting that allows you to continue the conversation — with someone who you already know is interested. No matter what business you're in, you can find creative ways to exchange information with your customers.

Newsletters

One option is to publish a free — but subscription-based — monthly (or more frequent) newsletter. You can sign both customers and prospects up to receive news about new products and special events. Note that prospects who request the newsletter have explicitly identified themselves as interested in you.

Newsletters have several features that make them a particularly attractive marketing option. First, they can be published via e-mail, making them extremely cost effective to produce. E-mail also makes it easy for people to sign up. As a general rule, people are more willing to share their e-mail addresses than their home addresses. E-mail is slightly less invasive. Plus it simply doesn't take as long.

But even if you decide to put your newsletter on actual paper, there are advantages to publishing one. For one thing, the newsletter does double duty as a customer-acquisition tool and as a customer-retention tool.

Recall Chapter 10's discussion about customer-retention strategies and ways of keeping customers engaged. A newsletter is an excellent way to do exactly that. A newsletter is, in and of itself, an ongoing conversation with the customer.

Product information guides

Another popular approach is to offer more elaborate introductions to your products via a pamphlet, video, or other physical medium. Because this medium needs to be mailed, it allows you to capture the address of the person raising their hand.

Frequently these campaigns utilize something called *direct-response TV* (DRTV) — the use of TV commercials that ask the viewer to call or go online to order a product. Often they're used as lead-generation tools. The viewer is asked to order a free video, CD, or some other physical information packet.

You don't need to use DRTV. You can offer these informational materials online. You can also use print or even radio to solicit requests. Virtually any marketing or advertising channel can be used to drive hand-raisers to identify themselves to you in order to learn more about your products.

DRTV campaigns are used quite frequently in the pharmaceutical and medical device industries. In these industries, consumer database marketing is particularly tricky due to legal restrictions on the use of medical record data in marketing. By getting potential customers to request information, you can develop high-quality prospect lists without running afoul of regulations related to consumer data.

The use of CDs and videos is also quite popular in the travel and entertainment sector. Many popular vacation destinations produce material showing the wide array of attractions available, from beaches to theme parks to restaurants. Sometimes these materials are produced by the local Chamber of Commerce or other group of businesses. But many resort businesses produce them on their own.

Encouraging shoppers to register on your website

If a customer is browsing your website, that's a good indication that they're interested, at some level, in your products. This is classic shopping behavior. The problem is that much of this shopping is done anonymously. You can't follow up with these customers if you don't know who they are.

One solution to this problem is to get them to register on your site. If they're logged into your website while they're shopping, then you know who they are and what they're looking at.

But even if they don't log in every time they shop on your site, you may still be able to recognize them. Websites leave cookies on each user's computer. *Cookies* are small files that are used to keep track of user profile information. I talk more about cookies and their use in online marketing in Chapter 13.

You can drop a cookie on a user's machine when they initially register on your site. Then when they come back to your site, even if they don't log in, you can recognize them by the information in the cookie (assuming, of course, that the user hasn't deleted the cookie). A significant number of users do delete cookies. Estimates run as high as 40 percent. These estimates are a little murky, though, due to some nuances related to cookies. I discuss this subject in more detail in Chapter 13.

Incenting registrations by offering content

Earlier I mentioned newsletters as a vehicle for collecting e-mail addresses. You can publish your newsletter online rather than mail it out. In fact, requiring readers to register on your website to view the newsletter can provide you with a steady stream of new prospects. One advantage of this approach is that it comes with a built-in opportunity to advertise your newsletter — and in turn, your brand — online. You can place links to the newsletter on various web pages. And you have some control over what web searches will return a link to your page. I talk in more detail about marketing online in Chapter 13.

The same approach works for other content that you may want to publish online. Some companies have blogs that are partly intended as lead-generation tools. Similar considerations apply to social media marketing. For a much more detailed discussion of this topic, check out *Social Media Marketing For Dummies* (Wiley, 2012).

Incenting registrations by providing enhanced website features

In Chapter 3, I describe an experience that my wife and I had when buying new furniture. We were shopping around online. One company's website had a particularly slick application that allowed us to enter the dimensions of various rooms. We could then click on various pieces of furniture and move them around the room to get a feel for how we wanted to arrange things. We had to register on the website to use this feature, which we were happy to do.

Offering access to enhanced website features in exchange for registration can be a very effective way of identifying shoppers. People who register in order to use these features tend to be very good prospects. What's more, in using these features, those prospects become even more engaged with you. The longer these potential customers spend using your website, the more likely they are to follow through with a purchase.

I've seen an interior decorating site that allows you to upload pictures of your house. You can then select different paint colors, curtains, light fixtures, and other options. The site then gives you a virtual view of how all those options would look in your house.

I noticed another campaign being run by a home improvement store. Customers were encouraged to register so that they could keep track of past purchases. The hook was that you buy some things — like water filters, for example — quite infrequently. If you're like me, you never remember which one of the 50 filters available actually fits your refrigerator. By registering on the site, you make this information available in the store, either through your own mobile device or by having an employee look it up for you.

Restricting access to content is also an effective way to drive registrations. This *gated content,* as it's called, is made available only online and only to registered users of the site.

I rarely register on websites for content. But I recently registered on a site called lockerpulse.com. By logging in, I get access to every news story about Michigan Wolverines sports that appears on the web. And I get it every day.

This is more information than I could possibly keep track of, but it does appeal to my rabid college sports fanaticism. It also illustrates a point about content-driven registrations. The content had better be good if you're going to get people to sign up for it.

Clearly, the features and content you choose to offer on your website in exchange for registration are highly dependent on your type of business. But given the flexibility of the web and a little creativity, the possibilities are endless.

Not a Snap Decision: Understanding Your Customer's Mindset

Some businesses rely heavily on impulse buyers. The businesses who pay to have their products placed in the grocery store checkout lane, such as chewing gum and candy bars, fit this mold. I don't think I've ever gone into the grocery store planning to buy a candy bar. But I occasionally give in to an impulse while I'm standing in line.

Other products tend to require a good deal more thought on the part of the customer. Very few people take out a mortgage impulsively. A mortgage is a complicated and expensive product. Different banks offer different rates and fees, and fixed and variable rate products are available. Shopping for a mortgage is frequently an arduous process for the consumer.

You need to understand how your customers go about deciding to buy your products. Knowing where they are in their planning or research process allows you to help them along with relevant information. You also need to understand how far ahead of their purchase your customers begin investigating and planning. This allows you to time communications and offers effectively.

The decision-making process

Marketers tend to divide the process of making a purchase into four distinct phases:

1. **Awareness:** The consumer recognizes that they need or want something.

2. **Research:** The consumer investigates what's out there and compares different products or services that might meet their need.

3. **Purchase:** The customer makes the purchase.

4. **Post-purchase:** Because customer retention is so important, marketers also focus on a follow-up phase.

Guiding the decision making

My wife and I recently needed to replace our water heater. We browsed a few plumbing supply websites. We'd gotten interested in a tankless water heater that heats the water as you use it. Problem was, we didn't know much about how these systems compared to regular water heaters.

One website had done a very good job of anticipating our mindset. The website offered to send us a free pamphlet outlining the advantages of these tankless systems and describing the various types of systems that were available. We signed up to receive the information and did some more research.

About a week later, we received a follow-up offer from the supply store. They were offering a 10 percent discount on a particular brand of tankless water heater. By this time, we were convinced that this was the way to go. So we took them up on the offer.

When it comes to getting hand-raisers or shoppers to complete a purchase, I've found it helpful to focus on two distinct customer decisions. First, the customer is deciding whether to buy something. Do I really need a new car? Once the customer is past that decision, they move on to deciding whether they should buy the product from *you*. The way in which you talk to your shoppers changes, depending on which of these decisions they're trying to make.

If you're like me, you're put off by high-pressure sales pitches. One reason for this is that many high-pressure pitches gloss over the difference between the two different decisions I just mentioned. Once you decide to buy a new vehicle, for example, you want some time to do your homework. You want to get comfortable that you're making the correct decision.

Understanding the timeline for purchase decisions

If someone goes to your website and starts shopping for shoes, they're probably going to make a purchase pretty quickly. You don't have a very wide window of opportunity to get them to buy from you. You need to get your offer in front of them quickly.

Your strategy in this case would be to serve up content or offers on your website related to what the customer is doing. For example, you may notice that a customer browses your site and then jumps to a different site. If the customer comes back to your site a few minutes later, it's a good indication that they're interested in your product. At this point, you might decide to sweeten the pot by serving up a discount or some other offer during their session.

Other products have a more involved or time-consuming purchase cycle. As I mentioned, almost no one takes out a mortgage without shopping around. People tend to be very focused on rates. And rates change daily.

In the case of mortgages that are being used to refinance as opposed to purchase a house, the purchase decision is all about the rate. A customer may shop around for mortgage rates and then wait weeks or even months until rates go down enough to justify the cost of refinancing.

This means a consumer who's shopping your website for rates may not be ready to refinance at that time. This situation makes re-contacting the shopper at a later time a viable option. One approach you might take is to offer to send the shopper an e-mail alert when rates drop. You could even allow the customer to tell you what rate they're looking for. This approach guarantees that the timing of your communication will fit the customer's needs.

Another aspect of purchase decisions is related specifically to planning. You typically don't reserve a hotel room at a vacation resort the day before you leave. Vacations are planned months in advance. Cruise lines and resort hotels know far in advance when they have potential occupancy problems.

This advance notice gives these businesses the opportunity to craft discounted offers to fill potential gaps in their reservation volume. Understanding the typical planning timeline of their customers also allows them to avoid discounting their product until they recognize that sales are soft.

So Why Didn't They Buy? Overcoming Purchase Barriers

People consider a variety of factors when they shop for a product. What does it cost? How easy is it to buy? Is it high quality? If you're trying to convince a shopper to go ahead and purchase your product, you need to understand what might prevent them from doing so. Your strategy for marketing to shoppers will be largely defined by the *purchase barriers* you're trying to overcome.

Identifying purchase barriers

Some purchase barriers might be obvious to you. If you sell a high-end product, you probably know that price is an issue for many potential consumers. You may have a new product that hasn't been sufficiently advertised, making consumer awareness an issue. The American auto industry suffered for years with a perception issue. Many people viewed American cars as being of inferior quality compared to their Japanese and European competitors.

Some barriers may not be immediately obvious to you. Your frontline sales staff is an excellent resource for helping you understand why customers shop but don't purchase. Because they're dealing directly with customers, they typically know where the sale breaks down.

Similarly you may be able to learn something about purchase barriers by analyzing the way customers use your website. For example, what was the last thing the customer looked at before they abandoned your website?

 Survey research is a particularly effective tool for learning about purchase barriers. Small focus groups can also provide some insight because they allow the interviewer to dig deeply into consumer attitudes. Customers know why they didn't buy. So ask them.

Types of barriers

I think about purchase barriers as being in one of three general categories:

- ✔ **Cost:** Pretty much everyone checks the price before buying.
- ✔ **Perception:** This relates to how the consumer views your product and how it fits in with their needs.
- ✔ **Convenience:** This relates to how easy it is for the consumer to purchase the product.

In this section, I expand on various barriers. I also talk a little bit about strategies for overcoming these barriers.

Cost-related barriers

As I discuss in Chapter 7, some people are extremely price sensitive. They look for sales and discounts and rarely purchase anything without some financial incentive. You probably need to offer some sort of discount to incent price-sensitive shoppers to make a purchase.

Another group of consumers are more oriented toward quality or service levels. These consumers are willing to pay top dollar for premium benefits. Your approach to shoppers in this category should be to communicate those benefits. You want to show them what they're getting for the money.

Frequently, you won't have information on the price sensitivity of your shoppers. In these cases, a hybrid approach may be your best option. You could first contact your shopper with a message highlighting the value they're getting for the price. If that doesn't work, send a follow-up offer with a discount or some other promotional rate.

With shoppers, the first step is to get them to do business with you. Once you do, you can work on expanding your relationship with them. In Chapter 10, I talk about a variety of ways to upsell and cross-sell products to your customers to increase their profitability. Given the potential future revenue stream, using discounts to attract shoppers is effective and easily justifiable.

Introductory offers are sometimes quite effective at overcoming price-related barriers. Having recently moved, I've had to make decisions about choosing various service providers. My TV service provider, for example, sent me an offer to receive premium movie channels for free for several months if I bought their basic package. This type of approach doesn't just help to get customers over the price hump. It also positions you to upsell the customer later. We got hooked on a couple of shows that were broadcast on the premium channels. So when the free offer expired, we went ahead and paid for the premium service.

Perception-related barriers

One type of perception-related barrier is actually a *lack* of perception. Consumers may not even be aware that you sell a certain type of product or service. For example, I had no idea that I could deposit money into my online trading account at a mail and shipping store until they sent me an e-mail.

Perception-related barriers often have to do with negative views of your product, such as the troubles of the auto industry related to quality concerns. Overcoming preconceptions about quality can be quite difficult, especially if the perception is rooted in fact.

When you address quality concerns, it is a good idea to let someone else do the talking. The credibility of your brand is what's at issue. Customer testimonials are one way to do this. Another is to communicate positive results of customer satisfaction surveys. Still another is to play up awards that your products have received.

This approach played a large role in the resurgence of the American automotive industry. When the roots of their quality issues were addressed, these companies began to get some positive reviews. And they played them up for all they were worth. They're still doing it, in fact. I can't remember the last time I got a flyer from an auto dealer that didn't contain customer satisfaction ratings or an image of a trophy or both.

Another dimension of perception barriers is people's sensitivity to what's "in." There's an expression I hear once in a while related to country music: "I was country when country wasn't cool." The country music industry has been incredibly successful at overcoming negative sentiment related to the genre.

Whether it's the latest tech gadget, fashion craze, or book, people like to feel like they're cool. One of my favorite authors, who has since been wildly successful, got his big break when one of his books was spotted in the president's hand as he strolled across the White House lawn.

In positioning your product as socially relevant, images are very helpful. Use pictures of "cool" people using your products. Social media is also very useful.

The convenience barrier

Another type of barrier relates to convenience. The entire fast-food industry is based on our being in a hurry. Whether it's short lines, streamlined applications, or easy checkout, you need to communicate these conveniences to your customers.

Many companies have lost business by not keeping up with the advances in e-commerce. Going into a bank to fill out a paper loan application is much less convenient than doing it online. For me, it's doubly inconvenient because I invariably forget to bring some document or other critical piece of information.

A few months ago I was shopping for a gift for a relative. I knew she wanted a certain type of roasting pan. So I did a web search and clicked on the website of the first brand I recognized. From there I proceeded to spend ten minutes trying unsuccessfully to find the product I wanted. The web site was so poorly organized that I gave up and went somewhere else.

Social media and purchase barriers

Not a day goes by when I don't see a post on Facebook asking for a recommendation for some product or other. A friend will be travelling to New York on business and want some restaurant suggestions. Another will be shopping for a new car and want to know if anybody has purchased a given make or model. Many won't make a major purchase without consulting their Facebook friends.

And it's not just Facebook. My wife routinely peruses the customer feedback posts on websites before she's comfortable with decisions ranging from appliance purchases to hotel reservations.

A whole host of consumer ratings websites have sprung up over the last few years. Many specialize in a particular type of product. Tripadvisor.com has testimonials about practically every travel destination in the world. Carfax.com offers service audits for used vehicles. Angieslist.com gives ratings on local businesses based on customer experiences. The ratings on Angie's List have been extremely helpful to my wife and me as we've moved around the country. It's tough to know which plumber to call if you don't have any experience in the area. It's been said that the best advertising is word of mouth. Social media and consumer ratings sites can be your best friends in this regard.

Social media also forces you to be hyper-sensitive to customer service issues. Every bad experience a customer has with you can potentially end up being broadcast across the web. This makes it important to resolve issues quickly and to the customer's satisfaction.

Chapter 12

Crafting Your Marketing Message

. . . .

. . . .

Much of this book focuses on the mechanics of database marketing tactics. I talk a great deal about analyzing data to identify target audiences and measure results. But the customer data that underlies all this analysis can also be helpful in crafting the messages that you want your customer to hear.

In this chapter, I talk about using what you know about customers to make your communications more relevant. Given the current state of technology, it's possible to craft communications that are highly customized and personalized to individual customers. This personal touch helps immensely in getting your message heard.

Getting Your Message Heard

The first step in getting a customer to respond to your marketing communication is getting them to pay attention to it. This is actually a two-step process. It has to first avoid the recycling bin. Next it has to be read. Only then will you have any hope of coaxing your customer into action.

Getting past the recycling bin

First impressions are lasting impressions, as the saying goes. The first decision a customer makes when they receive a communication from you is whether or not to immediately recycle or trash it. In most direct marketing campaigns, the bin wins more often than not. For that reason, it's important to put some thought into how you *wrap* your message.

Whether you're communicating via direct mail or e-mail, you have limited opportunity to create a first impression regarding your communication. There's only so much you can do on an envelope or catalog cover to encourage people to open it. In the case of an e-mail, all people see is the sender and the subject line.

Identifying yourself

Every spring, it seems, I get a series of solicitations that are intentionally made to look like tax return checks. They come in a brown envelope with a clear plastic window. They have some variation of "Department of Revenue" in the return address window. And they often have some crafty, but meaningless, legal mumbo-jumbo printed on the envelope. In short, the whole package is dishonest.

I've learned to spot these things pretty quickly. And they always end up in the recycling bin. But I tend to open them first. My philosophy is that some business has been kind enough to inform me of their dishonesty. I'd be foolish not to actually take advantage of that information and avoid them.

It's important to identify your brand clearly. Trying to fool people into thinking your communication is from someone else is not a particularly effective strategy. It may get them to open your communication, but it actually makes them more likely to discard the letter or e-mail. And the impression you leave with the customer is that you're dishonest.

If you're not proud of your brand, then it might be time to look for another one.

This is equally true of e-mail. In fact, with e-mail it's even more important to be forthright about who you are. You can be thrown into the spam list with literally a click of a button. And once you're spam, you have lost your connection to the customer who put you there.

Making the most of the "envelope"

Personalizing your direct mail helps to get it opened. Or more precisely, not personalizing mail pieces helps get them tossed. I almost never open an envelope addressed to *Resident* or that contains the bailout phrase *or Current Occupant.*

You can also use the envelope to help entice the customer. Giving a hint of what's inside can be an effective way of getting them interested in your communication. Discounts or special offers, in particular, should be announced somehow on the envelope.

E-mail and other electronic channels provide less flexibility. In these channels, your envelope is essentially the subject line of your e-mail. You don't have a lot of space to work with. This makes it particularly important for you to put some careful thought into what goes in the subject line.

Some marketers are fond of including the recipient's name in the subject line of the e-mail. The idea is that this makes the communication seem more personal. My own take on this is that it seems a little contrived. People know that marketing e-mails are not "just for them." Besides, subject line space is limited. I've always felt that it could be used more effectively to generate interest in the communication.

Making sure your message is effective

Once your communication gets past the recycle bin, you've got an opportunity to be heard. Books have been written on the subject of creative work and copy development for marketing campaigns. Advertising and direct-marketing service providers employ stables of people to craft communications. But when you're evaluating a direct mail piece, there are a few things you should be looking for.

Does the message reflect your marketing strategy?

It's sometimes easy to get caught up in the look and feel of a direct-mail piece. The folks who develop marketing collateral are talented artists in their own right. And they can put together some dazzling and visually stunning work.

But you have a specific business goal in mind. Impressive graphics can distract from that goal. You need the message to be simple and clear. Being visually appealing is good, but not if it distracts from the goal of your campaign. Keep the communication on strategy.

Is the offer clear and concise?

You want your offer to be immediately recognizable. And you want it to be clear. Don't clutter up the mail piece or e-mail with a bunch of unnecessary buildup. Your offer needs to be the star of the show. You will often hear the offer referred as the *hero* of the message.

One common mistake is to get too cute with your offer. As a general rule, you don't want to confuse the customer by making several offers at once. If you get your customer comparing different offers, you've distracted them from the interest in your product that your communication is trying to create. For example, if you're trying to sell car leases, feature the monthly payment prominently. Don't confuse your audience by also featuring the payment on a five-year loan. This gets them wondering if either one is really a good deal.

Don't forget the call to action

Every marketing communication needs to be clear about what you're asking the customer to do. Be explicit about how the customer is to take advantage of your offer.

It's okay to give the customer options. You can tell them to visit your store or go online to take advantage of this discounted offer. In fact, most marketing communications these days contain a reference or link to the company's website. It's become routine practice.

In addition to being explicit about your call to action, you need to create a sense of urgency. Expiration dates for offers are an effective way of doing that. It's also common to reference limited inventory with phrases like *while supplies last*. However you do it, you want to plant a seed in the customer's mind that there is a downside to waiting.

 Direct marketers all learn, some sooner than others, not to overdo the call to action. Decades of evidence from marketing campaigns across all industries points consistently in the same direction. Straightforward is better than clever. Simple is better than complicated. Clear is better than subtle. Understanding your call to action should not require an intellectual effort on the part of the customer.

Using Technology to Customize Communications

It used to be that printing your customer's name in the salutation line of a letter was considered personalization. Those days are long gone. Your ability to customize and personalize your communications is almost endless now. Everything from images to copy can be presented to the customer based on information from your marketing database.

In this section, I talk about the process of customizing both online and offline database marketing communications. Technology has reached the point where you can make your messages as unique as snowflakes. By inserting content based on unique customer attributes, it's possible to create a campaign where no two messages are exactly alike.

I focus on e-mail and direct mail in this section, but customization opportunities exist across all customer touchpoints. In Chapter 13, I address the use of customer data in the online and mobile world. And in Chapter 17, I talk about using customer data in call centers and at the point of sale. The sort of *you know me* experience that customization and personalization provide to customers is now expected.

Customizing e-mail messages

It's probably not all that surprising to you that e-mail messages provide a great deal of room for customization. These messages are constructed out of frameworks that allow for content to be dropped in based on various parameters.

A simple example of customization relates to the links to your website that you include in your e-mail. Online marketers have learned there are much more effective ways to direct customers to their websites than to simply send everyone to their home page. For one thing, websites have gotten huge. And no matter how well they're designed, they take at least a minimal effort by users to learn their way around.

If you send out an e-mail advertising a back-to-school discount on clothes, why not send the customer directly to a page on your website that shows children's apparel? What's more, you don't need to send everyone to the *same* page. If your database happens to contain data on the ages of the children in each household, you can actually vary the links based on the ages. High school students wear very different styles and sizes than kindergarteners.

This same thought process applies to images. When a customer opens an e-mail, the images that are associated with that e-mail are not inside the e-mail, so to speak. What the e-mail contains is links, or pointers, to a server where the images reside. That's what allows users to block images. They tell their e-mail service not to download those linked images.

But there's an advantage to this architecture: You don't have to point all customers to the same image. Based on individual customer information, you can place different links in different e-mails.

And there is nothing special about images. You can do the same thing with text. Rather than including text in an e-mail communication, you can embed it in what amounts to an image. You then place a link in your e-mail that points to the particular version of your message which you think is most relevant to your customer.

An ancillary advantage of treating text this way is that it gives you greater control over how the text actually appears in the e-mail. Text files don't give you nearly as much flexibility (or control) over how your message appears. But you have all the flexibility in the world if you embed it in a linked file.

Customizing offline communications: The power of digital printing

As with online content, you have a great deal of flexibility in the way you construct your printed communications. Printing has come a long way since Gutenberg. It's now quite cost effective to use color digital printing to customize and personalize your offline communications.

Constructing a printed marketing piece is very similar to constructing an e-mail. You put together a framework that contains the basic text or outline of how you want the piece to look. This framework contains placeholders for where you want to customize content.

The digital printing press has access to the universe of images that you want to include. It also contains your customer list along with the data that drives the customization. As it pages through your customer list, it uses each individual customer's attributes to choose which images to print on the mail piece. As with e-mails and online content, you can customize images or text in your printed pieces.

There really is no limit to your ability to customize printed content. Even catalogs and magazines can customize their content based on customer attributes. Magazines in particular can benefit from customizing their advertisements to specific consumer segments. This is a selling point with advertisers because they know they are reaching the audiences they want to reach.

Using Images in Your Messages

A standard rule of thumb in direct marketing is that the copy in a communication is what sells, not the images. The offer and the call to action need to be explicitly stated. But that's not to say that images don't have their place. In this section, I give a couple examples of effective ways to use images in your direct marketing communications.

Integrating your message with advertising campaigns

The first challenge in marketing to consumers is to make them aware that you exist. Much of your company's marketing budget is spent doing exactly that. Advertising is largely concerned with establishing brand recognition and keeping your brand top of mind for consumers.

Advertising, particularly TV advertising, is largely a visual medium. Companies regularly employ celebrity spokespeople precisely because people recognize them. Others use well-established cartoon characters or develop characters of their own to build recognition. Animals are popular as well. MetLife has adopted Snoopy and even given him his own blimp. I've kept a lifetime tally of how many sports trivia questions posed by the AFLAC duck I've gotten correct. (My total stands at one.) One of the more endearing examples is the Travelers Insurance dog, Chopper. I'm told that Chopper was rescued from an animal shelter by an employee of the advertising company that produces the TV ads.

Take advantage of this association. By putting your company logo or iconic advertising image on your mail piece, you gain instant recognition. In the case of direct-mail pieces, put it on the envelope. Prominently displaying your logo on your communications is better than any introductory paragraph you could write.

Using customized images in your communications

One commonly referenced hurdle that marketers need to address is convenience. You need to make it easy for the customer to do business with you. Many marketing communications reference some variation of *visit a store near you.* In the case of direct-marketing communications, you can do better than that.

If you're trying to drive customer traffic to "a store near them," show them where it is. If you're mailing a postcard or letter, you know where they live. And you know where your stores are. So give them a map. Including a link to a mapping website is standard operating procedure with e-mails. But in the case of a direct mail piece, it's still possible to print a map that will get them where they need to go.

Being relevant to the customer is another key marketing challenge. You can use images in this regard as well. Including images that reflect their past purchases is a good way to be relevant. It shows that you understand and value your relationship. This idea is best illustrated with a couple of examples.

Every once in a while, my wife and I get postcards or letters regarding our cars. The messages vary. Sometimes they want to buy them back or take one on trade for a new car. Others are service reminders.

The communications that really impress me are the ones that actually show a picture of the car we have. One company in particular actually gets the color right. They also reference the make and model and even the year in the text of the solicitation — but the image really drives home the point that they're paying attention to who they're talking to.

Another example that impressed me relates to a recent cruise that I took with my wife. A few months after we booked, we got a notification that it was time to book our shore excursions. The e-mail contained a list of the available excursions on that particular cruise.

But the e-mail also contained images that portrayed those particular excursions. In this case, the images actually sold us. The majestic landscapes that were portrayed got both of us thinking, "We've gotta see that!"

Getting the Product Right

To be effective, you need to clearly define the goal of your database marketing campaign. That goal needs to be specific. But usually it's not so specific that it's limited to a particular product. You may be trying to sell cars. But you probably aren't going to run a campaign to sell 2013, black, four-door sedan hybrids with leather interior and chrome wheels. You have a more general goal of selling your brand of cars.

You have some flexibility in what particular products you feature in your messages. As with practically every other aspect of database marketing, your customer data can help.

Past purchases are the obvious place to start. To continue with the automobile example, you can customize your messages according to what type of car each customer is currently driving. If someone is currently in a high performance two-door convertible, featuring a picture of a pickup truck is probably not going to resonate. And vice versa.

As I mention earlier in this chapter, when you communicate using e-mail, you have some flexibility in the links you include. This is a situation where you can take advantage of that flexibility. You can send each individual customer to a page that reflects their current taste in automobiles.

If you don't have past purchase data, you can still customize your product messages. Your customer profiles give you a good sense of the demographics associated with different product types. Minivans are popular with families with children. Pickup trucks are popular in rural areas. Sports cars are popular with single women and middle-aged men.

You know a lot about your customers' preferences. You may know directly from past purchases what your customers are interested in. Or you may infer it from analyzing customer profiles. In either case, use this information in deciding how to position your product offering in your message. As always, being relevant to the customer is what drives the success of your marketing campaigns.

Using Customer Profiles to Craft Messages

Designing database marketing collateral, crafting e-mails and direct mail pieces, and writing copy require specialized talents. Most companies have dedicated resources for these tasks. Often external agencies are hired to do this work. So you probably won't be the one doing the so-called *creative development*.

Your interaction with your creative team generally revolves around something called a *creative brief*. This is a document that lays out the business opportunity, goals, strategy, and other details of your campaign. It's beyond my scope here to discuss how these briefs are developed. There's quite a bit of literature available on this subject, including a section in *Marketing For Dummies* (Wiley, 2009) that lays out the process.

My point here is that your customer data plays a significant role in the development of these briefs in two ways:

- ✔ It's important for whoever is developing the creative content to clearly understand the target audience.

- ✔ To create customized versions of the communication, the developer needs to understand what data is available to drive customization.

Speaking to the target audience

Understanding the target audience is fairly straightforward. You can be quite specific about it, in fact. This is one advantage that database marketing has over other marketing — and especially advertising — channels. You don't have to rely on market research or inferred profiles of your audience. You know precisely what rules were used to pick your target.

The definition of your target audience also constitutes a profile of that audience. And it's central to the messaging strategy. You speak very differently to families with young children than you do to retired grandparents, for example. Even if you're trying to sell them the same product, the emotional connection you attempt to make is different.

This example points out a common occurrence. Your target audience will frequently be made up of more than one customer segment. In the case of products — toys, for example — that are targeted at young children, the child isn't the one making the purchase. But both grandparents and parents buy presents.

This means that both these segments are perfectly viable audiences for a campaign marketing a particular toy. As I say earlier, the messaging strategies for these two audiences will be different. So you need to customize different versions of your communication to different segments in your overall target audience.

Customizing the message

Your audience selection criteria are critical to your messaging strategy. But these criteria aren't the only information you have available about your customers. Earlier in this chapter, I point out the value of varying the product message based on past purchase history. This sort of versioning can be extended to a wide range of customer data.

A number of years ago, I was involved with a customer-retention project for a company that owned a number of resort hotels. They were concerned about their cancellation rates for booked rooms. They didn't really have an interest in trying to address the problem through discounts. So they tried a different strategy.

The strategy was to create a communication stream that was intended to build up excitement about the upcoming vacation. It included notifications about various entertainment and dining options available in the area. But the flagship component of this stream was a letter that was triggered by the initial reservation.

This communication was vastly more than a simple confirmation letter. It was a high-quality, highly customized, full-color, glossy introduction to the resort the customer had booked. It took full advantage of the digital printing technology mentioned earlier in this chapter.

Everything in this letter was customized. A cartoon character greeted the family by name in a speech balloon. The restaurants described in the letter were specific to the particular resort that had been booked. The activities that were suggested were based on whether or not the reservation included children.

Even the images in the communication were customized to the reservation. The room photos reflected not only the booked resort, but the booked room class. Even the photos of the swimming pools varied according to the travel party details. Families with young children were shown the children's pool. Adults traveling alone were shown the pool with the swim-up bar.

And it worked. We quite quickly experienced a significant drop in cancellations. By being extremely relevant to the customers' particular attitudes and expectations for a vacation, we managed to build and maintain excitement about the trip. And we got a lot of positive feedback from guests strongly indicating that our communication stream had an effect.

As a side note, this example is relevant to a topic I discuss in several places throughout this book. The subject is data gathering. In this case, much of the data that we wanted to use to customize some of our messages was not being captured anywhere. To really get this project off the ground, we had to first make some changes in the information that was being gathered when reservations were being made.

The story of my involvement in this campaign has an epilogue. Years later, I was on the golf course hundreds of miles away from my old employer. I had been paired up with another golfer that I didn't know. We got to chatting as people do in that situation.

Quite at random, the subject of one of those resorts came up. And it came up in the context of the communication stream that I describe above. Apparently that campaign was still being used. And this guy couldn't say enough about how impressed he was with the attention to detail. Furthermore, he said that his first vacation had been so awesome that he and his wife were going back next year.

Needless to say, I gave myself a little pat on the back for our efforts. I then proceeded to hit a high, arcing drive directly into the lake.

Chapter 13

Using Customer Data Online

In This Chapter

▶ Understanding how to use e-mail effectively

▶ Serving up web content based on customer information

▶ Recognizing your customer online

▶ Being visible through search engines

The so-called *virtual world* has evolved at lightning speed over the last couple of decades. Search engines are often the first place consumers go when they want to shop for some product. *Google* has become a verb in virtually every language. E-commerce has overtaken traditional in-store purchases in many industries. I haven't been into a bank branch in years.

The virtual business world is vastly different than the brick-and-mortar world. Change happens much faster — you can set up a website in a matter of hours. Website content is constantly undated, and functionality is enhanced all the time. Perhaps the most significant difference, though, is that websites serve as marketing and advertising platforms as well as cash registers that process sales transactions.

The latest big change online is the flood of mobile devices. The Internet has gone mobile big time. This shift creates both challenges and opportunities for marketers. The world of smartphones and tablets is, if possible, even more dynamic than that of the traditional web.

Because of their ever changing nature, the discipline(s) of online and mobile marketing have developed largely outside other traditional marketing disciplines like advertising and direct marketing. New decisions are made on a daily basis, and the overall culture in these fields is one of experimentation.

I knew an Internet guy a few years back who had a sign on his door that read "Informed trial and error outperforms detailed planning every time." And that rings true. Waiting until you're sure you've got everything perfect is a sure way to fall behind.

Another feature of the online world is the blurring of the distinction between marketing and operations — particularly sales. As a database marketer, you don't have to pay attention to what is happening at the checkout counter of your stores every day. But your online team does. Typically they direct both marketing and e-commerce because the two things are so tightly intertwined.

This chapter introduces you to some basic ideas related to the online world that touch on customer data. I don't have room to address online and mobile marketing in great detail here. If you'd like to explore this topic in more detail, check out *Web Marketing For Dummies* (Wiley, 2012).

There's More to E-mail Than You Might Think

When e-mail first became a popular marketing channel, it started as an inexpensive alternative to direct mail. A direct marketing campaign using e-mails costs a small fraction of what printing and postage cost. In the early days, e-mail campaigns followed the same general principles of more traditional mail campaigns. They were designed and executed following the same mass mailing model.

The use of e-mail in marketing has become a good deal more sophisticated over the years. Due in part to the negative reaction of users to the early overuse and abuse of e-mail addresses (called *spamming*), marketers now have to be much more careful about how and when they use e-mail to communicate. At the same time, they've developed more and more insightful ways of tracking the success of their e-mail campaigns.

Chapters 10 and 11 talk about some of the ways that marketers use e-mail in their database marketing campaigns. Here I discuss some aspects of e-mail marketing related to collecting and managing your e-mail addresses. I also talk about how to track responses to e-mail campaigns.

Understanding how customers deal with spam

Because mass mailings through e-mail are so inexpensive, these campaigns don't need to have very high response rates to generate sales. It was this fact that led inevitably to the abuse of the channel. People's distaste for spam or unsolicited e-mail, especially in large volumes, led to all kinds of technical and legal developments designed to block e-mail solicitations.

In other words, people have gotten to the point where they simply tune out much of the marketing related e-mail that comes to them. They can flag an e-mail as spam and never see another e-mail from that sender again. E-mail service providers block e-mails all the time.

My wife and I have a separate e-mail account that we use for only one thing. We make a lot of purchases online, and they invariably require us to provide an e-mail address. Because merchants need an actual e-mail address (yes, websites can check this), we created what amounts to a dummy account to receive the inevitable follow up e-mails. We reserve our real e-mail address for companies that we frequently do business with. This is becoming a common tactic for online consumers. I talked recently with someone in the online marketing business who suggested that as many as 15 percent of the e-mail addresses in marketing databases are being used this way.

In Chapter 4, I discuss allowing your customers to opt out of hearing from you — this is standard practice when you collect a customer's e-mail address online. Usually it involves offering a check box for them to indicate whether they want to receive special offers and other marketing communications from you in the future.

Respect their decision. You are actually legally mandated to do so per the CAN-SPAM law mentioned in Chapter 4.

There is a loophole in the CAN-SPAM law which allows you to communicate with existing customers. If the communication is related to your relationship with them, you can use e-mail. Shipping information on a recent purchase is an example of such an acceptable use. Confirming a password change is another.

Collecting e-mail effectively

You will no doubt want to send e-mails as part of your traditional direct-marketing campaigns. They are very effective as follow-up reminders to special offers that you may mail out, for example. An e-mail telling your customers that they only have three days left to take advantage of a discount not only serves as a reminder but creates a sense of urgency.

But e-mail is only effective if it gets read. You want to be careful about how often you use this channel. All it takes is a single mouse click, and a customer can block your e-mails and never see them again. In Chapter 5 I talk about the importance of developing an explicit contact-management policy to avoid overcommunicating with your customers.

All e-mail addresses are not created equal. You want to focus on quality over quantity. This means you want to be sure your customer really wants to hear from you before including them in a marketing campaign.

As I discuss in Chapter 11, offering newsletters, product guides, or other informational material can be an effective way of collecting e-mail (or home) address information from your customers or prospects. When a customer makes the request, they are implicitly opting in to hearing from you. But this interest may only be related to the particular information you are offering.

You can improve the quality of your e-mail lists by taking this opt-in process one step further. You can require a second, more explicit, opt in from the requester. Typically this is done by sending an e-mail to confirm the request before sending out the requested information. This *double opt-in*, as it's called, has the additional advantage of confirming that the e-mail address is real and is being checked by the customer.

Over time, your database has accumulated e-mail addresses that have been collected in a wide variety of ways. The quality of those addresses also varies widely. Some may no longer be active. Some are opted in. Some are opted out. You will even find some that have done both. Still others never were given the opportunity.

A one-time mass-mailing version of the double opt-in approach can be used to clean up your e-mail address list. By *clean up,* I mean dramatically pare down the list. In addition to ensuring compliance with CAN-SPAM, doing this occasionally confers a few other advantages:

- ✓ It improves response rates.
- ✓ It lets you purge e-mail addresses that are no longer active.
- ✓ It keeps you out of trouble with your e-mail service provider.

E-mail service providers are extremely sensitive to being used as vehicles for spammers. They are the ones holding the smoking gun if the Federal Trade Commission should come calling about CAN-SPAM violations. If a large number of your customers are reporting your e-mails as spam, then you will eventually be dropped by your provider.

Speaking of e-mail service providers, choosing one is among the most important decisions you will make. You'll rely heavily on your ESP — not just to execute e-mail campaigns, but to ensure CAN-SPAM compliance and e-mail address deliverability. The ESP will also provide reporting on which e-mails have been viewed and which customers have clicked links in them. The best ESPs provide this information in real time on the web. A good ESP can also provide this data back to you at the customer level so that you can incorporate it into your database for analytic purposes. Because you rely so heavily on your ESP, you should get proposals, including client recommendations, from several providers and evaluate them carefully before making a decision.

Tracking e-mail effectiveness

As I say in Chapter 2, it's important for marketing campaigns to have a clear call to action. You need to communicate exactly what you want them to do. In the case of e-mail campaigns, you typically direct the customer to your website. In fact, most campaigns contain a link to your website in the e-mail itself.

The simple way to think about responses to e-mail campaigns is that the customer proceeds in a straightforward fashion. They click the e-mail. They read the e-mail and become interested. They proceed to your website and potentially end up making a purchase.

I discuss the purchase piece of the puzzle later in this chapter. In this section, I want to talk a little about the click part.

Who is getting to your website? Open and click-through rates

Customer behavior is actually a good deal more complex than a nice linear progression from clicking your e-mail to purchasing. They may read your e-mail on their smartphone and wait until they get home to browse your website on a larger computer screen. They may click the link to your site but visit it several more times before making a purchase. Some customers may be registered on your website and others not. Customers can take vastly different paths to finally making a purchase.

When analyzing the success of an e-mail campaign, one thing you will want to know is what percentage of people who received the e-mail actually opened it. This is known as an *open rate.* Of the users who do open your e-mail, you also want to know what percentage actually clicked the link to your website. This is called the *click-through rate.*

Your e-mail service provider will be able to tell you both these things. Open rates and click-through rates are standard metrics in e-mail marketing. Even these simple-sounding methods can be a little tricky, though. You — or more accurately, your service provider — need to avoid overcounting. Reporting of these rates must take into account multiple views of the e-mail as well as multiple clicks on the link.

What are they doing on your website? View-through analysis

More recently marketers have gotten interested in diving deeper into what customers are doing after they click a web link. This sort of analysis is known as *view-through* analysis. Be aware, though, that this term means slightly different things to different people.

If you're running an online advertising campaign involving streaming video, you'll obviously care how many clicks you get asking to view the video. But more importantly, you'll be concerned with what percentage of those viewers actually watched the whole video. This second number is referred to as a *view-through rate.*

The term *view-through* is also used in the context of website traffic analysis. In the case of e-mail campaign response analysis, it is an extension of click-through analysis. After a user lands on your website, they have a lot of options. They can search for a specific product, for example. They can browse products by price. They can simply wander around exploring various pages. Or they can leave.

Understanding view-through behavior can be very helpful in designing future e-mail campaigns. In particular, knowing what products your customers are searching for and viewing helps you to focus future messages on what's most relevant. In Chapter 11, I discuss the importance of understanding barriers to purchase. What is it that's preventing the customer from buying? View-through analysis can be very helpful here as well. When a customer abandons your website, you can tell what they last looked at. You can also tell where they went.

Many websites, particularly ones that sell retail products, allow you to view products by price ranges. A user might be looking at refrigerators in the lowest price category and then immediately jumps to a competitor's website. This would be a good indication that you have a price-sensitive consumer. You may decide to offer this customer a discount on a higher-quality model. The assumption is that the customer didn't see anything in their price range that was satisfactory. Bringing a slightly higher end model into that price range might be enough to get them interested.

View-through analysis can also help in another way. Nobody ever said that when you embed a link to your website in an e-mail, it has to point to your home page. If you understand what pages users are gravitating toward, why not send them directly to what they're interested in? Making the shopping and purchase experience convenient is a key part of making a sale.

Creating customized landing pages turns out to be a very powerful tool in your e-mail campaign tool kit. These pages are easy to create and they can be modified almost in real time based on the data you receive from your ESP. If the products you feature on your landing page don't seem to be capturing many clicks, you can change them very quickly.

Serving Up Web Content Dynamically

Your web page is an ideal place to personalize and customize content and messages to your customers' preferences and needs. Whether the user is logged in or not, you have a large amount of information at your disposal. This information can be used to make decisions about what content, advertisements, and links are displayed to the user.

Selling even when they aren't buying

Every few months I have to buy flea-prevention medicine for our cats. The stuff we use is kind of expensive (and we have a lot of cats), so I'm a little sensitive about the price. On the other hand, I'm also a little mistrustful of ordering pet meds over the internet. Nevertheless, before I go to the vet, I generally check the online price of the medicine. I'm just trying to keep my vet honest about his prices, you see.

Now because I don't actually buy anything from the websites I check, they really don't know anything about me. But when I search for my brand of flea medication for cats, the web sites often return advertisements for other cat-related products. The interesting thing is that they often return ads for the very brand of cat food that we buy.

The reason for this is that my wife spoils the heck out of our cats (okay, both of us do). Only the best is good enough. It's no surprise that the websites know to serve up ads for cat food as opposed to dog food. They know that from my search. But some of them also recognize that I'm searching for the most expensive flea medication they sell. So they serve up ads for the most expensive cat food they sell. And if the price is right, I sometimes take them up on their offers.

Web analytic platforms are also an important part of your online marketing tool kit. These platforms provide detailed analysis regarding website traffic, page views, click streams, keyword searches, and everything else that leaves a data trail online. These platforms provide information not only on your site but on search engines and sites that you buy advertising on. Google Analytics and Omniture (which is now owned by Adobe) are two of the big players in this space.

Using information about browsing behavior

Chapter 10 talks about event-triggered marketing tactics. These are communications that are sent out based on the occurrence of specific events. The way you serve up content on your website is event-triggered marketing on steroids.

As soon as a customer lands on your website, everything they do can be tracked by the site. This means that every mouse click and search query can potentially be used to determine what they see next. Even if you know nothing else about the user, this browsing information is useful.

Chapter 10 also explains the notion of cross-selling. The idea is that certain products are bought in bundles or are otherwise similar in some way. So when a customer buys one product in that bundle, they are likely to buy another. One extremely common online cross-selling technique is to respond to purchases or even views of a product by immediately serving up images of similar products. You've no doubt experienced the "People who bought this book also bought these" pitch.

In addition to content related to your own products, your website may contain links to other websites. You may even sell advertising to other companies. You can control the links and ads that you choose to display by monitoring how the user is navigating your website.

So far, I've been talking about information related to a particular browsing session. There is actually a good deal more information available to you that can help you customize your web content.

Using information about the customer

The problem with data collected during a particular browsing session is that once the session ends, you lose the connection to the customer. This data is still useful for analytic purposes. But it can no longer be used to steer the conversation with the customer who created it.

Personalizing your website

If the user is registered on your website and logs in to view it, then this problem disappears. You have full visibility not only to past browsing history, but also to preferences and personal information the customer has provided.

Many websites, particularly those that have aspirations to being home pages, allow registered users to fully customize what they see. I've been using Yahoo! mail for years. By logging into the site, I can use MyYahoo! to essentially create my own personal web page. I can choose background colors and themes as well as page formats. I can insert links to other sites. I can choose what news stories I want displayed, and so on.

Another way to personalize your website is to tailor it around your relationship with your customer. Online banking is a classic example. When I log in to my bank's website, I land on a homepage that is literally my own personal web page. This page contains information on all the accounts I have. It allows me to drill down to view details of individual accounts, even to the transaction level. It also allows me to open new accounts.

This last feature is no accident. The bank uses information about my accounts and how I use them to serve up ads on "my" website that it thinks I might be interested in. After we sold our last house, we paid off the mortgage we had with this bank. We went with a different lender when we bought a new house. But the bank, being astute, started to serve up ads to me regarding home equity lines of credit.

If a customer logs in to your website, it makes personalizing content easy. But there is another solution to this problem that doesn't require the user to register or log in.

Linking web sessions together

Linking browser sessions together is done through the use of *cookies*. I talk more about cookies in the next section, but essentially, cookies are just small files that your website stores on a user's computer. Cookies contain information that you want to remember and are a way of making information from one web session available when a user returns and initiates another session.

For me, like many people these days, the web has taken the place of the newspaper in my morning coffee routine. I have a news site that I check every morning. I haven't bothered to register on the site and set up any preferences, but the site seems to know a great deal about my morning routine.

For example, during baseball season, I always check the Detroit Tigers' box score and the Central Division standings. At the beginning of the season, I had to click the sports page and then click the MLB tab and so on to see what I wanted. Now, when I click the sports page, this information automatically appears.

The same thing is true on the financial page. I have a group of stocks that I look at every day. I no longer have to enter each ticker symbol to check the price. The ticker symbols and prices are all neatly displayed when I land on the finance home page.

This is all being done via cookies. The website has written notes to itself (on my computer) to remind it of what I have done in the past. It then serves up content accordingly.

Recognizing Customers Online

In a perfect world, every time a customer visited your website, they would log in and therefore identify themselves. But you know from your own web browsing experience that this is the exception and not the norm. In fact, the vast majority of web browsing is done anonymously, or at least without the user being logged in to your website. But unregistered browsing sessions aren't completely anonymous. There are a number of ways of getting at least some information about users that visit your website. I briefly describe a few common techniques in this section.

Recognizing where they are: IP addresses

Whenever a user initiates a web session, the web needs to know the location of the machine requesting access in order to route content to it. This location information is known as the machine's *IP address*. (IP stands for *internet protocol*.) When a user visits your website, their IP address is available to you. This means that (theoretically) you know where the user is located.

Location data can be quite useful in customizing web content. If a customer is shopping for pizza delivery, you may be able to use their IP address to point them to locations that are close by. If your business is selling college logo sweatshirts, you could serve up images depicting the logos of nearby colleges. In Chapter 7, I talk about a number of ways to use geographic data. These strategies apply equally well to customizing the web pages and images that you serve up to users of your website.

Location information is often used to aid in security and user verification. Whenever I'm away from home, if I try to log in to my online banking account, I have to go through an extra layer of security. I get asked one of my security questions before the site will let me in. The website recognizes that I'm not where I normally am (home) when I typically do my banking.

But wait! It isn't quite that simple

Earlier I said that you *theoretically* know where your user is located. This last example points up a subtlety that you should be aware of. Actually a lot of subtleties surround the subject of IP addresses and how data is routed around the World Wide Web. The inner workings of the web are vastly complex and far beyond the scope of this book.

The particular subtlety I'm talking about is that IP addresses do not actually reflect the location of the user's machine. They reflect the location of the device that's actually accessing the internet. If you're accessing the Internet from home, this means your modem. If my wife and I are both browsing the same site at the same time, both sessions will be associated with the same IP address — that of our modem.

There are a number of situations in which IP addresses can provide misleading or just plain wrong location data. One has to do with web sessions that are initiated from work rather than home. Many — in fact, most — companies make use of internal networks to connect computers, printers, and other devices. All the computers attached to these internal networks may not be in the same place. In the case of large companies, they may be spread out all over the country or even the world. But the Internet access devices that they're using may not be nearly that spread out. Users may be remotely accessing the Internet devices, and so their actual locations may not be reflected by the IP address that shows up at your website.

IP addresses and cellular networks: Geolocation

When users access your website via mobile devices, IP addresses are particularly untrustworthy. As if directing traffic on the web weren't complicated enough, mobile devices that use a cellphone network throw a whole other level of complexity into the mix. Mobile devices are just that. And they do move. Even when they're stationary, the cellular network may be routing and rerouting calls through its system of towers, fiber optic lines, and various other network components. This means that the actual Internet access point may wander around during a session. Depending on traffic patterns, the actual IP address associated with a smartphone may be hundreds of miles away from the actual device.

Luckily, you have another location option for mobile devices. Virtually every mobile device is equipped with geolocation capabilities. Typically, the user has the option of turning those services off, but many people leave them on because they're critical to a number of popular apps. Maps, searches for nearby restaurants, even keeping track of the local time while you're traveling all depend on the mobile device knowing where it is.

As Chapter 2 explains, customer privacy is a sensitive issue. It's particularly sensitive when it comes to collecting location data from mobile devices. The legal environment surrounding geolocation data is evolving quickly. You need to stay abreast of the legislation that's coming down the pike. An example of such legislation has been proposed by Congressman Ed Markey of Massachusetts.

Recognizing who they are: Cookies

Chapter 3 discusses constructing a customer (and ultimately a household) record. The data you have about your customer is spread out across your enterprise, and not all of it is easily associated with individual customers. If your website is designed as an e-commerce site — that is, customers can purchase online — then many of the problems of the offline world go away. There isn't a problem linking transaction data to the customer profile that is created when a customer registers. But identifying users, even if they are registered, can sometimes be a problem.

Using cookies to identify users

As mentioned earlier, a *cookie* is a file that a website deposits on a user's machine. It's basically the website's way of writing itself a reminder note about something. Sometimes cookies are used to facilitate the login process on your website. When a user registers on your site, you can drop a cookie on their machine that remembers the username they registered under. Then when the user returns to your site, you can serve up a login page that has the username prepopulated. Cookies can also be used as a routine security check. If a registered user tries to log in from a machine that doesn't contain your username cookie, you can prompt them to answer a security question to validate that they're really who you think they are.

Earlier in this chapter, I talk a little bit about using cookies to link together information about different browsing sessions. Knowing what the user typically browses for allows you to serve up relevant content. Ideally you would like to have the user registered, because that gives you a full picture of their contact information and preferences. But there is a situation in between. For example, I can register on your site and provide you all the information you want. But if I log off and later return, I may not bother to log in.

In this situation, a cookie can be very helpful. When I come back to your site, the cookie remembers my username, even though I haven't logged in. This allows you to access my information in the customer's registration profile and serve up content accordingly. If I decide to make a purchase, you need to get me to log in to verify that it's really me. But while I'm shopping, there's nothing wrong with looking up my registration information and addressing me as Mr. Semmelroth, as opposed to dave3784.

The deleted cookie problem

Cookies aren't a magic bullet for identifying and tracking web browsing behavior. Many users choose to delete cookies for one reason or other. Different browsers treat cookies differently. It's also possible for users to completely block websites from depositing cookies.

Estimates of the percentage of users who delete or block cookies run as high as 40 percent. But there are some nuances to cookies that make these types of estimates a little hard to interpret. First of all, cookies come in a couple different varieties. Your online banking website probably deposits cookies on your computer to aid in security and identification and to allow you to customize certain features of your session. These cookies, deposited by the website you're visiting, are known as *first-party cookies*.

Most people don't generally block or delete these cookies. Deleting them frequently makes sites more inconvenient to use. For example, if I blocked or deleted cookies on my machine, I'd have to re-enter my location every time I checked the weather forecast rather than having it appear automatically. The stocks I follow, the baseball scores, and a host of other things that appear automatically when I visit certain sites would all have to be re-entered on every visit without these first-party cookies.

The cookies that are more frequently blocked or deleted are *third-party cookies*. These are cookies that are placed on your machine by websites other than the one you're visiting — typically websites who are paying for advertising or tracking web surfing behavior. People are far more likely to block these cookies altogether. In fact, Apple's Safari web browser blocks all third-party cookies by default.

Most of the studies that have been done regarding cookie blocking and deletion take this third-party versus first-party cookie distinction into account. These studies also have a time frame associated with them. For example, the 40 percent estimate I mention earlier actually means that 40 percent of users either block third-party cookies altogether or delete third-party cookies at least once a month. In contrast, users rarely block first-party cookies because that makes web surfing difficult.

The device problem

Fully understanding your customer's online behavior requires knowing what they're doing on all their devices. This is no small task. In my household alone, we have two laptop computers, three tablets, and three smartphones, not to mention a box for streaming movies from the Internet.

These devices are all connected to our private wireless network and from there to the Internet. And that's just while we're at home. When we're away, eight of those devices can be connected to the internet via wireless hotspots, and six of them frequently use cellphone networks to access the web.

It's extremely difficult for marketers to connect the myriad browsing, shopping, and purchasing behavior among all these devices and access points. There is no magic bullet for it. The most effective way of tying customer browsing behavior together is still to get them to log in to your site when they're browsing. Short of that, you need to take advantage of the browsing information that you do have available.

Another challenge related to mobile devices is that content needs to be designed differently. It isn't just a matter of serving up web content on a smartphone. Companies create separate, pared-down, "mobile friendly" websites for smartphones and tablets, for example. These sites typically have limited content compared to the full-blown website.

This aspect of online marketing is evolving very rapidly. A huge amount of valuable customer data is associated with these devices. It's important for you to understand how these challenges are being approached and what solutions are emerging in the marketplace. It's also important for you to understand how privacy law is evolving to address the concerns of consumers.

Customer Data and Search Engines

When it comes to using analytics to serve up web content, search engine sites are at the top of the heap. This is their bread and butter. Many of the browsing sessions initiated on your website come from a search engine page.

This means it's extremely important for you to make sure that your website gets displayed prominently when potential customers are searching for information related to something you sell. *Search engine optimization,* or SEO, as this process is called, is a subject unto itself. Most medium to large companies have a team dedicated to doing nothing else. But your customer database plays a role.

In its simplest form, SEO involves identifying keywords you think are relevant to your product offerings. If you own a resort hotel, for example, you would want your website to appear in searches that include words and phrases like *vacation* and *spring break* in addition to searches of your company name.

In the good old days, search results were primarily based on search history. The search engine looked at where users went after doing a similar search and served up the websites in order of popularity. Search engines now take into account the customer profiles of their users. Search results are informed by an individual's previous searches as well as other past web browsing behavior.

More and more of the screen space on the results pages of many search engines reflects sponsored search results. There is an ongoing bidding war for sponsored search engine placement. And by *ongoing*, I mean *continuous*. Your website can appear at the top of the list for a given search one day and disappear from the first page of results the next.

Search engines do a great deal of customer profiling based on search behavior. When your search optimization team is bidding for prime real estate on a results page, they have the opportunity to bid on particular customer segments as defined by the search engine profile.

Here's where you come in. You too have a great deal of customer profile information. In Chapter 7, I talk about profiling customers and creating customer segments. The customer segments you create from your data can be mapped to search engine profiles. This allows your optimization team to focus their bidding efforts on the right customers.

Part IV
The Feedback Cycle: Learning from Experience

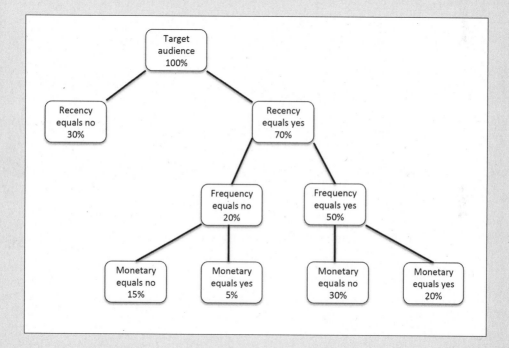

Find out how true, scientific marketing research is conducted in a free article at
www.dummies.com/extras/datadrivenmarketing.

In this part . . .

✔ Learn what sets scientific marketing experiments apart from wishful thinking and fooling yourself.

✔ Understand how to measure your marketing campaigns — and how to avoid potential pitfalls.

✔ Explore the power of some advanced analytical methods available to you and your data driven marketing program.

✔ Find out who else in your organization is interested in customer data and how sharing it across the enterprise can help the company as a whole.

Chapter 14

Learning Curve: Setting Up a Testing Plan

*I*n many ways, marketing is more art than science. Experience and intuition play a large role in the development of marketing and advertising strategies. It's an age-old lament among marketing executives that they know only half of their marketing budget is effective. The problem is they don't know which half.

At any given time, your company is running a variety of marketing and advertising campaigns. It's complicated, and to some extent impossible, to figure out whether a customer purchased your product because they saw a TV commercial or because they saw an ad in the newspaper.

Marketers can measure a lot of things. You have a general sense of how many people see your TV commercials. Television viewership is well tracked. You know how many people subscribe to the newspapers you advertise in. But it's difficult to connect this information to actual purchases.

As a database marketer, you're in a unique position with respect to understanding the success of your campaigns. You know exactly whom you are communicating with. You also have at your disposal a number of ways of tracking exactly who responds to your campaigns.

In Chapter 15, I talk in detail about response tracking and measuring campaign results after the fact. But first I want to discuss the steps you need to take *before* you execute your campaign that will allow you to effectively measure them.

Several of the topics in this chapter are fundamentally technical in nature. The ideas related to *random sampling*, *control groups*, and *statistical confidence* require some statistical acumen to be fully appreciated. My goal in this chapter is to make you aware that these ideas play an important role in analyzing marketing campaigns. The actual implementation of these ideas generally requires the assistance of technical resources who have some advanced knowledge of statistics.

Using the Scientific Approach

We've been taught since grade school that scientific discovery proceeds through disciplined experimentation. You observe something that sparks your curiosity. You ask a specific question. Then, in the critical step, you formulate an answer to that question. That answer is called your *hypothesis*. You then proceed to test this hypothesis by doing an experiment.

You can apply a version of this scientific approach to your database marketing campaigns. In database marketing, the steps you follow look like this:

1. **Identify a marketing goal:** This may involve generating sales of a particular product. It may involve addressing customer-retention issues. Whatever it is, this goal represents a problem you are trying to address. The question you are trying to answer is: How can I meet this marketing goal?

2. **Come up with a strategy:** You dig around in your data for a way to achieve your goal. This may involve customer profiling or other more advanced analytic techniques. This is the heart of database marketing. Your strategy will include the definition of your target audience as well as the messaging approach you will take.

3. **Formulate a hypothesis:** Your hypothesis is essentially an educated guess as to what your campaign will achieve. This campaign will increase purchases by 5 percent among the target audience, for example.

4. **Design a test:** It's critical to set yourself up to properly test your hypothesis. Chapter 6 introduces the notion of a control group. Your test design typically involves holding out a random portion of your target audience. It also involves understanding how responses will be tracked. I talk about both these things in more detail later in this chapter and in Chapter 15.

5. **Execute:** Run your campaign.

6. **Analyze the data:** The last step is to analyze your response data. This is where you evaluate your hypothesis. Were you really able to increase purchases by 5 percent?

This chapter is about steps 4 and 5. Forming your hypothesis and designing an effective test both require some careful thought. In what follows, I introduce you to some considerations that will help you to learn as much as possible from your database marketing campaigns.

Lesson Plans: Deciding Beforehand What You Want to Learn

Every database marketing campaign is an opportunity to learn something. You certainly want to be able to tell whether your campaign works. But you also want to be able to learn *why* it's working, if it is.

Don't mistake the goal of your marketing campaign for the hypothesis that you want to test. The goal of your campaign may be to sell more widgets. But in doing so, you may want to test the effectiveness of direct mail versus e-mail. Or you may want to compare the response rates of two different target audiences. All aspects of your campaign, from audience to message to offer, are potential subjects of your hypothesis.

Offers are a frequent subject of marketing experiments. You may routinely mail out back-to-school offers in the late summer. And you may have a pretty good sense of how well they work. But the eternal question is: How large a discount do you need to offer? Ideally, you'd like to give as small a discount as possible while still generating sales. By sending out several different offers and comparing the response rates associated with each, you can start to get a sense of where your sweet spot is.

You can't test everything

As with many things in life, simple is usually better. Trying to test everything all at once is a recipe for learning nothing at all. As I discuss later in this section, you need to have a sufficient number of data points to get a meaningful read on what is and isn't working.

In its traditional form, the scientific method admonishes you to test one thing at a time. In marketing experiments, the strategy is to break up your target audience into two groups. This is often referred to as an *A/B split*. You then send one communication to group A and another to group B. The difference in the communications is what you want to test.

The thinking behind the A/B split design is pretty straightforward. Suppose you send out one communication with a discounted offer to young families.

You also send out a non-discounted offer to retirees. Now suppose the first offer dramatically outperforms the second. What have you learned? Have you learned not to market that product to retirees? Or does this suggest that you need to offer them a discount? The truth is, you haven't really learned anything from this experiment.

There are two ways you can improve this experiment. One is to test only one thing at a time. Test a discounted offer to both audiences, for example. Or test both a discounted offer and a non-discounted offer to one audience.

The other way is to test all four possible combinations. You could test both offers against both audiences. This essentially means do two different experiments. One experiment would be an attempt to learn about the offer's effectiveness with young families. The other would be the same experiment repeated for retirees.

Audience size plays a key role in how much you can learn from your marketing experiments. If you get too many experiments going at once, the individual A/B splits will get too small to be meaningful when you analyze your results. Later in this chapter, I talk in detail about the importance of audience size when it comes to setting up control groups. Those considerations apply equally to any A/B split that you may want to implement.

At the beginning of this section, I said simple is usually better. There are more advanced methods of designing experiments that can sometimes allow you to test several different things at once. In fact, *design of experiments* is itself a sub-discipline of statistics. One approach in particular is used in marketing. This involves actually developing an equation that relates various components of a campaign to the response rate. This approach can be effective, but it is loaded with landmines and requires a good bit of statistical expertise to implement.

Tracking responses

All your database marketing campaigns are designed to evoke some sort of response. You may be trying to drive purchases. You may simply be trying to drive web traffic or registrations. I make the point repeatedly throughout this book that a key component of your marketing message is a clear *call to action*.

That call to action is central to almost all of the marketing experiments that you design. This means that in analyzing the results of your experiments, you will typically be looking at the response rate. Loosely speaking, a *response* is an answer to your call to action. To learn anything from your campaign, you need to be able to recognize when a customer has responded.

It's critical to identify, up front, how you are going to track responses to your campaigns. This involves connecting responses to the target audience of your campaign. If your call to action directs a customer to a retail store to make a purchase, you need to find a way to track that purchase back to your campaign. If customers make their purchases anonymously, your experiment is a bust.

Identifying responders

In many cases, figuring out which customers have responded to your campaign is not all that difficult. If your purchase process requires customer to identify themselves and provide their address, then it's fairly easy to connect their purchase back to a direct-mail campaign. Airlines, hotels, banks, car dealers, and a host of other industries require a good deal of information from their customers at the time of purchase.

Tracking is also relatively straightforward for online transactions that are generated from e-mail campaigns. As long as the customer enters the correct e-mail address to receive a purchase confirmation, you can track that purchase back to the e-mail address used in your campaign. If your online purchase process requires the customer to register and log in, then you're golden.

In other cases, you need to get a little more creative. One common way of doing this is through the use of promotional codes. You give the customer a code that they provide at the time of purchase (preferably a short code, though I've seen some doozies). This code allows the customer to take advantage of a discounted offer. It also allows you to connect their purchase back to your campaign.

One problem with this approach is that these offer codes can grow legs. People sometimes share the codes with their friends. In some cases they find their way onto the Internet. At some level this is a good thing, because it does generate business. But at the same time, it complicates your experiment.

A simple refinement of the offer code approach solves at least part of this problem. You can actually generate individualized offer codes that can only be redeemed once. I sometimes get plastic discount cards in the mail that actually have a magnetic strip on the back that can be swiped at the checkout counter. This ties my transaction more directly to me. I can give the card away, but it still generates a unique purchase.

This technique doesn't require the use of physical cards. It's just as easy to create individualized offer codes that you can serve up to the customer in an e-mail. In fact, the plastic cards that I receive can actually be used this way as well. They have a code printed on the back, much like a credit-card number.

Defining your response window

Another aspect of your marketing experiment involves what you're willing to treat as a response. More specifically, you need to decide *when* a response can be legitimately associated with a particular campaign. Your *response window* is the period of time over which you can reasonably assume customer behavior is really caused by your communication.

Many campaigns involve time-sensitive offers. In these cases, your decision is pretty obvious. The response window closes when the offer expires. But not all situations are this simple.

In other cases, you might need to put a little thought into how long you want the response window to stay open. Later in this chapter, when I talk about control groups, I describe a simple technique for getting some idea of when your campaign is no longer working.

But the basic idea is that, even if it doesn't come with an explicit expiration date, your offer or message has a limited shelf life. You don't want to be counting purchases that happen a year later, for example.

You also need to be a little careful about the beginning of your response window, particularly when you're using direct mail. You need to allow time for the mail to be delivered. If a customer buys a product on the day you dropped the mail, there's a pretty slim chance that your mail piece had anything to do with it. How much lag time you allow will depend on the geographic scope of your mailing as well as whether you are paying first class or standard bulk rates.

Taking a Random Sample

In Chapter 6, I talk about the importance of *random sampling*. This process is essential when it comes to setting up A/B splits. Both A and B groups need to have the same characteristics if you want your experiment to be meaningful.

When you ask for a mail file to be pulled, that file is never in random order. Often you'll ask for it to be sorted by household and address. Even if you don't, the file may be sorted according to the order in which records were added to the database — oldest records first, for example. There are many ways that your file may be sorted. But make no mistake, some kind of sorting has been done.

This sorting means that if you want to split your target audience into two equal size groups, you can't just cut it down the middle. If you do, then you've generated an A/B split that is made on the basis of how the file was sorted. The two groups will be inherently different.

When you split a sorted file, it makes comparing the two groups problematic. For example, many databases are naturally sorted according to when customer records were added. This means that when you pull a file, it may well contain older, more loyal customers at the top. Suppose you're testing the effect of two different discounts. You decide to mail the smaller discount to the top half of the file, namely your best customers. This half of the file may well outperform the higher discount that is sent to your newer, less loyal customers.

These results will leave you scratching your head. But if you don't recognize that the results are due to a sampling problem, you risk coming to an incorrect conclusion about the effect of discounts. Bad information is actually worse than no information.

This situation can be avoided by ensuring that your A/B splits are chosen randomly. In the next couple of sections, I explain two common ways that random samples are generated.

Selecting every nth record

One simple approach is to just grab records that are separated by a regular interval. If you want to split the file in half, you simply select every other record. This solves the sorting problem that I describe above. Each group in your split contains records from the beginning, middle and end of the file. This approach, called an *nth selection process*, can be used to pull any size sample that you want. If you want to pull out 5 percent of your file, you just pull every 20th record. It's a technical nuance, but you should pick your starting point at random among the first 20 records. Otherwise you haven't completely eliminated the effects of the way the file is sorted.

One advantage to *n*th selection is that it's simple to implement. In the early days of direct marketing, when computer resources were at more of a premium, this approach was appealing because it's also fast. You just zip through the file once, and there's no need to make any calculations.

But this approach does have some drawbacks. Though it solves the problem of sorting, it is vulnerable to another sort of structure that may appear in your file. It's vulnerable to patterns in your mail file that tend to alternate.

Think about street numbers, for example. Suppose you're trying to randomly split a file that's been sorted by address. Addresses alternate, even numbers on one side of the street and odd numbers on the other. If you're splitting a file in half, you run the risk of creating your A/B split based on which side of the road they live on.

I live in a neighborhood on a lake. If you split this neighborhood down the middle of the street, you'd find one group all owned lakefront property and the other group didn't. You wouldn't consider splitting a file based on home values for an experiment! But in this example that's exactly what has happened.

I'll fess up to having my fair share of mathematical snobbery. Along those lines, I have a personal bias against using nth selection techniques. Simply put, there are a lot of ways of creating a 5 percent random sample from a mail file. Billions and billions of ways, to steal a phrase from Carl Sagan. My attitude is that a truly random approach should make all these samples equally likely to be selected. The nth selection process can only ever produce n different samples depending on where you start. If you're splitting a file in half, there are only two ways the nth select can possibly do it.

Nth selection will do in a pinch. But given its drawbacks and the availability of computer power and advanced random-number generators, I recommend a different approach, which I outline below.

Flipping a coin

Okay, not literally flipping a coin. But the idea is the same. You use some kind of kind of random-number generator to simulate flipping a coin for each member of the target audience to determine which group that customer will belong to.

All statistical-analysis software as well as database-management software contains some sort of random-number generator. Even spreadsheets have them. Each time you invoke a random-number function, it returns a value between 0 and 1. By invoking this function, you can assign each customer record its own personal random number. These random values can be used in a variety of ways to generate a random split.

If the random number generator is invoked repeatedly, the values tend to spread out evenly over the interval from 0 to 1. Just as a fair coin will come up heads about half the time, the random number generator will produce values between 0 and 1/2 about half the time.

If you simply want to split your mail file in half, you can simulate a coin flip by generating a random value for each member of your target audience. If the value is less than 1/2, then you put the record in group A. If the value is greater than 1/2, then you put the record in group B. (Technically you need to account for the possibility that the value is equal to 1/2, but you could do database marketing for a thousand years and never see this happen.)

This approach can be easily modified to generate any sample size you might want. If you want a 5 percent sample, for example, you simply adjust the ranges to include in group A only random values between 0 and .05.

TIP There's nothing special about the particular range you specify. The determining factor for sample size is the length of the range. Including values between .27 and .32 will also generate a perfectly good 5 percent sample.

TIP There is one situation when being able to use different random number ranges is particularly helpful. Sometimes marketing databases store a random number on each record. Because many simple reporting tools don't possess random-number functions, this allows samples to be taken without the need for more advanced programming skills.

But these random numbers are only updated occasionally. As I discuss in Chapter 16, there will be times when you want to be able to take multiple samples from your database. If you do this based on a prepopulated random number, you get the same set of records every time you use a given range.

For example, suppose you want two distinct 10 percent samples of household records. Selecting households whose random number is in the range 0 to .10 will produce exactly the same results every time you make that selection based on pre-populated random numbers. To get a different sample, you need to choose a different range.

Getting Significant Results: Sample Size Matters to Confidence Level

The goal of all this design, preparation, sampling, and so forth is that you report the results of your marketing experiment with some degree of confidence. In fact, *confidence level* is actually a statistical term. It's a measure of how likely it is that the results of an experiment happened purely by chance.

In the vast majority of cases, your marketing experiments will be designed to test a hypothesis involving response rates. Families with children responded at a higher rate than retired couples, for example. Or a 10 percent discount generates more responses than $50 off your next purchase.

More about flipping coins

These sorts of hypotheses have something fundamentally in common with a simple experiment. Suppose you wanted to demonstrate that a coin was biased. Flipping the coin once isn't going to tell you. Nor will flipping it twice. Even if the coin is fair, you expect to see either heads or tails come up twice in a row about half the time.

But what if you flipped the coin 10 times and it came up heads only 4 times? Do you have reason to believe the coin is biased? This question can be answered in a very precise way. You can actually quantify the likelihood of this outcome. This in turn gives a way of measuring the confidence you would have in declaring the coin biased.

In the case of 10 coin flips, there is actually a 20 percent chance that you will observe exactly 4 heads even if the coin is fair. More importantly, there is an almost 40 percent chance that a fair coin will come up heads fewer than 5 times in 10 tosses. If your hypothesis is that the coin is fair, this experiment doesn't give very solid evidence to the contrary.

Your *confidence level* in the result of an experiment is the probability that it didn't happen by chance. This is known in statistics as an experiment's *p-value*. In the preceding experiment, there is a 40 percent chance that the result happened by chance. Conversely, there is a 60 percent chance that it didn't. That is, there is a 60 percent chance that the coin isn't really fair. In this case you would say that you are 60 percent confident that you have a biased coin. Not terribly convincing.

Typically, experiments are not considered particularly meaningful until their confidence level reaches 95 percent. In marketing applications, sometimes results are reported as significant if the confidence level reaches 90 percent.

If you had flipped the coin 50 times instead of 10 times and gotten the same 40 percent result, the situation changes dramatically. In this case, your confidence level soars to almost 90 percent that the coin is biased. If you flip it a hundred times and the same result occurs, your confidence level passes 97 percent. In general, as the number of flips increases, the more confident you become in the result.

Intuitively, this makes sense. The more times you observe something, the more likely it is that you are observing a persistent pattern.

Sample size and confidence levels

So what does all this coin flipping have to do with marketing, you ask? A lot, as it turns out. In your marketing experiments, you're essentially trying to determine whether response rates are different between two groups of customers. You can use a similar statistical approach to assigning confidence levels to the results of these experiments.

Statistical techniques allow you to quantify the likelihood that two response rates really are different. There is always at least a small possibility that response rates differ purely by chance. You want to set up your experiment to make that possibility as small as possible.

The main tool at your disposal is that you can control, to some extent, the size of your A/B splits. As I explain in the preceding section, your confidence in your coin flip results increases as you flip the coin more times. Similarly, the larger the groups whose response rates you're measuring, the more likely it is that you will see meaningful results.

Determining the optimal sample size for your splits is a technical exercise. As I explain in the next section, getting a "big enough" sample depends on a number of factors. Your statistical geek can help you to understand the tradeoffs in each specific case. For a more thorough examination of the technical aspects of confidence levels, I refer you to *Statistics For Dummies* (Wiley, 2011).

Other factors that influence confidence levels

When trying to determine the appropriate sample size for an experiment, you need to take two factors into account:

- ✔ The response rate you expect to get
- ✔ How small a difference in response rates you want to be able to detect

Expected response rate

Because of the subtleties of the mathematics involved, the overall response rate to your campaign directly affects your confidence levels. The reason for this connection is beyond the scope of this book. But there is a fairly simple rule of thumb that you may find useful.

For reasons that I will leave mysterious, your required sample size will go up as your response rates go up. Once response rates pass 50 percent, the required sample sizes begin to go down again.

In other words, differences between response rates are harder to detect at significant levels when the response rate is close to 50 percent. One place you may see evidence of this fact is in polling data around election time. When a race comes down to two candidates, especially a close race, poll results hover somewhere in the neighborhood of 50 percent for each candidate. The margin of error reported in these polls is typically quite large, sometimes several percentage points wide.

In your database marketing campaigns, it's the other end of this spectrum that typically comes into play. If you're running database marketing campaigns that are generating 50 percent response rates, then you're my hero. Typically response rates are much lower than that. And it affects sample sizes dramatically.

Suppose you want to be able to say with statistical confidence that a 25 percent response rate is better than a 23 percent response rate. Then you need to have a sample size just north of 3,500 to reach 95 percent confidence. However the difference between a 1 percent and 3 percent response rate requires a sample size of only a few hundred to reach the 95 percent level.

When deciding on sample sizes, it's important to think carefully about what response rates you expect to see. Because of the reverse relationship between confidence levels and response rates, it's better to err on the high side. This means that for purpose of sample sizes, you should overestimate your response rates.

How big a difference do you want to detect?

Another factor that greatly influences your optimal sample size is the level of precision you want to have in your measurement. This factor is a little more intuitive than the response rate effect covered earlier. Smaller differences are harder to detect and therefor require larger sample sizes.

In my experience, the precision issue is the biggest driver of large sample sizes. Many marketing campaigns are targeted at large audiences. This means that even a small improvement in response rates can be extremely valuable. What's more, because these large programs cost a lot to execute, their sponsors want to be able to say with confidence that they're worth it.

I've worked on mailings in the credit-card industry where overall response rates were expected to be less than 1 percent. In a case like that, even improving those rates by 0.2 percent would be well worth the effort. In order to be able to detect this level of difference, our A/B split sample sizes had to exceed 30,000 consumers.

Performing confidence level analysis carries with it many pitfalls. This is one reason why it's important for you to have access to someone who is well versed in statistical methods. Analyzing confidence levels is a fundamental part of understanding the success of your marketing campaigns. You want to make sure you're getting it right.

need to hold out a separate control group for each offer. Because the audiences are the same, one control group will give you a baseline against which you can compare all three offers.

Being careful: A couple of warnings

Control-group design should be done with the help of your resident statistical geek. A trained expert can help you avoid a number of traps you might otherwise fall into. There's nothing worse than getting to the end of your campaign and finding that your results are meaningless. In the next section I point out a couple of mistakes that I've repeatedly seen people make over the years.

Don't get caught up in percentages

Many marketers are in the habit of speaking in relative terms about control groups. It's easier to refer to a 10 percent sample instead of talking about a sample of 7,256 customers. In fact I've been talking that way throughout this chapter. But it's important to understand that the usefulness of your control group depends only on the actual number of customers it contains. The percentage of your target audience doesn't matter a bit.

The number of customers that you put in your control group depends on three things and three things alone. Notice that in all three cases, better news comes at the cost of a larger control group:

- ✔ **The response rate you expect to see:** The *higher* the response rate, the larger your control group needs to be.

- ✔ **The precision with which you want to detect differences in response rates:** The *smaller* the difference, the larger your control group needs to be.

- ✔ **The confidence level with which you want to be able to report results:** This is typically set at either 90 percent or 95 percent. The *higher* the confidence level, the larger your control group needs to be.

Testing different target audiences

As I've said, your control group can potentially perform multiple duties. When you're testing different offers, messages, or even channels, a single control group can serve as a basis of measuring all of your variations.

Never use a single control group to test targeting strategies. The value of a control group lies in its similarity to your target audience. It is *only* valuable to the extent that the members of the control group meet the same selection criteria as those in the target audience.

Mission Control: Using Control Groups

As I mention throughout this book, one of the great advantages you have database marketer is your ability to measure the success of your campaig Without a doubt, the most frequent hypothesis you will be asked to test comes down to "Did this campaign work?" In Chapter 15, I talk about how measure the success of database marketing campaigns and put that meas ment into financial terms. All of that analysis depends on a particular kind A/B split known as a *control group*.

Control groups and measurement

As Chapter 6 explains, a control group is basically a random sample of yo target audience that you *don't* communicate with. It's like the use of place in pharmaceutical testing. The idea is you want to get a bead on what wou happen if you didn't do anything. The thing that happens if you do nothing is what you need to control for. Your ultimate goal here is to compare the performance of the mail group to that of the control group. It's the differer between the two groups that represents your success.

You have other marketing communications and advertisements running virtu all the time. There is a chance that some responses to your direct-marketii campaigns would have come anyway based on these other initiatives.

By holding out a portion of your target audience, you can get an idea abou how many responses fall into this category. If you design your experiment correctly, you will be in a position to clearly and (statistically) confidently show exactly how much business you were able to produce.

In the previous sections, I discuss in detail the use of random sampling and sample size in the context of designing marketing experiments. That entire discussion applies hook, line, and sinker to designing control groups. Contro groups are just a special case of the A/B splits discussed throughout this chapter.

You may want to test any of a number of different factors, as I've mentioned before. Comparing the success of different offers, different message strategies, or different targeting strategies are all potentially informative experiments. But you'll also be asked to include control groups so that you can evaluate the overall success of your campaigns.

In many cases, your control group can do double or triple duty. If you're tes ing three different offers to the same target audience, there is absolutely no

When testing different targeting criteria, you need to create a different control group for each audience split. These multiple control groups need to be sized on their own. In other words, they each individually need to be large enough to give you the confidence level you want. If you try to cobble together a control group containing members from more than one audience, you completely negate your ability to get a clean read on the success of your campaign.

Out of Control: Reasons to Skip the Control

There are times when you'll be forced to abandon the idea of a measurement strategy for your database marketing campaigns. Despite your best intentions, there are situations in which it just doesn't make sense to hold out a control group. Sometimes this is caused by a statistical issue. Other times it's dictated by larger corporate priorities.

Small target audiences

Some marketing campaigns are just too small to allow for a useful control group design. When I say small, I mean that the target audience isn't big enough to give you the kind of precision you would need to do a meaningful analysis of your campaign. You need to be aware of one situation in particular.

If your geek comes back to you recommending a control group size that is getting close to half your overall audience size, then you might be in trouble. Whenever you're setting up an experiment, the recommended control group size applies to not just to the control group. It applies to the group you're measuring as well. If your control group needs to include 10,000 customers, then that implicitly means that you need to mail at least 10,000 customers as well.

You need to be aware of this fact because your geek may perform your control group sizing before your mail counts are final. As I discuss in Chapter 5, you perform a number of steps before you send out a mailing which have the effect of purging customers from your target audience. I've seen cases where this purging of records has dropped the actual mail file below the size of the control group.

Lost opportunities

Control groups come with a cost. To the extent that a database marketing campaign is successful, anyone you don't mail represents a lost opportunity. In other words, control groups mean lost revenue.

I use the example of pharmaceutical companies testing drugs several times in this book to explain some of the basic ideas around control groups. Here again, that industry provides an insightful example.

Some drug trials are wildly successful in demonstrating the effectiveness of a treatment. In some cases — especially ones involving particularly nasty or even fatal conditions — this success creates a moral conflict between the science of medicine and the practice of medicine. In these cases, it is generally considered wrong to continue the drug trial and withhold an effective treatment from the control group. The trial is then suspended, and patients who had been receiving the placebo are given the actual drug.

Most marketing executives buy into the idea that the information that comes from well-designed tests is worth the cost in lost revenue. But cases will arise when this is not true.

One situation where it really is a little pointless to keep holding out control groups is for well-established marketing campaigns. If you've been running the same campaign to the same audience year after year, you may already have a pretty good idea of how much that campaign is driving to the bottom line. There really isn't a compelling reason to keep verifying that contribution.

Control groups often go out the window in times of trouble or heightened concern about company performance. If your CEO gets concerned about the company meeting its quarterly or annual sales goal, your marketing executives will feel the pressure. And they'll do everything in their power to squeeze as many sales as they can from their marketing budgets. Control groups are an easy target (pardon the pun).

Chapter 15

Getting to the Bottom Line: Tracking and Measuring Your Campaigns

*A*s I say repeatedly throughout this book, your ability to measure the success of your campaigns sets your database marketing efforts apart from other marketing disciplines. Other disciplines can measure costs and, to some degree, the benefits associated with their efforts. But you can use your database to give very precise financial results.

This ability arises from your use of the scientific method discussed in Chapter 14. You approach your campaigns as experiments. This means that you form a hypothesis and then proceed to test that hypothesis in a systematic way.

In this chapter, I examine some of the most common metrics that are used to evaluate database marketing campaigns. Ultimately, I discuss the assignment of financial metrics that allows you to clearly and convincingly measure your contribution to your company's bottom line.

Defining Responses Clearly: A Couple of Things to Keep in Mind

In Chapter 14, I talk about creating a tracking mechanism when you set up your campaigns. You want to clearly define what counts as a response. And you want to be sure that you can connect responses back to the target audience for your campaign. This needs to be done before you execute your campaign.

But you need to keep in mind a couple of things after the fact. In this section, I talk about some pitfalls related to counting responses. I also explain a method for using response data to figure out how long you should wait before you stop counting customer behavior as being in response to your campaign.

Counting responses

The expression *the devil is in the details* is particularly true when it comes to counting responses to database marketing campaigns. If you're not careful, it's easy to overstate or understate the number of responses you've received to your campaign.

Be clear about what counts as a customer

Part of the confusion comes from the fact that people tend to be a bit sloppy when they talk about target audiences. I refer liberally to *the customer* or *the consumer* throughout this book. But if you want to get nitpicky (and when it comes to response data, you definitely do), I don't always mean the same thing when I use these terms.

In some cases, I really do mean an individual person. But often — particularly when I speak about traditional direct mail — I really mean the household. In the case of e-mail or online marketing campaigns, I really mean an e-mail address or a website registration. Failure to clearly make these distinctions can lead to over- or undercounting responses.

My wife and I recently bought a new car. I'd received an offer in the mail saying that the dealership would like to buy back my car and apply the balance to a new one. Because we had just moved from the South to the North, I was actually concerned about the car my wife was driving because she didn't have any experience driving in the snow.

So we went into the dealership and ended up buying a new car for her, and I started driving her old car. Because the new car was hers, we put it in her name. My name appeared nowhere in the transaction. Now here comes the question: Does this purchase count as a response to the direct-mail campaign that was sent to me? The answer is unequivocally yes.

Another variation on this example occurs in catalog retailing. If you send a catalog to my house, it's perfectly plausible that both my wife and I will separately make purchases from it. She may order a new suit, and I may order a new pair of shoes a few days later. Again, both purchases can be reasonably associated with that catalog campaign.

You want to be a little bit careful in this situation, though. You may credit the revenue from both purchases to your campaign. But you probably don't want to count these purchases as two separate responses. A *response* is usually defined as a household that makes at least one purchase.

In the case of direct-mail campaigns, responses should generally be assigned at the household level. Families know what's relevant to whom in the household and will pass offers around regardless of whom the offer is actually addressed to. As long as you've removed duplicate addresses from your mail file, as I discuss in Chapter 5, you can assign responses at the household level quite easily.

Be careful with online data

In the online world, householding is a good deal trickier. If you're dealing with an audience of registered web users or have some other way of knowing their home addresses, then assigning responses at the household level might be possible. But you rarely have such a clear picture of your entire target audience.

The online world is more complicated in other ways as well. In the case of e-mail campaigns, responses are usually tracked back to the e-mail address. Other online marketing campaigns may be tracked back to registered users. Even anonymous users can be tracked by dropping cookies on their machines when they visit your website, as I discuss in Chapter 13.

In the case of direct mail, the usual challenge is to make sure you count everything you can as a response. You're trying to avoid undercounting. Online, the challenge is frequently the exact opposite: There are a lot of ways to overcount if you're not careful.

It may seem to you that a purchase is a purchase, so how could you overcount them? One answer is that you may attribute the same purchase to two different people.

Here's an example: Suppose you send an e-mail offer to a target audience. Some of that audience is registered users of your website, and some aren't. You decide that you're going to track results at the e-mail level.

Now suppose further that both my wife and I receive your e-mail offer. She's registered on your site, and I'm not. So you have no way of knowing that we're in the same household. She ignores your e-mail, but I bite. When I go to your website, I use my wife's login credentials. When I make the purchase, I enter my own e-mail address to track the package.

Here's where the problem comes. You now have two different e-mail addresses associated with that purchase, mine and the one my wife used when she registered. And you mailed your offer to both of them. Which one do you associate with the purchase?

It doesn't really matter which one you choose. The critical thing is that you choose one or the other to avoid counting the purchase twice. Because of the complexity of behavior relating to web surfing and e-commerce, thinking through the various possibilities that can arise is important. When evaluating your tracking methods, you should make a serious attempt to break them. In other words, you should try to invent an example where double-counting would occur.

Closing the tracking window: How long do you wait for responses?

You can't wait forever to evaluate the success of your database marketing campaigns. A limited amount of time can pass during which you can reasonably attribute purchases or other responses to a particular campaign.

If your campaign includes an offer that expires after a given period of time, then you obviously only track responses that occur during that offer window. But in cases where there's no inherent time limit to the offer, you need to put a little more thought into how long to wait before you consider the campaign over. In Chapter 14, I hint at a way to use your control group to do this.

Your *control group* is a randomly selected sample of your target audience, remember. The control group is held out from your campaign — in other words, you don't contact customers in the control group. The basic idea is that the behavior of the control group represents what the target audience would have done had you not contacted them. This allows you to measure the effectiveness of your campaigns, as I explain later in this chapter.

At first glance, you may think that eventually "responses" will simply stop. That your response rate will drop to zero. But you're not operating in a vacuum. There are always other advertising and marketing campaigns out in the marketplace that are driving customers to purchase, register, or whatever else you might want them to do. This means that you'll continue to see purchases among your target audience that are unrelated to your specific campaign.

I have on occasion used control groups to get a sense of when to stop counting responses. The idea is to track response rates separately over relatively short time periods — daily or weekly in most cases. Over time, as the effect of your communication wears off, the response rate of the target audience will tend to decline until it reaches the same level as the control group. When this happens, your campaign is no longer having an effect.

When comparing response rates between your target audience and control group, you need to check with your statistician regarding the significance of the differences between these response rates. In Chapter 14, I talk about the relationship between the size of your control group and your confidence in your measurements. Those considerations apply here as well. What you're looking for is the point at which the response rate from the target audience is statistically indistinguishable from the response rate of the control group.

Getting a Handle on Costs: Some Common Metrics

When evaluating your campaigns, you obviously need to understand their costs. In fact, you need to understand costs even before you execute your campaigns. You have a limited budget and you want to make sure you're using it effectively.

In most cases, these cost metrics relate to costs that are specifically tied to a given campaign. You typically won't try to factor in the cost of your salary or the department copy machine into your analysis of marketing campaigns.

The costs you'll focus on have to do with the production and delivery of your marketing messages. In the case of direct mail, creative development, printing, and postage costs are taken into account. In the online world, development costs, production costs for videos, and e-mail delivery and tracking charges are typical examples of costs that are assigned to campaigns.

Most finance teams are comfortable with partial cost accounting in relation to marketing campaigns. They generally focus on the types of costs I've listed here. That is, they're only concerned with the costs directly associated with executing the campaign. There are times, though, when labor or product development costs need to be included. For example, if a call center needs to add staff to process orders related to a campaign, that cost will often be borne by the marketing campaign. In any case, it's good practice to get agreement from your finance folks up front about which costs will be included in your evaluation of campaign results.

Database marketers have inherited some traditional cost metrics from the broader disciplines of marketing and advertising. These are very simple calculations that you'll see (and make) again and again. In what follows, I explain these calculations and how they're used.

Cost per thousand: CPM

An extremely simple but extremely common way of measuring costs is to calculate what it costs to reach a thousand customers. This is known as your *cost per thousand,* usually abbreviated *CPM.* The roman numeral M represents one thousand.

Using CPM in database marketing campaigns

To calculate this metric, you need only know the total cost of your campaign and the size of your target audience. CPM is then calculated using the following equation:

$$CPM = 1,000 \times (\text{total campaign cost / target audience size})$$

As with many common marketing terms, the phrase *cost per thousand* is used in slightly different ways depending on who's doing the talking. Frequently, mail houses and e-mail service providers will quote their rates on a CPM basis. Advertising is often measured on a CPM basis. In both cases, the costs they're referring to are generally not fully loaded with creative development or production costs. They relate specifically to the cost of getting the message delivered.

Don't get confused: A similar metric in advertising

In the case of advertising, costs are typically reported based on the size of a TV or radio audience or on the basis of the subscriber base to a newspaper or magazine. This type of reporting is also common in online advertising, when banner ads or popups are purchased, for example.

In this situation, advertisers speak about the cost per thousand impressions. An *impression* essentially means someone had a chance to see the ad. It amounts to the number of times that an advertisement was put in front of a customer, regardless of whether they actually saw it or not.

For a newspaper advertisement, the number of impressions would be the newspaper's circulation. For an online popup ad, it would be the number of times the ad popped up.

In these cases, the *cost per thousand impressions* or CPMI are calculated by replacing the target audience size with the number of impressions, as follows:

$$CPMI = 1,000 \times (\text{advertising cost / number of impressions})$$

Using CPM to compare campaigns

The main advantage of CPM metrics is that they make it easier to compare costs among different types of marketing campaigns. Your marketing executives are constantly balancing the trade-offs between different marketing and advertising strategies. CPM metrics give them a sense of the relative costs of reaching consumers through different channels.

CPM metrics all represent costs for a standard audience size of 1,000 consumers. This means they can be compared head to head without having to take differences in audience size into account. They represent a way of comparing the efficiency of different marketing programs.

When using CPM metrics to compare database marketing programs to other marketing and advertising campaigns, it's important to make sure you're including the same costs. You may be asked to compare the efficiency of a direct-mail program with a magazine ad. When doing so, make sure that both metrics either include or don't include costs associated with creative development, for example.

Cost per thousand is no magic bullet when it comes to measurement and comparison of campaigns. But it's useful. Many marketing and advertising channels have limited ability to track their effectiveness. CPM metrics can be almost universally applied. This means that they're a core strategic tool.

Measuring Marketing Effectiveness in the Online World

When you communicate using direct mail, you're basically in the dark from the time the mail drops until the customer heeds your call to action. The only real feedback you get in between has to do with whether your mail piece actually got delivered. If you pay for return service, you can use the return mail to clean up your database, but that's about it.

Your online marketing presence, on the other hand, generates one heck of a lot of data about consumer behavior. This means that there's also one heck of a lot of ways to approach measurement online. Whether you send an e-mail or recognize a visitor on your website, you can see everything that's going on.

In this section, I explain a few common metrics that are used to understand consumer behavior online. I point out (repeatedly) some pitfalls related to overcounting transactions online. I also discuss some of the advantages and shortcomings of various ways of looking at this data.

Getting the customer to your website: Metrics related to e-mail campaigns

When you execute an e-mail campaign, you almost always include a link to your website. You may be trying to increase website registrations. You may be trying to drive purchases. You may simply be trying to increase website traffic. In any case, you can see every interaction the customer has with you from the moment they open your e-mail.

The metrics I describe in this section, along with many others, should be available from your e-mail service provider. Most of these metrics can be tracked in real time via a website that's maintained by your provider. But there are sometimes subtle differences among vendors in how they calculate certain metrics. It's a good idea to go through these metrics in detail with your vendor to avoid confusion about what the data really means.

Did the e-mail get delivered? Understanding bounce rates

When an e-mail fails to be delivered, it's said to have *bounced.* Your *bounce rate* — the percentage of your e-mails that bounce — is a measure of the quality of the e-mail addresses in your database. And it's something you need to pay attention to.

An e-mail may bounce for a couple different reasons. The first reason, known as a *soft bounce,* is when an e-mail server is busy, down for maintenance, or otherwise simply can't process a delivery request. These aren't particularly problematic, and many e-mail service providers will simply queue these soft bounces up and re-send them later.

The more problematic situation is when you e-mail an invalid, expired, or nonexistent e-mail address. These *hard bounces* need be removed from your database.

Chapter 4 talks about complying with regulations regarding e-mail spam. If you appear as though you might not be complying, your e-mail service provider will simply stop servicing you.

One thing these service providers look at is your bounce rate. Spammers do not generally do any verification or quality control of their e-mail addresses. In fact, sometimes they just make them up. This means that if your campaigns consistently show high bounce rates, you'll be suspected of being a spammer.

Did the customer opt out? Understanding retention rates

If an e-mail hard-bounces, the address is no longer of any use to you. Another way e-mail becomes useless is through opt-outs.

It's standard practice in e-mail marketing, to include a link at the bottom of the e-mail message that allows the customer to opt out of hearing from you. If they click this Unsubscribe link, then they have effectively removed their e-mail from all future mailing lists. These are known as *unsubscribed* e-mail addresses.

Clearly a customer unsubscribing isn't a positive outcome. You'll want to keep track of unsubscribe rates for your campaigns. High unsubscribe rates are a sign of trouble with your marketing strategy. Ideally, you want these rates to be in the low single digits. The problem could relate to your messages being irrelevant or annoying. It could relate to your pestering the customer with too many e-mails. Or you may just not be choosing your target audience very well. In any case, you need to investigate.

Unsubcribes are used in a common metric that measures how much your e-mail list shrinks due to a campaign. Because you'll invariably have bounces and unsubscribes in any campaign, any campaign has the effect of reducing the number of e-mail addresses available to you. The *subscriber retention rate*, which I abbreviate SRR, measures how many e-mail addresses survived your campaign. Here's the calculation:

$$\text{SRR} = 100 \times (\text{target audience size} - \text{bounces} - \text{unsubscribes}) / (\text{target audience size})$$

Did the customer see the e-mail? Understanding open rates

Another widely reported metric related to e-mail campaigns is the *open rate*. At first blush, this may sound like an incredibly simple metric. It's just the percentage of e-mails that you send that are opened, right? Wrong. It's actually a little more involved than you might think.

First of all, you want to calculate the open rate as a percentage of delivered e-mails. You exclude bounces from your open rate calculation. Second, the definition of *opened* requires a little explanation.

When tracking open rates, e-mail marketers use the term *open* as shorthand for the technical term *tracked open*. To count as a tracked open, the customer has to do more than just open the e-mail. The customer needs to interact with the e-mail. One way to interact with the e-mail is to click a link in the e-mail.

But there's another way that an e-mail is counted as a tracked open. If the customer downloads the images in the e-mail, it counts as an interaction. I usually have my e-mail account set up to block remote images. If I open an e-mail and then click the Download Images button, that e-mail counts as tracked open. If I don't, it doesn't.

One problem with this metric is that not everybody disables images in their default e-mail settings. This means that every e-mail they open automatically downloads images. For these folks, every e-mail they open will count as a tracked open and contribute positively to the open rate. This means that not all tracked opens are created equal. Some are *passive* views and others represent *requested* views.

Typically, you want to count an e-mail as opened only once. What you're interested in is how many e-mails got seen. If someone opens an e-mail three different times, this may tell you something about their interest. But you don't want to count it three times toward your open rate. In other words, *open rate* usually means *unique, tracked opens*.

So with all that in mind, here's the formula for calculating the open rate for an e-mail campaign:

> Open rate = 100 × (unique tracked opens) / (target audience size – bounces)

Open rates give you a sense of how many customers you're actually reaching with your message. But they're also your primary tool for evaluating the effectiveness of the subject line of your e-mail. You can actually use open rates to test different subject lines to see what's most effective at grabbing the customer's attention.

I confess to being puzzled by a small technicality related to unsubscribes and tracked opens. My issue is this. If I click an Unsubscribe link in an e-mail, I will count, by definition, as a tracked open. Because tracked opens are supposed to be a good thing, it seems to me that unsubscribes should be excluded from the tracked open total. But this doesn't seem to be standard practice. It's a subject worth bringing up with your e-mail service provider.

Did the customer bite? Understanding click-through rates

Your e-mail campaigns are generally designed to drive customers to your website. You usually include one (or more) website links in your e-mail campaigns. So it's only natural for you to want to understand what percentage of your target audience is actually making it to your website. This metric is called *click-through rate* or CTR.

One again, I need to bring up the double-counting issue. What you're really interested in here is how many customers you're actually driving to your website. A customer may click multiple links in your e-mail. Or they may come back to your e-mail multiple times and click through to your website. In both cases, you want to count that customer as only one click-through.

What you're really interested in is *unique* click-throughs. The traditional way of calculating click-through rates is by dividing unique click-throughs by the number of e-mails that are delivered:

CTR= 100 × (unique click-throughs) / (target audience size – bounces)

There's another, related, metric that's sometimes used to understand how effectively an e-mail campaign is at driving web traffic. This metric, known as the *click to open rate,* or CTOR, compares unique click-throughs to tracked opens rather than to delivered e-mails:

CTOR = 100 × (unique click throughs) / (unique tracked opens)

Understanding browsing behavior: Some simple web metrics

As I point out in Chapter 13, click-throughs don't tell the whole story. Once a customer lands on your website, a whole other world of behavior data becomes available to you. Understanding what customers are doing on your site once they arrive can give you clues to what is and isn't working. A number of companies offer these services. The largest is Google, which offers many metrics free of charge. Omniture (now owned by Adobe) charges for these services but also customizes the reporting platform to integrate it with your other data.

In this section, I describe some simple metrics that measure, to some degree, how interested a customer is in your website. These metrics all represent some sort of rate or average for a given audience. When describing these calculations, I refer generically to *site visits,* or the number of visitors to the site.

However, a user can land on your web site in a number of different ways. They can click an e-mail link. They can click a banner ad or popup ad. They can click a link from another site. They can click a link served up by a search engine. In all these cases, you'll have visibility to how they got there.

This gives you wide latitude to define exactly what site visits you're interested in when you calculate browsing metrics. You can compare these metrics between and among different audiences based on how they landed on your website.

Understanding what a web session is

Most web metrics depend to some extent on a couple of simple ideas. The first is the notion of a *page view.* This means exactly what you think it means.

An individual user clicks on a link and a particular web page appears on their screen. Tracking page views is a central part of doing analysis of users' web-browsing behavior.

Another fundamental concept is a *site visit,* sometimes called a *web session.* Your intuitive understanding of this term is also correct. A site visit starts when the user lands on a website and ends when they leave. But it's important for you to understand the nitpicky definition of what a site visit actually is.

A site visit, or web session, is actually defined as a set of page views that are requested by a single user. A session is deemed to be over when the user has stopped requesting pages. The user is deemed to have stopped requesting pages when some (arbitrary) time period has passed since the last request. A 30-minute time limit is common but by no means universal.

One of the original metrics that was used to evaluate a user's interest in a website involved looking at how long a web session lasted. Metrics about session duration are still used. But many marketers now prefer other methods of gauging user interest.

Because of the way a session is defined, you don't have to worry about situations where a user leaves the browser open and goes to bed. You won't get metrics back saying that a user browsed your website all night. But there's still confusion about how session duration is defined.

The duration of a web session is defined as the time between the first page request and the last page request in that session. There's then a 30-minute time period that elapses before the session is considered over. These 30 minutes do *not* contribute to the duration of the session.

Another common confusion about web sessions is that they don't require a user to remain on the site the whole time. They can browse another site and come back to yours without being deemed to have ended one session and begun another.

Did they bother to stay? Bounce rates

The simplest and clearest signal that a customer isn't bowled over by whatever page they've landed on is that they immediately leave. The way this is generally measured is by looking at web session data.

Each web session contains a specific number of page views. If a user lands on your page and never requests another page view, then the number of page views is 1. This single page view session is called a *bounce.* Your bounce rate is calculated as follows:

Bounce rate = 100 × (single page view sessions) / (site visits)

I've been told that the English language has more words than any other language on earth. Despite this fact, marketers have chosen to call sessions that contain only a single page view *bounces*. Because this term is also used to refer to e-mails that cannot be delivered, there's some potential for confusion. It might seem that the word *abandon* might have been a better choice, but alas, that word means something else in online marketing.

In the context of web-browsing metrics, the term *abandonment rate* refers specifically to shopping cart abandonment. In fact, it's often called the *cart abandonment rate*. It measures the percentage of users who get so far as to place an item in their shopping cart, but fail to actually complete their purchase.

How interested were they? Understanding the depth of their visit

As I mention earlier in this chapter, one common measure of how interested a user is in your website is how long they stayed on your site. But many marketers have come to prefer page view counts over time to measure interest. Page views indicate interaction with the website which is more clearly associated with a user's interest.

There are a couple of simple metrics associated with page view counts. One is the average number of page views per site visit. This is called *average page depth*.

$$\text{Average page depth} = (\text{page views}) / (\text{site visits})$$

There are some variations on how this metric is used. Often, you'll be interested in how long (in terms of page views) it takes a user to get around to doing something in particular, like registering or making a purchase. It's easy enough to modify this metric to do that. For example, you could make the following calculation:

$$\text{Page depth per purchase} = (\text{page views before purchase}) / (\text{purchases})$$

Another metric related to page views measures the percentage of your sessions that reach some threshold. You may notice that most purchases don't happen until a certain number of pages have been viewed. For the sake of this example, let's say that number is 7. You might then be curious how many sessions last that long. For example, you might make this calculation:

$$\text{Seven-page visit rate} = 100 \times (\text{seven page sessions}) / (\text{site visits})$$

There's seemingly no end to the metrics that are potentially available to help you understand how users are using your site. Many of these metrics are also available from search engines to help you understand how users are managing to find your website. In the online world, change is continual and fast. So stay abreast of what new data and metrics are being developed.

How Did You Do? Assigning Value to Your Database Marketing Campaigns

Chapter 14 talks at length about setting up your campaign as an experiment. The key component of that experiment is your control group. You've held out a random sample of your target audience from your communication. You've executed the campaign and collected the response data. Now it's time to put that control group to use.

Understanding lift: Calculating your net response rate

In controlled experiments that test medications, the placebo effect is well documented. Some patients who receive a placebo — meaning they *don't* receive the actual treatment — still show signs of improvement. This placebo effect needs to be taken into account when the effectiveness of the drug is reported.

You're in a similar situation with respect to measuring your direct-marketing campaigns. You can't take sole credit for the responses to your campaign. Advertising campaigns and other marketing efforts have contributed to your customers' awareness of and interest in your products. But you can take sole credit for *some* of it. This is what that control group is for.

Gross response rate

The first thing you need to do is calculate the overall response rate, called *gross response rate,* to your campaign. Suppose you sent out 100,000 communications and 6,000 consumers in your target audience actually responded. They bought something from you. Your gross response rate is the ratio of these two numbers — in this case, 6 percent. The formula is this:

Gross response rate = 100 × (total responders) / (target audience size)

You need to be careful about distinguishing a *responder* from a *response.* A particular household might make two different purchases at two different times. That counts as one responder. But when you get around to attaching revenue to this responder, you can count both purchases.

Net response rate

Once you have your gross response rate in hand, you need to look in on your control group. What were these folks doing while your campaign was in market?

To continue my example, let's suppose that your geek had recommended that your control group contain 5,000 households. Of these 5,000 households, 250 made a purchase that would have qualified as a response to your campaign. That means the control group response rate is 5 percent. Your control group response rate is calculated the same way as your gross response rate:

Control group response rate = 100 × (control group responders) / (control group size)

Now comes the key to your being able to take credit where credit is due. The difference between the gross response rate and the control group response rate is all you. This difference is known as the *net response rate* — or more commonly, the *lift* — associated with your campaign:

Lift = (gross response rate) – (control group response rate)

This lift represents the proportion of the responses that can be attributed specifically to your communication. The only difference between the target audience and the control group was whether or not they received your message.

Once you calculate the lift, you need to check with your geek again regarding its significance. Chapter 14 talks at length about the notion of statistical confidence. Essentially, you need to make sure that this lift is large enough to be meaningful given the size of your control group.

In this example, you had a 6 percent gross response rate and a 5 percent control group response. This gives you a lift of 1 percent, or 1,000 responses that you can take sole credit for. A check with your geek will confirm that this lift is *significant* — well above the 95% confidence level, given the 5,000 members in your control group.

The bottom line: Net revenue and return on investment

Now that you've calculated your lift and hopefully verified that it's significant, it's time to calculate your contribution. (If you don't have significant results, then you can't justify claiming any contribution.) This calculation depends on two additional numbers. You need your total campaign cost and the total revenue that's tied to your campaign.

Suppose your campaign cost was $350 per thousand, or 35 cents per piece. This is actually pretty typical of a large postcard campaign. In this case, your total campaign cost would be $35,000:

Total campaign cost = (cost per piece) × (target audience size)

Your total revenue is simply the sum of all the purchases made by your responders. Remember that it's okay to count multiple purchases made by the same responder as long as those purchases fit your definition of a response.

Let's say that your 6,000 responders purchased on average $100 worth of merchandise. That means your total revenue came out to $600,000. This is usually referred to as the *gross revenue* associated with the campaign. Your *net revenue* is simply gross revenue minus campaign cost.

Now you're ready to claim credit for your share of that revenue. That share, or the *incremental revenue* associated with your campaign, is calculated by applying your lift percentage to net revenue:

Incremental revenue = lift × [(gross revenue) – (campaign cost)]

The net revenue turns out to be $565,000 ($600K minus $35K). Because your lift is 1%, you can take credit for a $56,500 contribution — a pretty good return on a $35,000 investment. And in fact, campaign results are often presented exactly that way. Your *return on investment* or *ROI* is calculated as follows:

ROI = 100 × [(incremental revenue) – (campaign cost)] / (campaign cost)

In the example, this turns out to be a little over 61 percent. This example isn't particularly outlandish. Database marketing can be an extremely efficient way to spend marketing dollars.

Chapter 16

Putting Your Geek to Work: Analyzing Campaign Results

. . . .

In This Chapter

▶ Understanding and working with different types of data

▶ Profiling marketing campaign responders

▶ Using decision tree techniques to understand responses

▶ Building response models

. . . .

Chapter 15 explains how you go about measuring the success of your database marketing campaigns. Ultimately, you can assign a specific value to your campaign's financial contribution. Once you've done that, it's time to roll up your sleeves and see what you can learn from that campaign.

Analysis of marketing campaigns has become quite sophisticated over the years. Statistical software packages such as SAS and SPSS are incredibly advanced and easy to use. If I'd had one of these packages when I took undergraduate statistics, I could have done the entire semester's worth of homework in an evening. In Chapter 19, I talk more about selecting statistical software.

Some of these packages actually have software modules specifically designed to analyze marketing campaigns. The convenience of this tool set is a great asset. I encourage you to explore and use these packages. But there's a lot going on beneath the surface, and you need to be a little careful with these tools.

In this chapter, I explain some basic types of data that you typically see in customer databases and database marketing campaigns and talk about how to properly use that data. I go on to describe some analytic techniques that can help you to learn from your campaigns and apply that learning to future campaigns. These techniques range from simple reporting to more advanced modeling.

Measurement versus Classification: Numeric Data and Categorical Data

All your marketing data falls into one of two categories. The first is numeric data. *Numeric* data essentially measures something, like age or revenue. The second type of data is categorical data. As the name suggests, *categorical* data simply separates consumers (or households or products) into categories. Whether a customer responded to a marketing campaign or not is a typical categorical variable. They either did or they didn't.

This distinction may sound pretty trivial, but it's one you need to keep in mind when you start analyzing data. In particular, you need to be sure that you recognize which type of data you're really dealing with. It's easier to make a mistake than you might think.

A silly example might make my point. I'm a baseball fan. Every morning during baseball season I pore over box scores and statistics while I sip my coffee. Batting averages, earned run averages, and every other kind of numerical data you can imagine are available on players and teams.

Every player has a number on the back of his jersey. But I've never seen statistics reported on the average jersey number per home run. Why not? Well, because that's a meaningless calculation. The jersey numbers aren't really numeric data. They don't measure anything. They simply identify an individual player.

I told you it was a silly example, but bear with me for a second. The jersey numbers represent categorical data. The categories they identify are categories with only one member, but they're categories nonetheless.

As I point out later in this section, it's always possible to turn a numeric variable into a categorical variable. But you can't go the other way. It leads to nonsense.

In marketing databases, many categorical variables are masquerading as numerical variables. In the next section, I point out some examples of this. I also explain in a little more detail how to determine whether a variable should really be considered a numeric variable and treated as a measurement of something.

Understanding Numeric Variables

All numeric data isn't created equal. As my jersey number example illustrates, just because you have data that looks numeric doesn't mean you can perform calculations with it. The jersey numbers are not numeric data at all. They're just names. But even if you have actual numeric data, you can still run into problems.

Interval and ratio data: When averages are meaningful

Numeric data can take a couple different forms. Financial data is an example of robust numerical data that supports statistical calculations. The feature that makes this data robust is that a dollar is a dollar. The difference between a $10 purchase and a $20 purchase is exactly the same as the difference between a $100 purchase and a $110 dollar purchase.

This feature turns out to be exactly what's needed to make the calculation of averages and other statistics meaningful. You need your data to have the property that different intervals are comparable. Age differences, income levels, purchase sizes, and any data that's measured on a fixed scale have this property. Such data is called *interval* data.

There's actually another level of robustness related to data types, known as ratio data. Most of your marketing data will have this property if it's interval data (meaning that different intervals can be meaningfully compared according to their length.) You don't really need to worry too much about the difference between ratio and interval data except when you're defining data types in your statistical software. Essentially, *ratio* data depends on the existence of some absolute 0 starting point. The classic example of interval data that's not ratio data is Fahrenheit temperature. The difference between 32 degrees and 33 degrees measures the same amount of energy as the difference between 100 and 101 degrees. But 0 degrees doesn't mean a total absence of heat. In fact, we observe temperatures below 0. For this reason, you can't meaningfully say that 100 degrees is twice as much heat as 50 degrees.

Ordinal data: When averages aren't meaningful

There's a kind of numerical data that falls short of meeting the interval data requirements described in the preceding section. I'm talking about something called ordinal data. Ordinal data is fairly common in marketing databases. *Ordinal* data measures the degree to which something is true. Essentially, it sorts things.

Ordinal data appears frequently in survey results. You see it all the time when you're shopping online. The 5-star rating system that seems to have taken over user ratings for everything from movies to pet-sitting services is an example of ordinal data. And it's also an example of ordinal data being misused.

Typically, the results of these online surveys are reported as an average. This movie got 3.5 out of 5 stars, for example. Technically, this calculation isn't justified. Why not? There's no reason to assume or believe that the difference between 1 star and 2 stars is the same as the difference between 4 stars and 5 stars. In fact, it isn't at all clear what a star is actually measuring.

Ordinal data should be reported according to the number or percentage of responses that, in this case, received a given number of stars. You would also be justified in reporting the percentage of responses above or below a certain level because there's an implied order to the ratings.

In the case of product ratings, reporting averages based on this ordinal data isn't terribly problematic. These calculations are really just used to compare one movie to another. Where you get in trouble with ordinal data is if you use it as input to another statistical procedure. When building a response model, for example, your statistical software will perform a lot of calculations on numeric data. If the data doesn't support those calculations, your results will be compromised.

Ordinal data often appears in the results of survey research and polling. When customers and people who are polled are asked to rank preferences, the data is typically ordinal. Questions that ask someone to rate their agreement with a given statement on a scale of 1 to 5 or 1 to 10 also should be treated as providing ordinal data. In the next section, I talk about a method of converting measurement data into ordered subsets called *deciling,* which also produces ordinal data.

Whenever you set out to analyze data using your statistical software, the program will ask you about your data. Most packages make assumptions about data types based on a cursory look at your data. But they also allow you to explicitly define the data type associated with each variable. It's well worth your time to look through these data types in detail to make sure they accurately reflect what's going on.

Analyzing Response Rates: The Simple Approach

When you begin to dig into the response data for your campaign, you start by trying to get a sense of who responded to your campaign. The first step is to build a profile of responders. You do that by looking at a wide variety of variables to see which ones effectively differentiate between responders and non-responders.

Some simple graphical techniques are very helpful in this regard. These techniques are supported by even the most rudimentary statistical software. In fact, they can even be applied using basic spreadsheet functions. They provide easy-to-interpret insights into the customer characteristics that are associated with responders. In this section, I outline a couple of common approaches to visualizing your campaign results.

Response distributions

In Chapter 6, I talk about a common graphical representation of data called a histogram. Histograms show how a variable is distributed. Figure 16-1 shows what a histogram charting the distribution of the number of children per household might look like.

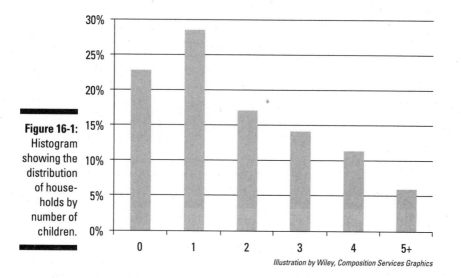

Figure 16-1: Histogram showing the distribution of households by number of children.

Illustration by Wiley, Composition Services Graphics

Histograms are extremely useful tools for data visualization. They can be combined with your response data to give you a picture of where responses are coming from.

For example, suppose you've just completed a database marketing campaign designed to drive sales of minivans. If you combine your response data with the data on number of children pictured in Figure 16-1, it might look like Figure 16-2.

The darker bars in the chart in Figure 16-2 represent the percentage of responses that came from households with the given number of children. Notice that for families with 2 children or more, the percentage of responders is actually higher than the percentage of households that fall into those categories. This means that number of children is actually a useful differentiator between responders and non-responders.

If you add up the numbers for these larger families, you see that families with at least two children account for about 50 percent of the audience. But they account for 75 percent of the responses.

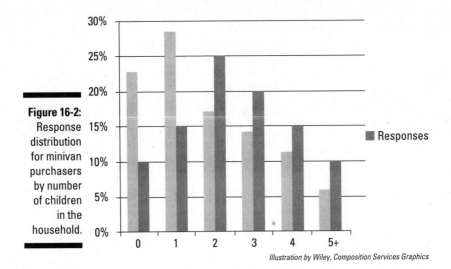

Figure 16-2:
Response distribution for minivan purchasers by number of children in the household.

By applying this technique to a wide variety of variables, you can start to build a picture of the typical traits shared by your responders. Not all variables will show this level of differentiation, or lift. What you're looking for is groups of customers where the responders appear in disproportionately high numbers.

In Chapter 6 and again in Chapter 15, I stress the importance of making sure that you report results that are statistically valid. The idea is that when you compare response rates, you want to make sure that the differences you report actually hold water. That statistical rigor should not be forgotten when you do response profiling (though it very frequently is overlooked).

Analyzing non-categorical data

Histograms are especially well suited to categorical data, especially data that contains a relatively small number of categories, such as number of children, marital status, or home ownership. But when you have measurement data, like age or income, it gets a little harder to differentiate responders from non-responders.

When building responder profiles, you'll no doubt run reports on things like average age of responders versus non-responders. You may even discover that the average age does differ significantly between the two groups. Such a discovery could indicate that age may be playing a role in response behavior. But this fact by itself isn't all that useful.

One way to dig deeper into this relationship is to simplify your age data. In the next section, I describe a technique for doing that which standardizes the data into equal sized groups. This essentially makes the data look more categorical (although technically these groups are really ordinal).

Rank ordering your data

We've all been subjected to the stresses of standardized testing in school. Whether it's college boards or achievement tests, the results of these wonderful little exercises are reported in the same way. The number you focus on is your *percentile rank.*

Your percentile rank is simply a measure of how many people scored lower than you did. A percentile rank of 50 means that half of the test takers scored lower and half scored higher than you. A percentile rank of 95 means you're pretty doggone smart.

You can use a similar ranking technique to help you get your arms around some of your marketing data, particularly data that involves measurements. Because age, income, and other financial data is spread out, it sometimes helps to simplify it by expressing it as percentiles.

Actually, there's nothing magical about percentiles. Percentiles are implicitly based on a scale of 0 to 100. But even this is still too granular to really be considered a simplification. You can actually break up your data into any number of groups you want.

The trick is simply to sort the data from lowest to highest and then split it into equal sized parts. These parts are referred to as *quantiles,* which is the generic term for percentiles. And you can choose any number of parts you want. The four most common ways of splitting groups are into 4 parts (*quartiles*), 5 parts (*quintiles*), or 10 parts (*deciles*).

If you divide a target audience into income deciles, your distribution might look like Table 16-1. The income associated with each decile represents the bottom of that range.

Table 16-1   Typical distribution of household income by decile

Decile	Income ($)
1	0–17,999
2	18,000–24,999
3	25,000–34,999
4	35,000–41,999
5	42,000–53,999
6	54,000–66,999
7	67,000–83,999
8	84,000–106,999
9	107,000–144,999
10	Over $145,000

You can see that the income ranges associated with these deciles are not at all uniform. The second decile ranges from $18K to $25K. This is quite narrow compared to the eighth decile, which ranges from $84K to $107K. What's uniform about this distribution is that, by design, each group contains exactly the same number of households.

Using rank ordering to analyze response rates

When you use histograms to graphically analyze responses, you need to calculate the percentage of responses that come from each category on your graph. Just reporting the response rate by category is misleading because the categories are not all the same size.

This actually becomes problematic for categories that are very small. Here's an extreme example: Suppose you end up with a category that only contains one household, and that household actually responded. You would show a response rate of 100 percent in that category, despite the fact that a single response is merely a drop in the bucket.

The fact that deciles (and other types of quantiles) are all the same size makes creating a useful graph a little easier. You can just report the response rates by decile. Figure 16-3 shows a (completely contrived) response report by decile for a campaign that's designed to drive sales of luxury sedans.

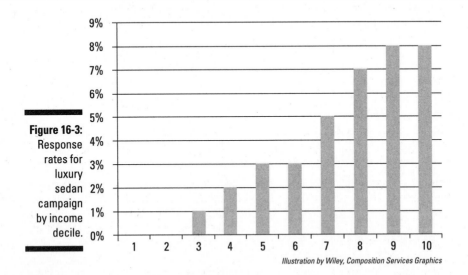

Figure 16-3: Response rates for luxury sedan campaign by income decile.

Illustration by Wiley, Composition Services Graphics

Because the reporting categories are all exactly the same size, the response rates in this graph are directly comparable. This graph clearly shows that income is a barrier to luxury sedan purchases.

Counting total responses

There's another common way of viewing this same data that's even more compelling. Figure 16-3 clearly shows that response rates are going up as you move up the income rankings. One thing you'll want to think about is what income level you should use as a cutoff for future target audiences.

To do that, reverse the order of the deciles. Then graph the percentage of responders that fall into incomes above each successive decile. Here you're measuring the cumulative response. Figure 16-4, which is called a *gains chart*, illustrates this approach.

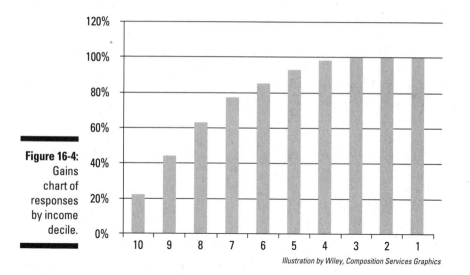

Figure 16-4:
Gains chart of responses by income decile.

Illustration by Wiley, Composition Services Graphics

This way of viewing the data makes it even clearer where your responses are coming from. Note that by the time you reach down to the 6th decile, you've accounted for over 80 percent of your responses. This means that you could have cut your audience (and therefore your campaign costs) in half and still have generated the vast majority of the responses.

Gains charts are commonly used in evaluating the success of statistical models. I discuss the use of gains charts in this context later on in this chapter.

Advanced Approaches to Analyzing Response Data: Statistical Modeling

The previous section talks about some simple ways to analyze your response rates based on what you know about your customers. All those techniques involve looking at one variable at a time to profile your responders. But no single variable is going to tell the whole story.

A couple of advanced modeling techniques are commonly used in database marketing. I discuss those later in this chapter. First I want to introduce you to some key elements of the modeling process.

The problem with cross tabs

When you start drilling further into your data, your first impulse (at least my first impulse) is to start building cross tab reports that take more than one variable into account.

You may have discovered that marital status and number of children are both associated with responses to your minivan campaign. The natural thing to do is to combine the two variables and look separately at response rates for married and unmarried parents of two kids, for example.

 The problem with this approach is that it runs out of gas pretty quickly. What I mean is, the sizes of the individual cells that you're analyzing get small quickly. A cross tab report that looks at response rates for number of children versus income decile might have 50 or 60 different cells. And that only takes two variables into account. Typically, you'll find a half dozen or more variables that are relevant. Cross tabs become unmanageable (and statistically irrelevant) quickly as the number of variables grow.

What is a statistical model?

The primary function of modeling in database marketing is to help you predict who will respond to your marketing campaigns. A *statistical model* in this context is a set of rules that relate customer data to campaign responses.

I enjoy cooking, so a natural way for me to think about models is as recipes. A recipe for a particular dish requires a specific set of ingredients. But the relative amounts of each ingredient are important, and so is the way they're combined and prepared. Many different bread recipes call for basically the same ingredients. But the amount of baking soda you use and the temperature at which you cook the bread can dramatically affect the outcome.

In database marketing, your target audience plays the role of the dish you're trying to prepare. Customer data — the variables in your database — play the role of the ingredients. Your statistical model is the recipe. It tells you how to combine those data elements to select your target audience.

The model development process

Developing a statistical model is a technical exercise requiring some advanced knowledge of statistical methods. It's not my intent here to address the details of various modeling techniques. But I do want to point out some highlights of the model-building process.

Specifically, I want to familiarize you with three main stages in model development:

- ✓ **Preparing your data:** Your data as it exists in your database isn't ready for prime time when it comes to building models. You need to do a fair amount of cleanup and transformation of your data to maximize the quality of your model.
- ✓ **Building the model:** This actually turns out to be the easiest part because a lot of the work is done for you by statistical software.
- ✓ **Testing the model:** This step is extremely important. A number of things can go wrong when you build a model that you can catch with a good testing plan.

Though testing your model is the last phase of development, you need to set up a testing structure up front. That essentially involves holding out a portion of your target audience from the model development process to use later in testing. I discuss this process in a little more detail later.

Preparing your data

The first thing you need to determine is which variables you're going include in your model. The profiling exercise that you've already performed on your campaign results can help immensely in this regard. You already have a pretty good sense of which variables are most strongly related to campaign responses. These ingredients, or *predictor variables,* will form the basis for your model.

Some modeling techniques purport to select your variables for you. Some decision tree approaches discussed later in this chapter will do this for you. My experience is that even if that option is available to you, it's better to limit the number of variables you're using to ones that you already know are relevant. This reduces the likelihood that your model-development process will get off track and produce less than optimal results.

Once you've identified your variables, you want to get them model ready. You need to look at a couple of standard things.

Getting rid of outliers

In Chapter 6, I talk about very long-tailed distributions. I give an example related to season pass use, in which the vast majority of pass holders use their pass only a handful of times. But some pass holders use them hundreds of times.

These very high transaction users represent a tiny fraction of the pass holders. But their high usage numbers can skew your model. Get rid of 'em. In statistical parlance, they're known as *outliers*. It's standard practice to ignore outliers when you build a model. It actually improves your model quality because the model isn't trying too hard to take into account what amounts to misleading data.

Your statistical package will do this for you. There are a number of ways of identifying outliers. You also have some flexibility in how far "out" a data point has to be to consider it an outlier. Your geek can help you to determine what to leave in and what to leave out.

You may not want to get rid of outliers altogether. If you have a borderline target audience size you may decide that every scrap of data needs to be included to make your model successful. In this case, it may sometimes be appropriate to re-assign values to outliers that are more in line with the norm. In the case of the season pass example, you may decide to re-assign the visit count to 10 for all pass holders with more than 10 visits. Check with your geek about the consequences of doing something like this.

Making sure data types match your modeling technique

Returning to my recipe analogy, just knowing that a recipe calls for a particular ingredient isn't always enough. Sometimes the form of that ingredient is important. I've found this to be particularly true of spices. A teaspoon of mustard is ambiguous. Does this mean prepared mustard, mustard seed, or ground mustard?

A similar thing is true of models. Some modeling techniques work best on categorical data. Others require the data to represent comparable measurements. As I point out earlier in this chapter, you can't make a categorical variable into a measurement, but you can go the other way.

If you're using a technique that likes categorical data, you don't have to exclude measurement data from your set of predictor variables. You can use the rank-ordering technique described earlier to make your measurement data more model friendly. By converting measurement data into deciles (or any quantiles you choose), you can include this data in your model.

Paying attention to timing

When you build a model, you're looking at the past. You're analyzing the responses to a completed campaign. You need to make sure that the predictor variables you decide to use match up with the time period when the campaign was actually executed.

For example, suppose you pulled your mail file in May and responses were received through June. It's now July, and you've decided to build a model based on this mailing. One of the variables you look at is the previous month's purchases, because this variable was used in selecting your target audience.

What you're going to find is that this variable predicts responses perfectly. Because you're now in July, a purchase in the previous month is actually a *response* to your campaign. It's not actually predicting the future. It's predicting the past. Not terribly helpful.

Now this may sound like an obvious point, but I've seen it overlooked more than once. Because your customer data is always changing, it's not always easy to determine if the data that's currently in your database represents what was there when you pulled your mail file.

If you think you might later want to build a model based on responses to a campaign, it's a good idea to create an analysis file when you pull your mail file. You can include any variables in that file that you think might be useful down the road in understanding responses. This guarantees that you have a snapshot of the way the data looked when you pulled the file, which is what you want if you're going to build a useful model.

Making sure the distributions match your modeling technique

In the aftermath of the relatively recent meltdown in the banking and investment banking industries, you heard endless talk about *financial derivatives* being the culprit. These investment instruments are not only mind-numbingly complex, but they depend in a fundamental way on statistical models.

In particular, they way derivatives are priced is based on a series of advanced statistical methods. Those methods, like all statistical methods, rely on a complex set of assumptions about how the underlying variables are distributed.

What happened leading up to the financial meltdown, among other things, is that these pricing models were used in computer trading long after their underlying assumptions ceased to be true. Essentially, the pricing tools continued to be used long after they were broken.

When you build your database marketing models, you'll be using techniques that depend on assumptions about the distributions of your predictor variables. In particular, the most commonly used response models like to see nice, normal, bell-shaped curves. Your data doesn't look like this. That means that the data needs to be coaxed into shape.

There are lots of techniques available for doing that coaxing. They involve performing various mathematical operations on variables that change the shapes of the distributions. A relatively simple example is that taking the logarithm of a variable with a long-tailed distribution yields a much more bell-shaped curve. Performing these data *transformations* is definitely a job for your geek.

In my experience, this is the most commonly overlooked step in statistical modeling. And it's an important one. You wouldn't put granular sugar in a frosting recipe that calls for confectioner's sugar. Don't dump wacky variables into a model that calls for normal ones.

Building the model

Data preparation is by far the most involved part of building a successful model. Once you have the data right, getting a model built is largely the job of your statistical software. But there's a bit of an art to it as well.

The modeling techniques typically used in database marketing involve culling through your data multiple times. It isn't as simple as just calculating the right amount of each ingredient in the recipe. These techniques operate on a trial-and-error basis.

The basic idea is that the software keeps making guesses and then refining those guesses. This is where the art of modeling comes in. You have to tell it when to stop.

It's actually possible to overcook a model. Essentially what happens is that the model stops predicting and starts memorizing the data. This phenomenon is referred to as *over-fitting* the data. When that happens, the usefulness of the model is limited to predicting the behavior of the audience that was used to build it. It falls apart when you try to apply it to a different target audience.

There are various statistical ways of sticking a fork in your model while it's in the oven, so to speak. It requires some technical knowledge to interpret these statistics correctly. And experience plays a big role in knowing when to declare a model done.

Testing your model

Once the model is done, you do have a chance to taste it. (And here, mercifully, my recipe analogy comes to an end.) There's a standard operating procedure for model building that allows you to test the model before you roll it out in an actual marketing campaign. When you develop a model, you're using data from a previous campaign. As I point out earlier, it's a good idea to pull an analysis file containing all the data about your target audience that you might want to use to build your model.

The first thing you need to do with this file is split it in half. This should be done at random. In Chapter 6, and again in Chapter 14, I talk in more detail about how to do this. The important thing is that both randomly selected halves need to be representative of the whole. You set one half, your *validation file,* aside and forget about it until you reach the testing phase. You use the other half, the *training file,* to build or *train* your model.

Once your model is built, you can use your validation file to check how you did. You simply apply the finished product to that validation file and check to see how well it did at predicting responses. This is an excellent way of identifying problems with over-fitting. If the model doesn't validate well, it's back to the drawing board. But at least you haven't wasted the money on testing the model in an actual campaign.

Models typically don't perform quite as well during validation as they do on the training data. This is to be expected. But you'll also see some degradation in performance when you actually roll out the model in a campaign. For this reason, it's important to temper your expectations for actual response rates when the model is rolled out. There are no hard-and-fast rules for how much you need to temper them. Experience in your situation is the best guide.

Common Response Modeling Techniques

Response models are basically attempts to use statistics to identify target audiences for marketing campaigns. Statistical techniques are evolving all the time, and new ones continue to pop up in marketing applications. There are, however, a couple of techniques that have stood up well over time.

In this section, I introduce you to a couple of the more common techniques used in database marketing. Both these approaches use past campaign response data to identify and refine target audiences for future campaigns. But they differ fundamentally in the way they go about it.

Classification trees

Earlier in this chapter, I point out the shortcomings of trying to produce detailed cross-tabulation reports (cross tabs) on campaign responses. The number of distinct combinations of variables becomes quickly overwhelming. For a human. But sorting stuff like this is exactly what computers do best. The classification tree approach to modeling responses tries various ways of combining data elements in various ways until useful combinations are found. In essence, the approach looks for hot spots in your target audience.

RFM models revisited

In Chapter 8, I introduce the notion of RFM models in the context of analyzing transaction data. These models look at transactions according to their recency, frequency, and monetary value. They then categorize customers according to how recent, how frequent, and how expensive their transactions were. By comparing response rates to past campaigns among these different customer categories, these RFM models are able to identify the best prospects for future campaigns.

In its simplest form, an RFM model might only look at whether or not a customer has reached a given threshold with respect to each of these measures. In other words, each customer would be classified as yes or no with respect to recency, frequency, and monetary value. This model is actually a classification tree model. The name becomes clear when you look at the data visually. Figure 16-5 shows a visual representation of a simple RFM.

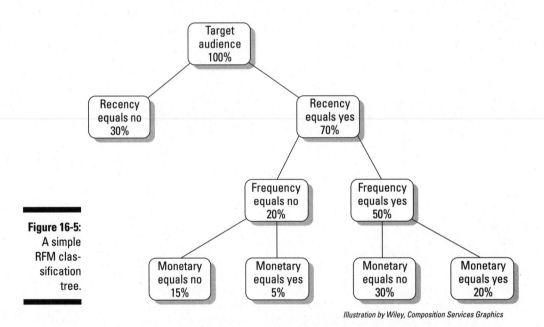

Figure 16-5:
A simple RFM classification tree.

Illustration by Wiley, Composition Services Graphics

In this tree, the percentages represent the size of the groups relative to the entire target audience. There are a couple of things to keep in mind about these trees. First, the boxes that have nothing below them, called terminal nodes or terminal leaves, add up to 100 percent of the target audience.

Second, the advantage of this method is that you can abandon a branch of the tree at any point. Because customers who didn't have a recent purchase aren't going to pop up as frequent or high value customers anyway, that branch is *pruned* (actually a technical term) in favor of focusing somewhere else.

By looking at the response rates associated with nodes of the tree, you can develop a targeting strategy. The idea is to focus your campaign dollars on nodes that have high response rates. In the tree shown in Figure 16-6, the hot spots are probably the two terminal nodes with monetary equals yes classifications. This represents a reduction in the target audience to a quarter of its original size.

RFM models are simple. This is both their strength and their weakness. It's a strength because they're effective and simple to build and understand. It's a weakness because they only look at three variables.

Building classification trees

There are a number of variations on how to go about building a classification tree. One of the first to be applied in marketing is a method called CHAID. This stands for *chi-squared automatic interaction detection*. Chi-squared ("chi" rhymes with "sky") refers to the statistic that's used to determine whether a difference between two groups is significant.

The *automatic interaction detection* part refers to the fact that this method determines all by itself how to set up the branches of your tree. You don't need to tell it which variables to look at. You can feed it a bunch of variables, and it will pick ones that are most effective at differentiating responders from non-responders.

As I mention earlier in this chapter, I'm not a big fan of letting statistical procedures pick my variables for me. I think it increases your risk of over-fitting your model. These types of processes can end up going down the proverbial rabbit hole if they're presented with too many possibilities.

But there's a very powerful advantage to using classification tree methods, automated or not. They can actually tell you the optimal way of re-classifying your data based on the categories of a particular variable. For example, your demographic data contains information on the number of children in a household. This data might contain values from 0 to 4 and another category of 5+. That's six different categories.

When presented with response data for a campaign, your classification tree software may come back and tell you that the only really relevant categories are 0, 1 to 2, and 3 or more. In this case, you've achieved a simplification by reducing the number of different cells by half. More importantly, the software has given you the "right" cells. These are the breaks that are most effective at distinguishing responders from non-responders.

Classification tree algorithms are particularly well suited to analyzing lots of categorical data. When preparing your data for a classification tree model, it's a good idea to convert measurement data into categorical data beforehand. You can easily do that using the rank ordering process I describe earlier in this chapter. Some software packages do this for you as part of the classification tree model development.

Creating response scores

Another common approach to modeling campaign responses is to try to estimate the probability of getting a response based on your predictor variables. This technique generally uses a procedure called *logistic regression*. This approach can take into account both categorical and measurement data. When such a model is applied to a given audience, the result is that each consumer is given a response score. Typically, this is a number between 0 and 1 and purports to measure the likelihood of that customer responding to your campaign.

It's been my experience that these response scores don't really resemble actually probabilities at all. In other words, if you just mail to people with response scores above .9, you're not going to get a 90 percent response rate. The important thing about them is that higher scores should be associated with higher response rates. In other words, these scores are a good sorting tool.

This brings me back to the notion of a gains chart, discussed earlier in this chapter. When you test your model against your validation group and again when you actually implement it, gains charts are a very easy way to visualize how the model is performing. The idea is simple. You sort your audience by response score from highest to lowest. Then you graph the percentage of total responses against the percentage of customers above each score level. Figure 16-6 represents a gains chart for a fairly successful model.

The model scores are represented along the bottom of Figure 16-6. These are the percentile ranks of the model scores. The leftmost 10 percent represents the top 10 percent of model scores. The vertical axis represents the percentage of responses that came from customers whose score exceeded a given percentile rank. For example, this graph is telling you that approximately 70 percent of responders came from the highest 30 percent of model scores.

When using a gains chart to evaluate a model, you're looking, qualitatively at least, for only one thing. You want it to be steep. The faster your total response percentage gets up close to 100 percent, the fewer customers you had to contact to get those responses.

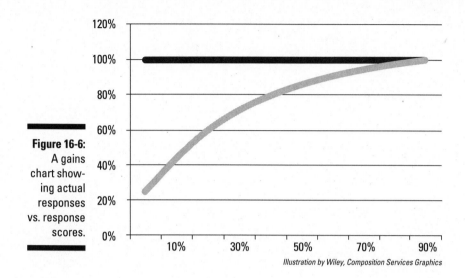

Figure 16-6:
A gains chart showing actual responses vs. response scores.

Illustration by Wiley, Composition Services Graphics

A common application of the information provided in a gains chart relates to sizing your audience for a campaign. When it comes time to select a target audience using your model, you can use the gains chart to figure out how many customers to mail to. In the earlier example, if 70 percent of your responses are coming from the top 30 percent of your model scores, you don't get many responses from the bottom 70 percent of your audience. Think about it from a cost/benefit perspective. Why spend 70 percent of your budget on the lower end of the audience when that's only going to generate 30 percent of the overall revenue? The precise point where you draw the line depends on the details of your campaign costs and revenue outlook. But gains charts are a powerful way of visualizing the targeting efficiency that models can provide.

Chapter 17

Sharing Customer Data Throughout Your Enterprise

In This Chapter

▶ Assisting with advertising and market research

▶ Using customer data to identify product gaps

▶ Understanding the role of customer data in pricing and revenue management

▶ Comprehending the role of data in customer relationship management

▶ Responding to law enforcement requests for data

*Y*our customer database is your stock in trade as a database marketer. You spend a great deal of your time and budget trying to build an accurate and comprehensive picture of your customers. This allows you to be very effective with tactical communications that drive revenue to the bottom line.

But that data you work so hard to compile has a wide variety of uses beyond simply executing database marketing campaigns. Everyone who's doing anything related to marketing or advertising has an interest in understanding your customer base.

And interest in your customers extends beyond just the marketing and advertising functions in your company. The role of customer data in making business decisions is expanding all the time. You'll experience a continuous stream of requests for data coming from a wide variety of sources.

Building strong partnerships outside the database marketing department is a core aspect of your job. Customer databases are expensive to build and maintain. By making your customer database a critical part of other departments' day-to-day operations, you open the door to getting some budget and resource help from those departments. This in turn improves your infrastructure, and everyone benefits.

In this chapter, I talk about some of the business functions that can benefit from access to consumer data. The way customer data is used both inside and outside marketing depends quite a bit on the nature of your business. This chapter points out some of the more common applications.

Customer Data and Advertising

As I discuss in Chapter 12, your overall marketing presence is most effective if it's coordinated. You want your company and brand to show a consistent face to consumers, regardless of how you're communicating with them. In part, this means keeping the messages and offers that you're communicating through database marketing campaigns consistent with the messages and offers being advertised through other channels.

But there's another way you can help to optimize your company's marketing presence. One of the big challenges for advertising is figuring out where and how to advertise. In a nutshell, this amounts to deciding what types of media to buy, when, and how much. Your customer profiles are very useful in this process.

Buying traditional media

Traditional media is an umbrella term that refers essentially to non-electronic channels. The typical examples are television, print, radio, and even billboards. The term *old media* is often used to distinguish these channels from *new media* like the Internet and social networking sites.

The cost of advertising in any given channel depends, quite simply, on the number of people that you can reach. The pinnacle of television advertising is the Super Bowl. The problem is that at a million dollars plus per minute, that air time is out of reach for most marketing budgets.

But for a million dollars, you can get a great deal of advertising done. Super Bowl commercials work because virtually everyone sees them. But as I point out in Chapter 2, your target audience is usually not everyone.

The companies that sell advertising in these traditional media generally have a pretty good sense of the audience they're reaching. Television stations, for example, get a lot of viewer demographic information from the Nielson surveys that have been run for decades. Magazines have demographic profiles of their subscribers.

The trick in purchasing advertising is to match up those audience profiles with the profiles of customers you want to reach. This is where you come in.

In Chapter 7, I discuss a number of ways to profile your customers. Among them, demographic profiles and geographic profiles tie most closely with the way advertising audiences are segmented. By profiling your past customers based on the types of data that define advertising audiences, you can help to get advertising in front of the consumers for whom it is relevant.

Television networks are just that. By definition, these networks have local affiliates. Advertising can be purchased selectively by geography. That means you can help focus this geographic exposure by segmenting your past purchasers based on their place of residence.

Demographics, particularly age and gender, play a huge role in TV audience profiles. But they also play heavily in describing the subscription base for print media, such as magazines. Put your marketing hat on and page through any periodical. You'll find an amazing uniformity in the types of ads that appear in it.

This uniformity is a reflection of demographic profiling. More specifically, it's a reflection of the matching up of demographic profiles. The periodical has developed subscriber profiles. The products that are advertised in its pages are targeted at consumers with profiles that are similar to those of the subscriber base.

Buying "new" media

Customer profiles play a similar role in the purchase of online and other electronically delivered advertising. But in the case of these new media channels, the profiles can be significantly more robust than those used in offline channels.

In Chapter 13, I discuss the use of data on the web. A tremendous amount of surfing data can be used to analyze consumer behavior online. For this reason, transaction-based customer profiles are central to deciding which ads to serve up and where. But this doesn't mean that more traditional demographic profiles don't have their place.

Getting your website to pop up on search engine pages is a major component of online marketing. Search engines are getting ever more sophisticated about serving up content based on more than just search terms. In particular, many search engines build consumer profiles based on past search behavior and which websites were actually viewed. They then serve up search results selectively based on a user's profile as well as what terms the user searched for. And you can buy sponsored search-result placement based on these profiles.

Social media websites are doing the same thing. They sell advertising placement based on customer profiles. These profiles are built using data from both user registration information as well as site usage.

Here again, you can be of assistance. It's been my experience that the marketing done via Internet and other new media is done largely independently of offline marketing databases. That's largely due to the rapid evolution of new media channels and the need to adapt quickly.

To the extent that your marketing database contains information that's not available online, you have an opportunity to help out your online partners. Profiles that you build based on offline transactions or demographics can still be useful in new media marketing efforts. Offline profiles are used more and more frequently to drive online prospecting. The idea is to look for new customers online who fit the offline profile of a profitable customer. And in most cases, it's beneficial to keep profiles consistent across channels. It facilitates a seamless customer experience with your brand.

I've observed one situation repeatedly over the years related to purchased demographic data: It often gets purchased twice. The Internet group buys demographic appends for their registered users. In the meantime, the same or similar data is being purchased for households in the marketing database. Because there's often a great deal of customer overlap between these databases, some money could be saved by coordinating these purchases.

Assisting with Marketing Research

Most companies do some level of consumer research. Surveys and focus groups are the two most prevalent forms of such research. Surveys, if they're well designed, provide data that can be analyzed using advanced statistical techniques. They can even be used to build customer profiles and segmentation schemes. For this reason, surveys fall under the category of *quantitative* research.

Focus groups, on the other hand, are used to get a sense of people's attitudes and decision-making processes. They don't really provide hard data that can be churned through by statistical procedures. They provide perspective and context. Focus groups fall under the category of *qualitative* research.

In both cases, however, your database can play an important role marketing research. Given the fundamentally quantitative nature of your database marketing efforts, you'll no doubt be more actively involved in quantitative research efforts (surveys). But you have a contribution to make on the qualitative side as well.

Selecting focus groups

On the qualitative side, your fundamental role is to aid in selecting the members of focus groups. Focus groups are small — usually only a handful of people at a time. And it takes time and expertise to facilitate a focus group productively. It's important that the members of the focus group are chosen well.

I used to work with a guy who was pretty skeptical of focus group research. His skepticism was based on a particular experience he had while doing marketing for a bank. He was asked to identify a group of credit card customers to be invited to participate in a focus group. This research was intended to gauge people's attitudes towards various fee and rate structures.

To get a clear picture of such attitudes, they decided they wanted to talk to customers who routinely carried balances on their credit card. I think their attitude was that if people weren't paying interest, they weren't going to have very strong opinions about interest rates. So, one of the key criteria for being invited to participate was carrying a balance on their credit card.

But when the subject came up in the focus groups, most participants claimed that they typically paid off their cards every month. These claims were the source of my colleague's skepticism about focus groups. I suspect that the social dynamics of the situation played a role in these claims. There can be a stigma attached to debt. But this example does point up the usefulness of using actual behavioral data in selecting members of focus groups.

Customer data and survey research

As in the case of focus groups, you may occasionally be asked to provide a targeted list of customers for the purpose of sending them a survey. But with survey research, your data plays a larger role than it does in focus group research.

First, the results of the survey questions can be combined with data from your marketing database to provide a more complete picture of the survey respondents. And you have the analytic tools to build profiles and models to aid in the analysis of survey results.

One common reason for doing surveys is to gauge customer satisfaction. It's become almost standard operating procedure for many companies to ask consumers to "answer a few questions about your recent experience" after a purchase is made. In many cases, this is used as a quality control check.

There are good ways and bad ways of doing this. I have a pet peeve about companies that use these surveys to financially punish their employees. This seems to be a particularly popular strategy among some auto dealerships. I have frequently been coached by the attendant to fill out the survey with no responses other than "completely satisfied" to prevent the attendant's pay from being docked.

The problem with this approach is that the surveys aren't really providing information about quality. Most people, even if they have a minor problem, aren't willing to throw an hourly employee under the bus. In that respect, I tend to think of these types of surveys as really being customer segmentation tools. They identify mean people. For my own part, I've simply stopped responding to them.

My point here is that by connecting the survey results back to your database, you can help validate that the survey is really measuring what it's intended to measure. If customers who aren't "completely satisfied" keep coming back to the dealership to get their cars serviced, then you might get suspicious of your survey methodology.

Another common reason for doing surveys is to build profiles of the customers who are most likely to be interested in your products. Once you understand what features define an interested consumer, you can extend this profile to your entire database of customers.

The survey results may contain information that's not directly available in your database. But like the response models I discuss in Chapter 16, this information can potentially be modeled based on data that you do have on hand.

Survey research is a two-way street when it comes to exchanging customer information. You can provide lists that fit the profile of the customers that will be surveyed. You can also learn from the results of these surveys and apply them to your broader customer base.

Customer Data and Product Development

Ideas for new products can come from a variety of sources. Engineers discover uses for by-products of a manufacturing process. Marketing research identifies new trends in consumer interests. Many companies have full-time research and development teams. Frontline salespeople make product suggestions based on their interactions with customers.

Your customer database can also be a source for new product inspiration. You have a unique perspective on which customers are buying which products. You've built customer segments and profiles that describe the primary audiences for your brand. Conversely, that means you know which segments *aren't* buying your products.

Marketers use the term *under-penetrated* to refer to customer segments or markets that don't buy products with the frequency they'd like. The term is frequently used in connection with age or lifestage segments. It's also used to refer to specific geographic markets.

A market or audience might be under-penetrated for a number of reasons. It may be a brand awareness issue, for example. But sometimes it's simply a consequence of your not having a product that's relevant to that particular audience. In any case, your marketing database may contain clues to indicate where a new product offering might be needed.

Sometimes price can be a big issue. Automobile manufacturers go to great lengths to make sure they have products available across a broad price spectrum. They've learned that being under-penetrated in the 20-something age group is ominous. If they don't develop brand loyalty early on, then it's much harder to attract customers later.

Fast-food restaurants have also done a good bit of product development based on under-penetrated markets. Twenty years ago, it would never have occurred to me to go to a fast-food chain to get a salad for lunch. They simply didn't offer them.

But as people started becoming increasingly health conscious, these restaurants began losing market share. The hipster crowd was becoming increasingly under-penetrated. So fast-food outfits started developing healthier menu options that would appeal to this under-penetrated segment. As a side note, it seems that simply offering these options is enough. They don't need to actually sell that many of them. More than once, I've talked my wife into pulling into McDonald's by reminding her that they offer salads. More often than not, she ends up ordering a Quarter Pounder with Cheese.

Keep an eye on your product sales data as it relates to your core customer segments. By monitoring the purchase volumes by segment, you can spot downward trends in market penetration. These trends are often signals that you have a product gap. Your product development team would very much like to understand and address such trends.

Customer Data and Pricing

Determining how to price your products is partly an exercise in basic accounting. How much does it cost to produce a product, and what is a reasonable profit margin? And this is only the beginning of the story when it comes to pricing decisions.

The science behind pricing actually gets quite involved. Sometimes discounts are necessary to address sales shortfalls. Sometimes certain products are sold at a loss in order to gain future sales. An understanding of customer behavior is central to making effective pricing decisions.

What is revenue management?

The discipline of pricing actually has a more technically flamboyant cousin known as revenue management. *Revenue management* is an analytic process that takes into account customer buying patterns and available inventory. This approach was initially developed in the airline industry. But its use has spread to many other industries as well.

The problem for airlines is two-fold. First, it's incredibly expensive to fly a plane. And it's incredibly unprofitable to fly an empty one. Second, once a flight is scheduled, the seats on that flight are perishable assets. Once the departure time arrives, empty seats mean lost revenue. There's no way to recover it.

Everyone who travels at all knows that airline ticket prices fluctuate constantly. Occasionally when I fly, I'll ask the person sitting next to me what they paid for their ticket. Often, the price is significantly different from what I paid.

A seemingly odd thing sometimes happens with connecting flights. I've sometimes been tempted to drive a couple of hours to a nearby airport in order to get a direct flight to where I'm going. But I've noticed that sometimes that very flight is actually less expensive if I pair it with a connecting flight from my home airport.

These price fluctuations and counterintuitive pricing structures are the result of revenue management techniques. Ticket prices are constantly balanced against available inventory — empty seats — using revenue management techniques.

The oddness of the pricing structure is a direct consequence of the mathematics that underlies revenue management. Essentially, they're looking to optimize their entire inventory. That is, they're trying to maximize their overall revenue. This can't be done by trying to maximize revenue for each individual seat.

All we as consumers see is a particular flight or small group of flights to a given destination. In the case of my example about a flight being cheaper if it includes a connection, the revenue that's being optimized is the total revenue for both flights. They may get less money from me that way, but they manage to fill up both flights with this strategy. In the big picture, this leads to more revenue.

One theme that comes up when I talk with revenue management folks is that they try very hard to avoid training customers to wait for a discount. If airlines consistently discount tickets the week before the flight departs, consumers will pick up on this pattern. And the airline will have for all intents and purposes lowered its fares.

So one technique they use is to offer discounts for early bookings. If there's one trend that's pretty recognizable in airfares, it's that waiting to book gets you a more expensive ticket. By discounting early, they're filling up their inventory. This in turn makes tickets for that flight a scarce commodity, and, according to the law of supply and demand, up go the prices.

Beyond the airline industry

The use of revenue management techniques has spread far beyond the airline industry. Naturally, its first expansion encompassed other sectors of the travel industry — namely, rental cars and hotels. I say *naturally* for a couple of reasons.

First, folks in the travel industry talk. Travel agents and travel planning websites are constantly bundling car and hotel offers with airline ticket purchases. The executives in those industries have a vested interest in cooperation. So it's natural that these industries would be the first to find out about revenue management success stories.

Second, the rental car and hotel businesses have something in common with airlines: perishable inventory. An empty seat on a flight can never be recovered after the plane leaves the gate. So too with rental cars and hotel rooms. Every day a car goes unrented or night that a hotel room stays empty is lost revenue.

Revenue management techniques have since been adapted to a wide variety of industries. Industries from financial services to retail apparel sales have found ways to apply the mathematics of revenue management to their pricing and discounting strategies.

In all these cases, revenue management techniques begin with customer data. In particular, customer purchase data plays a central role. How price sensitive are customers? What effects do various discount levels have on sales volume? How far in advance do customers book travel? All the customer behavior information contained in your marketing database is potentially relevant to advanced pricing analysis.

And it's not just behavioral data. Your profiles and segmentation analysis will also be of interest. Pricing decisions, particularly discounting decisions, can be made based on purchase channels as well as particular audiences.

In my experience managing a marketing database group, the revenue management and pricing folks were some of the more frequent visitors to my office. They tend to be pretty astute from an analytic perspective. And they're voracious consumers of data.

Customer Relationship Management

As promised in Chapter 1, I've thus far completely avoided the subject of customer relationship management in this book. You have enough to worry about in managing your database marketing efforts. But I'm sorry — the subject can't be avoided any longer. And you definitely have a large role to play in this arena.

What is CRM?

The term *customer relationship management,* usually abbreviated CRM, has become a marketing buzzword. It means slightly, sometimes vastly, different things to different people. For me, it's an umbrella term that refers to the integration and use of customer data throughout the enterprise.

When I was a kid, we lived in a small town. When I started to get an allowance for doing certain chores around the house, my father took me to the local savings and loan to open an account. We marched right up to the manager. He opened my account, handed me a passbook (I know, I'm dating myself). He told me that if I needed anything at all to just knock on his office door.

This manager knew my family. We were neighbors. He knew me and my particular financial situation. As I grew older and took jobs, bought a car, and eventually went to college, he remained my banker. Every time I walked into the bank, he greeted me and personally saw to my needs.

There are very few businesses that can still operate this way. But this example is my metaphor for what CRM should strive to be. It's a way of using customer data to re-create this personal customer experience.

A growing number of companies sell CRM software and services, such as Siebel (now Oracle) and SAP. These packages aren't all created equal. And they don't all do the same things. Many packages are designed to be used at call centers. Others are focused on the web. Still others are designed as sales force automation tools. When evaluating CRM software, be very persistent in understanding exactly what the software is designed to do and whether it fits in with your company's needs. The term *CRM* has become so widely used by software sales people that it doesn't really mean anything anymore. When exploring potential CRM implementations, stay focused on your business and your business processes. Don't get sucked into thinking it's all about software.

Sharing data across customer touchpoints

CRM is easier said than done. Doing it well involves getting customer data to everyone who interacts with the customer. This is a potentially huge data integration challenge. It takes significant investment and time. And it's not something that's really ever finished. It's implemented in an endless series of phases.

In that sense, CRM is as much a business strategy as anything. It's a commitment to doing everything you can to know your customers and interact with them on a personal level. In this section, I outline a few common components of a typical CRM strategy.

Your marketing database

In a sense, CRM is an extension of database marketing. Almost everything I talk about in this book is part of your company's CRM strategy. You're actively trying to understand your customers and engage them in the most relevant way possible.

Because CRM is based on knowing your customer, your marketing database lies at the center of your company's CRM strategy. The customer profiles you build are designed to help you implement database marketing campaigns. But they're also relevant to others who interact with the customer.

You've spent a great deal of time and effort integrating customer information from across your company. CRM is about pushing that integrated picture of the customer back out to where the data came from in the first place.

The web and new media

As I discuss in Chapter 13, there's a large amount of customer data available on how users are navigating the Internet. And with the advent of mobile computing, this data is growing all the time. Managing and using this data is another core part of your CRM strategy.

A key challenge is to try to integrate the customer experience across all of their access points. You want to show the same brand "face" to the customer whether they're browsing on a smart phone or on a laptop at the local coffee shop.

Another challenge is to integrate the customer experience throughout social media channels like Facebook, Twitter, and the various gaming sites. Because users are often logged in to more than one site at once, there's a constant tug of war to determine what content they'll see. The subject of social media marketing is a big one. Check out *Social Media Marketing For Dummies* by Shiv Singh and Stephanie Diamond (Wiley, 2012) for a full treatment.

The online customer experience is relatively easy to personalize and customize based on profile and usage data. For this reason, your online and new media marketing strategies will be a core part of your CRM strategy. The more customer interactions, sales, and service you can effectively conduct online, the better able you are to add a personal touch. But the key here is *effectively*. Online transactions need to be well integrated with other customer channels, like call centers, to be fully effective.

Customer service and call centers

One of the most obvious touchpoints is your call center. Customers call in to place orders, request service, or report a problem. It's extremely helpful for your call center representatives to have a clear picture of the customer relationship available while they're talking to them.

There's nothing more annoying to me than calling a number and getting routed to an automated phone system that doesn't allow me to do what I want to do. However, I do occasionally have a positive experience in that regard.

I recently had some trouble with my cable box. I discovered after some digging that the cable company was doing some upgrades related to converting to the new all-digital standards. The upshot was that every time they made a change, I had to reboot my cable box.

Now, my cable box is in an extremely inconvenient location because of the shape of my living room. Rebooting it myself involves a ladder and a screwdriver. So I called my cable company to reboot it for me.

Predictably, I was greeted by an automated system. But it did recognize my number and identified me and my account correctly without my needing to tell it. It then asked me if I wanted to reboot my box after asking me only one question to determine what I was calling about. The system told me it had sent the reboot signal and it would take a few minutes for it to complete its procedure.

So far, so good. I hung up, waited, and tried again. Still no dice. So I called back. This time the system recognized my number and immediately asked me if I was calling back about the reboot. I said yes and was connected with a live service agent who ended up helping me through the problem.

This is a pretty good example of a call center CRM system that's working well. They recognized me and what was going on. I didn't need to repeat my account information over and over again. In fact, I didn't even have to provide it.

Another aspect of CRM at the call center involves serving up offers based on previous or current purchases. In Chapter 13, I talk about serving up offers and content online based on browsing behavior and customer profiles. The same approach can be taken when a customer calls in to place an order. The more the call center agent knows about the customer who's calling, the more personal and relevant they can be.

Call centers frequently use scripts and structure decision trees in their CRM solutions. I admit that this approach can be useful for training purposes and for certain research calls. But I personally find it irritating to talk to someone who's feeding me canned responses that aren't really getting at what I need. It's far better to provide customer data to the call center agent and empower them to respond to that information in the most relevant way possible. No script can ever hope to anticipate all calls.

CRM at the point of sale

Getting customer data out to frontline sales people is one of the most effective ways to personalize the customer experience. At that point, it really is a personal interaction. Unfortunately, this is one of the more challenging aspects of CRM.

Grocery stores do it to some extent through the use of loyalty or rewards cards. But for the most part, the personalization that this enables is limited to choosing which coupons to print out based on your purchase patterns.

The Apple store has actually mastered point-of-sale CRM quite well. When you walk in, you can essentially log into your Apple account from any machine in the store. And the employees can process transactions while you're standing in front of the machine you're buying.

This fact alone is more powerful than you might think. Computers and other devices are expensive purchases. If you're forced to stand in line carrying a boxed-up computer and contemplating the price tag, you have time for buyer's remorse to set in. Not so if you're logged in and exploring the shiny new features of the machine while the salesperson is running your credit card and initializing your new device.

One effective strategy for moving in the direction of point-of-sale CRM is to let the customer bring their data. More specifically, you can take advantage of the fact that so many people are carrying their smartphones everywhere they go. By building apps that are useful to people at the store, you can effectively integrate your web and point-of-sale CRM approaches.

One example of this that I've found very useful is an app I found at Lowe's (www.lowes.com). It allows me to create a home profile to keep track of common purchases. I buy a number of things regularly: light bulbs, water filters, air filters, and fuses for various devices. But I don't buy them often enough to remember what size or model I need.

This Lowe's app allows me to look up what I bought the last time. It's organized by product type. And I can do it while I'm at the store. And I don't need to get up on a ladder or behind the fridge to extract the filter to figure out what I need and then again to replace it when I return from the store. CRM is about making things convenient, and this app fits the bill.

Customer Data and Law Enforcement

Believe it or not, you'll occasionally run across situations where someone in the law enforcement or legal community will take an interest in your customer data. Usually when this happens, your legal team is consulted first. But in any case, you should make sure you have their approval before providing any data.

Years ago, when I worked in the credit-card industry, there was a rather amusing legend in the company about a guy who worked in collections. The story (and I have no idea whether it was true) goes that somebody from the Justice Department showed up in the collections office to talk to him about a particular past due account.

The investigator was very curious about exactly how this particular collector had managed to get the home phone number of the person whose account was past due. The problem, as it turned out, was that the person in question was in the witness protection program.

I guess the situation wasn't all that amusing for either the witness or the people that had to relocate him. But it earned a promotion for the collector.

Customer data and criminal investigations

There are a number of situations in which customer records may be subpoenaed as part of criminal investigations. They may want to know whether someone was where they said they were at a given time. They may want to understand what purchases were made by a given person.

Because I've done a lot of work in the financial services industry, the most common law enforcement situations I've seen relate to financial records. The PATRIOT Act that was passed after 9/11 contains, among other things, some prescriptions for banks and other financial institutions related to the prevention of money laundering.

The focus of these rules relates primarily to large, anonymous monetary transactions. The airline industry is required to respect the no-fly list designed to prevent terrorists from boarding planes. But there's also a do-not-wire transfer list that banks need to check when they process these transactions.

Another type of monetary transaction that's tracked closely is large cash deposits. These types of transactions have been of interest to the IRS for a long time. They're sometimes signals that tax evasion is afoot. But they also are of interest as signals that more nefarious money laundering might be going on.

There's a tension in the legislative environment and legal environment around customer data. On the one hand, consumer privacy is a hot button issue. On the other hand, public safety concerns in the wake of 9/11 have led to some increased authority for law enforcement. The legality of law enforcement requests for data is not always cut and dried. You need to let your company lawyers handle such requests.

Customer data and civil suits

Another situation where customer data is requested is in regard to civil court cases. Divorces get nasty. Business deals fall apart. The whole spectrum of people's disagreements about money and property is fodder for the civil court system.

And when money comes up in civil court, financial records get subpoenaed. These subpoenas are generally pretty straightforward to deal with. But I repeat my admonition to check with your lawyers if one should arrive on your desk.

The more visible civil suits related to customer data involve lawsuits against the company with the database. As I mention in Chapter 3, you have a legal responsibility to keep your customer data safe.

Consumer credit lawsuits are a staple of the civil court systems. Inaccurate credit scores, unfair lending practices, and other violations of lending regulations produce a steady stream of court cases.

Another type of lawsuit that's fairly common involves data security breaches. You've no doubt heard a number of stories over the years about someone walking out of a company with a disk full of personal information about customers. In the age of identity theft, this obviously raises some hackles.

Still another common theme for lawsuits is violation of privacy. The sharing and selling of customer information between and by corporations is coming under increased scrutiny. As I mention in Chapter 3, it's important that you have a clear privacy policy and abide by it religiously.

Electronic devices, particularly mobile devices, provide a vast amount of customer data, including detailed location information. This data is a dream for predatory criminals if they can get their hands on it. This fact, combined with the widespread use of smartphones by children, is getting increasing attention in legislatures.

Part V
The Part of Tens

 For an extra Part of Tens chapter on the ten (or so) steps common to all database marketing campaigns, head on over to www.dummies.com/extras/datadriven marketing.

In this part . . .

- ✔ Get some practical tips on capturing customer-level data.
- ✔ Explore a variety of third-party resources available to boost your data driven marketing efforts.

Chapter 18

Ten (or So) Ways to Capture Customer Data

*B*its and pieces of customer data are spread out over virtually all the systems that your company uses. But this data is only useful to you if it's centralized and can be connected to customers. Much of your company's sales and transaction data is either summarized or cannot be directly traced back to individual customers.

There's also a lot of information that would be useful to you if it were actually captured. The conversations that occur between your sales staff and customers uncover a great deal of information about customer's attitudes and preferences. This information would be of great value to you if you could capture and store it.

In this chapter, I talk about some ways you can increase the amount of customer data in your database. When evaluating which of these techniques you might want to employ, you need to stay focused on how you plan to use the data. Capturing and storing data is costly — sometimes very costly. Before making that investment, make sure you know how you can use the data to drive revenue.

Identifying Customers with Loyalty Cards

Capturing customer-level sales data is particularly challenging for consumer retail businesses, especially those that operate physical stores. The problem is that almost all of their sales are made anonymously. Grocery stores, department stores, gas stations and a host of other businesses do not require customers to identify themselves in order to make a purchase.

But understanding customer purchase patterns is as important to these retail businesses as it is to anybody. One approach to getting at this data has been to implement loyalty programs. *Loyalty programs* operate by offering customers discounts in exchange for personal information. You fill out a form with the basic name and address information necessary to create a customer record in the company's marketing database. You're then given a plastic card that you swipe at the cash register when you make a purchase. The card swipe applies discounts or points toward a future discount to your "account." But it also ties the details of your transaction to your customer record.

When you implement a loyalty program, you want to get as many customers as possible to sign up. The more data, the better. Keep these things in mind:

- Make the application as simple as possible so that it can be filled out quickly.

- Make the discount meaningful. Being able to tell a customer that they can take $5 off this purchase if they fill out an application is a powerful motivator.

- Make the card easy to use. I actually have a half dozen mini-plastic cards attached to my key ring. This has the additional benefit of making sure that I always have my card with me.

- Actively manage your loyalty program. You should have a resource dedicated to actively monitoring and tweaking the program rather than simply putting it on autopilot. It's easy to fall into the trap of simply training your customers to expect discounts rather than actually building loyalty.

- Consult your accountant. Loyalty programs can have accounting implications related to the benefits that are promised to the customers. Some of these benefits need to be reflected on your company's balance sheet.

A Variation on the Theme: Rewards Cards

Rewards cards operate in a similar way to loyalty cards. In fact, many people use the two terms interchangeably. But there's a slight difference. The difference lies in the nature of the financial incentive. Whereas loyalty cards offer discounts on your company's products, rewards cards often offer discounts on *another* company's products.

The grocery store I usually use has a rewards card that earns me points toward discounts on gasoline. Every $50 I spend at the store earns me 10 cents off per gallon at a particular gas station.

In this case, the card is actually both a loyalty card and a rewards card. I also get discounts on certain products at the grocery store. But my purpose for making the distinction has to do with the cost of a rewards program versus a loyalty program.

Rewards programs serve the marketing needs of a partner company. This means that if you develop a rewards program, you share the cost of that program with somebody else. That makes it an attractive option, particularly for low-margin businesses. In the case of my grocery store card, the cost of the rewards are being borne by the relatively high-margin gas station/convenience store. The low-margin grocery store is reaping the data benefits.

Tracking Transactions with Offer Codes

You'll face another challenge related to associating purchases with particular marketing campaigns. Even if you can track transactions back to individual customers, it may not be clear whether a transaction is related to a specific marketing campaign.

For example, you might communicate that a discount is available for a limited time on a given type of purchase. But a customer may stumble onto that discount by noticing a good price while they're idly browsing the shelves. It's hard to tell whether your marketing communication had anything to do with the customer knowing about the offer.

One way around this is to include an offer code in your marketing communication. There are two ways of doing this:

- ✔ Use a generic offer code that's the same for everyone.
- ✔ Issue serialized codes that are unique to individual customers.

Issuing a single discount code makes implementing the program at the point of sale fairly simple. Your transaction system only needs to know about a single code. This means that the discount can be used multiple times. That's not necessarily a bad thing. But it does make measuring the campaign's performance a little tricky.

One disadvantage of this approach is that, personalized or not, these codes can be shared or given away. This makes it difficult to *fence* the offer. You can't restrict the discount to only price-sensitive customers, for example. This isn't as big a problem for individualized codes that can only be used once. But for generic codes, the door is wide open to discount sharing. There are actually websites out there dedicated to doing exactly that. Coupon fraud, like forged coupons, can also be a problem. A number of coupon clearing houses, such as NCH (which grew out of the Neilson empire), can help streamline and audit the administration of coupon programs.

Identifying Potential Customers with Newsletters

One way to generate lists of potential customers is to offer a newsletter. This approach has two advantages. First, in order to receive the newsletter, customers have to identify themselves. These days, the vast majority of newsletters are delivered electronically, which requires an e-mail address. And because the e-mail channel is so inexpensive, these newsletters can be delivered at very low cost.

What's more, these tend to be pretty good leads. By requesting a newsletter, the customer is signaling that they have some interest in your products. This means that when you design marketing communications to them, you know they already have an interest in what you have to offer. You don't have to waste your breath on brand recognition or product awareness messages. The newsletter does that for you.

Offering Physical Information Packets

You can expand on the newsletter approach by offering potential customers more actual physical collateral with information about your products. Videos, CDs, planning guides, or even product samples can be shared with your customers.

The advantage of sending a physical packet of some kind to the customer is that it requires them to give you their name and address. This is the core information that you need to create a robust customer record. And as in the case of newsletters, a request for such information signals an interest in your product. These are hot leads.

This approach is used frequently in connection with television advertising. So-called *direct response TV* advertising involves asking the viewer to call in to order a product. It can also be used effectively as a lead-generation tool. The viewer can be asked to call in to order their free information guide.

These advertisements are typically run on cable channels whose audiences have specific demographic characteristics. By targeting the advertisements to segments that fit your customer profile, the leads you get tend to be of very high quality. Another advantage is that you have additional demographic information on these leads that can help you design re-contact messages.

Encouraging Web Registrations

As I discuss in Chapter 13, a vast amount of data is available on how your customers use your website. You can learn a great deal about customer browsing behavior without requiring consumers to be registered or logged in on your site. But if you want to use this information to communicate with them directly, you need to have an e-mail address.

One of the biggest mistakes you can make in designing a registration process is to make it complicated. Because you can start a conversation with your customer using just their e-mail address, allow them to register with just an e-mail address. The more information you ask for, the more likely it is that the user will bail out of the registration process before completing it.

You can encourage this sort of "light" registration by simply restricting full access to content on your website. The pizza delivery store I usually use requires me to log in to see the weekly specials, for example. The newsletters and information requests discussed earlier in this chapter are also good ways of encouraging web registrations.

Once a customer is registered, you have a way of communicating with them. You'll have many opportunities to collect more data about that customer as the customer browses your website in the future. Detailed address data, for example, can be captured when the customer actually makes a purchase. In the next section, I discuss other ways of adding to your customer's online profile.

Building a More Robust Online Customer Profile

If a customer is registered, you can actually tie future browsing behavior to that customer record, even if the customer isn't logged in. As I discuss in Chapter 13, *cookies* are small files that you can place on a user's computer that allow you to tie browsing sessions together. Simply put, you drop a cookie on a user's computer when they register. You can then recognize the user every time they come back to your site, logged in or not.

Once the customer is registered, you have access to what pages they're looking at. You know what products they're searching for. You also know what ads they're clicking on. You can learn a lot from studying this behavior.

But you can learn more. One way is to allow the user to customize their preferences. Let them tell you what they want to hear about. Let them tell you how often they want to hear from you. Are they primarily interested in discounted offers? Do they have an interest in a particular type of product?

Another way of getting a broader picture of your guests' product interests is to provide planning tools or apps that assist them in doing business with you. I recently bought furniture from a store whose website allowed me to enter the dimensions of my living room. I could then drag and drop various pieces of furniture into the image and plan how I wanted to arrange the room. My home improvement store allows me to store information about my water filter numbers and air filter sizes so that I can access them at the store.

Customer Data and the Call Center

There's a great deal of information that's exchanged between customers and call center representatives. Making customer profile information available to your call centers can help your sales and service agents immensely. It can also cut down on the length of phone calls, which in turn brings down the cost of running the call center and improves the customer experience.

Conversely, it's very helpful to your database marketing efforts to have access to the information that call center reps collect from customers. Those reps can be trained to ask for key pieces of information about customers. If a customer asks a call center rep about a specific product, for example, that could trigger an offer from you. But only if you have access to this information.

A variety of software systems available for call centers facilitate the capture and sharing of customer data. These are frequently called Customer Relationship Management (or CRM) systems. They typically require a significant investment to implement, both in technology and training, but the investment may prove worthwhile.

When evaluating the possibility of implementing call center data capture systems, you'll need to understand the business case for doing so. When building the business case, take into account the value of the data that you capture as it relates to database marketing campaigns. But you also need to consider the benefits at the call center. The call center may (or may not) expect to shorten call times. But these systems can also be used to drive up sales efficiency.

Customer Data at the Point of Sale

Like call center reps, the frontline salespeople in your stores can also benefit from having customer data available. And you can benefit from the data that they might capture.

The grocery store loyalty swipe card connects my past purchase data to the transaction. This allows the point-of-sale system, by which I mean the cash register, to spit out coupons that are relevant to my buying patterns. This cross-selling technique is quite effective.

Auto parts stores do this very effectively. By collecting information on a customer's car, they can easily identify which parts are needed. They can also tell when certain parts are likely to need replacement. This information can trigger marketing communications to remind the customer to change their wiper blades, for example.

Purchasing Customer Lists

When all else fails with your lead-generation efforts, you can fall back on third-party list providers. You can buy lists of names and addresses of potential customers or e-mail addresses from a wide variety of companies.

These lists can be targeted in the sense that the consumers on the list meet certain criteria. Depending on the list provider, the level of targeting varies. The simplest (and cheapest) lists are simply geographically concentrated. You're selecting addresses within a given set of zip codes, for example.

But list providers can be a great deal more sophisticated. Age, income, marital status, presence of children, and other demographic profile information can be used to select lists that meet very specific profile requirements.

When you purchase a list, you are not really purchasing it. It's more like you're renting it. After a given period of time, the list vendor will expect you to purge the list from your database. They do this partly to make sure they keep up with data privacy and opt-out best practices. The exception to this purge requirement is that the names of consumers who actually purchase from you are yours to keep.

Purchasing Demographic Data

You can also buy demographic information on your customer base. Several companies compile consumer data from a wide variety of sources. They look at census data, public records, warranty cards — literally any data they can get their hands on. Several of the big players in this space have records on virtually every household in United States.

Because of privacy concerns, some of the data that these companies have cannot be provided to you at the individual customer level. They get around this issue in one of two ways. They either aggregate the data or they provide you with a targeted list of prospects (I discuss prospect lists in the previous section).

The aggregation I'm talking about involves using the individual customer data to create customer segments. These segments are relatively small groups of consumers who share deep similarities in their demographic makeup and purchase patterns. They create literally hundreds of such segments. They can even tailor customized segmentation schemes to your particular business goals.

What they provide to you is a classification of your customers according to which segment they belong to. They also provide a detailed description of each segment. By comparing these segments to your purchase data, you can identify hot segments from a targeting perspective. In addition, the detailed demographic descriptions of these segments can help you craft relevant messages for different segments.

Not all demographic data is created equal. And prices vary widely for this data. Sometimes, particularly with census data, it may appear that you are getting individual customer-level data. But this data may well be aggregated geographically. All the households in a city block or group of blocks may contain exactly the same data. It's important to understand at what level data is aggregated when you evaluate different data providers.

Chapter 19

Ten Resources for Information and Assistance

In This Chapter

▶ Getting information about direct marketing best practices

▶ Complying with privacy and opt-out legislation

▶ Understanding where to get data and marketing services

▶ Buying analytic tools

As you go about learning and applying the discipline of database marketing, you'll at times feel somewhat overwhelmed by all the moving parts. The good news is that you're not alone. There is a great deal of help available, if you know where to look for it.

In this chapter, I introduce you to some of the resources that are at your disposal. They range in nature from direct marketing best practices to the regulatory environment to software and services. I try to touch on the areas that are most likely to require some outside assistance.

Joining the Direct Marketing Association

The Direct Marketing Association, or DMA, is a non-profit organization that provides database marketing–related services and support to both consumers and businesses. If your company isn't already a member, you should strongly consider joining (www.thedma.org).

The DMA is the standard bearer for best practices in database marketing. It has a detailed set of policies and procedures that all members are expected to follow. These guidelines relate to all aspects of database marketing campaigns, from data privacy to the language used in marketing offers.

The DMA acts as an industry advocate in Washington. It lobbies for legislation that protects the rights of database marketers to use direct-marketing channels in a responsible and ethical way.

It's also the keeper of several national opt-out registries. These registries allow consumers to request that they not be marketed to. The DMA actively enforces compliance with these requests among their business members.

The DMA provides you with several useful tools. It keeps you abreast of what's happening with regulations that affect database marketers. In addition, it provides a steady stream of training and informational materials on new developments in the industry.

One key function of the DMA is to keep tabs on mail houses and other marketing service providers. It has a searchable database of vendors and marketing service providers that comply with its standards. Don't ever use a vendor that isn't on this list. If someone is selling database marketing services and doesn't bother to join the DMA, then something is wrong.

DMA membership costs are based on your direct-marketing budget. It charges a small fraction of a percent of your overall annual expenditures. Most companies that do a lot of direct marketing find that just being able to say that they are compliant DMA members is worth the cost of membership.

Subscribing to Industry Publications

Practically all industries have journals, blogs, and websites that are targeted specifically at that business sector. These resources can help you stay abreast of the issues and trends affecting your industry. Many are free. But most business sectors have a couple of best-in-class publications that are considered must-reads for industry participants. A simple web search for publications in your industry sector will give you plenty of options to evaluate.

Using Census Data

You'll frequently find yourself asking questions about the demographic makeup of various markets. You may be trying to get a sense of how big a given audience is. You may be trying to determine how deeply your penetration in a given market is.

One useful resource for answering these types of questions is the Census Bureau. Its website, www.census.gov, contains a wide array of data that can be viewed geographically. In addition to population data for the major metropolitan areas — data which is important to your advertising department — the Census Bureau also reports age and income data at various levels of summary.

Getting Familiar with the Post Office

If my mailbox is any indication, a huge portion of revenue taken in by the U.S. Postal Service is related to direct marketing. That motivates the USPS to keep direct marketers happy. It also motivates it to make processing direct mail as streamlined as possible.

The Postal Service web page, www.usps.com, contains a lot of information related to direct marketing, including links to publications outlining the address standards for bulk mail. It outlines in detail the advantages and costs associated with different methods of dealing with returned or undeliverable mail.

To avoid having to deal with large amounts of undeliverable mail, the USPS has strict standards for how bulk mail needs to be prepared. These standards relate not just to how addresses are formatted, but also involve matching the addresses to a standardized database of valid addresses. These standards are outlined in detail on the website.

You should know the process by which mail gets certified as complying with USPS standards. This is known as *Coding Accuracy Support System* (CASS) certification. CASS certification is necessary if you want to get bulk mail discounts. The way the post office does this is by evaluating the software and vendors that provide these services. It provides a list of certified vendors on its website.

Keeping Up with the Regulatory Environment

A variety of laws apply to your database marketing activity. Some of them revolve around privacy in some form or another. Some deal with the sharing of data. Others deal with honoring people's requests not to be contacted. The DMA can keep you informed about what legislation is out there and how to comply. But I always like to find out what the people enforcing the laws have to say about them.

The regulations that are most broadly applicable to database marketing relate to e-mail (CANSPAM) and the national Do Not Call Registry. The Federal Trade Commission is responsible for enforcing regulations regarding spam. You can find the FTC's take on the subject on its website, www.ftc.gov. The Do Not Call Registry is maintained through the website www.donotcall.gov.

There are some other industry-specific laws governing the use of customer data. Fair lending and other laws specific to the financial industry can be investigated at www.fdic.gov and www.federalreserve.gov. Even if you don't work directly in the financial industry, some of these laws may still apply to you. Offering payment plans or other types of payment deferrals may constitute offers of credit, for example.

There are also laws regarding the way data is used in the health care industry. These laws apply narrowly to the health care sector, but they're the most restrictive privacy laws out there. The main law is HIPAA or the Health Insurance Portability and Accountability Act. The Department of Health and Human Services, more specifically its office of civil rights, is responsible for enforcing these regulations. You can investigate at www.hhs.gov.

The Children's Online Privacy Protection Act (COPPA) is full of potential land mines for marketers as well. This law is actively enforced, and more than a few companies have found themselves paying large fines without realizing they were in violation of this law. The law essentially requires websites to detail privacy policies and to make efforts to obtain parental permission before collecting data on children under the age of 13. But the law has nuances. It's important for you to understand COPPA in detail. The website www.coppa.org contains the detailed text of this law, along with information regarding compliance.

I discuss the issues of legal compliance related to privacy and unsubscribe requests in Chapters 3 and 4, respectively. I also talk about the legal environment related to mobile messaging in Chapter 13.

Hiring Direct-Marketing Service Providers

A lot goes into the details of executing a direct-mail campaign. To take advantage of bulk rates at the USPS, several technical functions need to be performed. Addresses need to meet formatting standards. Addresses also need to be verified as being valid, which requires the use of software certified by the Postal Service. And the mail needs to be physically sorted.

On the e-mail side, there is also a fair amount of technical work to be done. But with e-mail, a great deal of this work has to do with tracking what happens to the e-mail. Did it get delivered? Did the receiver mark it as spam? Did the receiver open it? Did the receiver click the link to your website? The list goes on.

Most companies don't perform the mechanics of campaign execution in-house. It's far more efficient to farm these functions out to companies that do them for a living. Because they're distributing the cost of their infrastructure across many clients, these companies can perform these functions far more cheaply than you ever could. When selecting a vendor or vendors to perform these tasks, use the DMA (www.thedma.org) as a resource to check credentials.

Buying Creative Services

Many companies also choose to farm out their creative development. If your company does TV advertising, you already have a relationship with an advertising agency that facilitates media purchases. These agencies are frequently part of a larger marketing services company. They typically have sister companies that provide creative services, from copywriting to graphic design, that are necessary for your database marketing campaigns.

The larger agencies also have relationships with a variety of related service providers. They routinely work with printers and mail houses. These relationships allow for a smooth transition from campaign development through execution.

Grouping Your Customer Records into Households

In Chapter 3, I discuss the importance of collecting customer records together into households. There are two main reasons for this:

✔ Much of the demographic data that you use is only available at the household level.

✔ Your marketing campaigns are typically targeted at households rather than individuals. It usually doesn't make sense to send multiple copies of a message to the same address.

Most companies choose to purchase householding services from a third party. The advantage is that the vendors that perform these services have access to a vast amount of data that you don't have. Another advantage is that address updates and standardization are a core part of this process.

Householding can be performed in large batches. You can send your entire database of customers out annually or biannually to be scrubbed and house-holded. But most of these vendors actually allow you to submit small numbers of new customers daily, or even in real time, to be scrubbed and householded before you even add them to your database.

A few vendors out there have huge databases that essentially contain every household and address in the country. I've had positive experiences with three really big players in this space: Acxiom (www.acxiom.com), Epsilon (www.epsilon.com), and Merkle (www.merkleinc.com).

Third-Party Data Providers

To enhance the data that you collect in-house, you'll likely want to consider buying data from an external source. A wide range of demographic data is available that you'll likely never be able to get from your internal data sources.

The data you can buy falls into two general categories. The first is data that's tied to individual households. A fair amount of data has been compiled from a variety of sources, including public records. Home value, or at least the last sales price, is public record data, for example.

But data providers also have access to a large amount of data that's protected by privacy regulations and corporate privacy policies. Vendors can't provide this data to you at an individual household level. What they do instead is analyze their data with a view to creating small segments of customers that have similar traits. In other words, they use the data they have to identify groups of customers who share very similar demographic traits, product tastes and needs, and even psychological attitudes.

Even though they can't share the data they have on individuals, they can tell you which one of their segments each one of your customers falls into. This combined with a detailed description of the segment makes for a very useful marketing tool.

In the previous section, I mention providers of householding services — Acxiom, Epsilon, and Merkle. As it turns out, these companies also sell a broad array of demographic and customer segmentation data. The major credit bureaus have also jumped into the space of providing market-ing services. The data they provide is primarily consumer-segmentation data. Those agencies are Equifax (www.equifax.com), Experian (www.experian.com), and TransUnion (www.transunion.com).

When evaluating data vendors, be aware that they can typically customize the data that you purchase. You can often purchase data a la carte, depending on what's most relevant to your business. They also can create customized segments that take into account your customers' purchase patterns. In any case, it's a good idea to press for some kind of proof of concept before making a large investment in demographic data.

Analytic Software

Throughout this book, I talk about the role of data analysis in database marketing. Some of this analysis can be done with basic reporting tools and spreadsheets. But some of it requires an advanced knowledge of statistics—and software that can perform advanced statistical procedures on large amounts of data.

The phrases *marketing analytics* and *marketing analytic software* are used in a variety of contexts. When I use them, I mean statistical analysis. But these phrases also pop up when it comes to doing web analytics and website traffic analysis. And they're also used in the context of producing consolidated marketing performance reports, known as *dashboards*.

I briefly address web analytics in Chapter 13. But a detailed discussion of either web analytics or dashboard reporting is far beyond the scope of this book. Luckily, each subject has a *For Dummies* book all to itself.

In the context of statistical analysis, a couple of software packages are commonly used in the marketing industry:

- ✔ **SPSS:** Now owned by IBM, this software package has been a marketing industry standard since it first became available in the 1970s. Its widespread use in marketing applications began in the context of analyzing survey data and other marketing research applications.

- ✔ **SAS:** I think I've used SAS in every job I've ever had since college. SAS is actually a large software company that offers numerous data processing, analysis, reporting, and statistical tools. Many of SAS's products are customized to specific business applications, such as database marketing.

Neither SPSS nor SAS is particularly cheap. But they both have extensive capabilities. And in both cases, the vendors can provide you with training and support. They also provide consulting services in case you need to farm out your more advanced analytic projects.

Index

Notes

About the Author

David Semmelroth has spent the last two decades working with data and training people to work with data. He has witnessed and participated in the development of increasingly sophisticated techniques to collect, manage, and use data to drive business results.

Though his career started in Information Technology, he quickly developed an interest in how data can be utilized in marketing applications. Early in his career, his interest in customer data and his ability to find ways to pry it from databases caught the interest of a couple of his colleagues in marketing. They facilitated his transition into the world of database marketing, and he never looked back.

David has worked for several large companies over the years. More recently he's been doing consulting work related to customer databases and database marketing. His industry experience includes working with a variety of financial services companies, from insurance to retail banking. He also spent several years in the travel and entertainment industry.

Data Driven Marketing For Dummies is a natural extension of David's interest and experience in teaching. He's taught classes in statistics and mathematics at several colleges. And he's designed and taught a variety of data-analysis–focused courses for database marketers.

David earned bachelor's and master's degrees in mathematics from the University of Michigan. He wears the title of *geek* proudly, though he also prides himself on being able to communicate effectively with both business and technical partners.

Dedication

For my parents, Carl and Sara.

Author's Acknowledgments

I would like to thank my wife, Kelley. Her enthusiasm for this project has kept me going through my first attempt at writing a book. Her extensive marketing expertise hasn't hurt either.

I owe a huge thank-you to all the brilliant people I've worked with over the years. Your diverse talents and perspectives have been both inspiring and instructive. This book would not have been possible without you.

In particular, I'd like to thank Tom Boyles. He helped get me started in the marketing business and has been a pillar of support for many years.

Chris Crayner has also been a great mentor, colleague, and friend during my career. Database marketing is a small world, and our paths seem to keep crossing in the most unlikely places. Most recently, he's been instrumental in helping to edit this book.

Several people have been kind enough to share their time and insights on Internet and new media marketing. In particular, the team at Cramer-Krasselt was very generous. Julie Sheridan, Tim Mauery, Karen Glass, Christian Dodd, and Nick Papagiannis were also all quite generous in sharing their perspectives. My friend and colleague Carlos Figueroa was also kind enough to spend some time with me on this subject.

I would also like to thank my editor, Corbin Collins. His patience and encouragement, and perhaps most importantly his faith in me, have been critical to the successful completion of this project. Stacy Kennedy at Wiley also was critical in getting me up to speed on how to write a *For Dummies* book. I'd also like to thank my agent, Grace Freedson, who delivered this opportunity to me on a silver platter.

Publisher's Acknowledgments

Acquisitions Editor: Stacy Kennedy

Editor: Corbin Collins

Technical Editor: Chris Crayner

Project Coordinator: Katie Crocker

Cover Image: © Zoonar RF/Getty Images

Math & Science

Algebra I For Dummies,
2nd Edition
978-0-470-55964-2

Anatomy and Physiology
For Dummies,
2nd Edition
978-0-470-92326-9

Astronomy For Dummies,
3rd Edition
978-1-118-37697-3

Biology For Dummies,
2nd Edition
978-0-470-59875-7

Chemistry For Dummies,
2nd Edition
978-1-1180-0730-3

Pre-Algebra Essentials
For Dummies
978-0-470-61838-7

Microsoft Office

Excel 2013 For Dummies
978-1-118-51012-4

Office 2013 All-in-One
For Dummies
978-1-118-51636-2

PowerPoint 2013
For Dummies
978-1-118-50253-2

Word 2013 For Dummies
978-1-118-49123-2

Music

Blues Harmonica
For Dummies
978-1-118-25269-7

Guitar For Dummies,
3rd Edition
978-1-118-11554-1

iPod & iTunes
For Dummies,
10th Edition
978-1-118-50864-0

Programming

Android Application
Development For
Dummies, 2nd Edition
978-1-118-38710-8

iOS 6 Application
Development For Dummies
978-1-118-50880-0

Java For Dummies,
5th Edition
978-0-470-37173-2

Religion & Inspiration

The Bible For Dummies
978-0-7645-5296-0

Buddhism For Dummies,
2nd Edition
978-1-118-02379-2

Catholicism For Dummies,
2nd Edition
978-1-118-07778-8

Self-Help & Relationships

Bipolar Disorder
For Dummies,
2nd Edition
978-1-118-33882-7

Meditation For Dummies,
3rd Edition
978-1-118-29144-3

Seniors

Computers For Seniors
For Dummies,
3rd Edition
978-1-118-11553-4

iPad For Seniors
For Dummies,
5th Edition
978-1-118-49708-1

Social Security
For Dummies
978-1-118-20573-0

Smartphones & Tablets

Android Phones
For Dummies
978-1-118-16952-0

Kindle Fire HD
For Dummies
978-1-118-42223-6

NOOK HD For Dummies,
Portable Edition
978-1-118-39498-4

Surface For Dummies
978-1-118-49634-3

Test Prep

ACT For Dummies,
5th Edition
978-1-118-01259-8

ASVAB For Dummies,
3rd Edition
978-0-470-63760-9

GRE For Dummies,
7th Edition
978-0-470-88921-3

Officer Candidate Tests,
For Dummies
978-0-470-59876-4

Physician's Assistant Exam
For Dummies
978-1-118-11556-5

Series 7 Exam
For Dummies
978-0-470-09932-2

Windows 8

Windows 8 For Dummies
978-1-118-13461-0

Windows 8 For Dummies,
Book + DVD Bundle
978-1-118-27167-4

Windows 8 All-in-One
For Dummies
978-1-118-11920-4

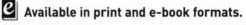

Available in print and e-book formats.